Contributions To Phenomenology

In Cooperation with The Center
for Advanced Research in Phenomenology

Volume 86

Scope

The purpose of the series is to serve as a vehicle for the pursuit of phenomenological research across a broad spectrum, including cross-over developments with other fields of inquiry such as the social sciences and cognitive science. Since its establishment in 1987, *Contributions to Phenomenology* has published more than 80 titles on diverse themes of phenomenological philosophy. In addition to welcoming monographs and collections of papers in established areas of scholarship, the series encourages original work in phenomenology. The breadth and depth of the Series reflects the rich and varied significance of phenomenological thinking for seminal questions of human inquiry as well as the increasingly international reach of phenomenological research

The series is published in cooperation with The Center for Advanced Research in Phenomenology.

More information about this series at http://www.springer.com/series/5811

Lisa Foran • Rozemund Uljée

Editors

Heidegger, Levinas, Derrida: The Question of Difference

 Springer

Editors
Lisa Foran
Philosophical Studies
Newcastle University
Newcastle Upon Tyne, UK

Rozemund Uljée
Institute for Philosophy
Universiteit Leiden
Leiden, The Netherlands

ISSN 0923-9545   ISSN 2215-1915   (electronic)
Contributions To Phenomenology
ISBN 978-3-319-39230-1   ISBN 978-3-319-39232-5   (eBook)
DOI 10.1007/978-3-319-39232-5

Library of Congress Control Number: 2016951438

Printed on acid-free paper

This Springer imprint is published by Springer Nature
The registered company is Springer International Publishing AG Switzerland

Contents

Introduction: Between Heidegger, Levinas, and Derrida

'I am, I think, I live', means that I am one human being among others in the world, that I am related to nature through my physical body, and that in this body my *cogitationes*, perceptions, memories, judgments etc. are incorporated as psycho-physical facts [...] *The essence of consciousness, in which I live as my own self, is the so-called intentionality.* Consciousness is always consciousness of something.

Edmund Husserl, *The Paris Lectures.*

The seismic shift in the philosophical landscape produced by the work of Edmund Husserl is easily comparable to Immanuel Kant's 'Copernican revolution'. Husserl's phenomenology revolutionised philosophy, producing a turn in thinking that spins on in the work of many of today's thinkers. This turn pivots, in many ways, on the concept of intentionality. Adapted from Brentano's psychological approach, Husserlian intentionality marks the very structure of experience as *relation* and makes the description of that structure the task of philosophy. In this, Husserl's phenomenology escapes solipsism and scepticism to assure itself of a firm ground for knowledge. However, this ground is called into question by the very fact that it is built upon *relation* and thus upon difference. And it is this question of difference which in many senses frames the rich, complex, and elusive relation between Martin Heidegger, Emmanuel Levinas, and Jacques Derrida.

Marrying Husserlian phenomenology with the hermeneutics of Wilhelm Dilthey, Heidegger's magnum opus poses the question of Being and answers with the ontological difference. This primacy of the question as the *hodos* or 'way' of thinking echoes in the work of Levinas, for whom 'one comes not into the world but into question'. Philosophy itself is the 'community of the question' for Derrida. A question presupposes difference: difference between call and response; difference between one and the other; and difference between saying and listening; and so on. Difference, as the condition of the possibility of the question, is thus also the possibility of philosophy itself insofar as the latter begins with the question. But how do these questions of difference pose themselves and multiply themselves between Heidegger, Levinas, and Derrida?

It was to this question that we initially sought a response when we organised a conference 'Between Heidegger, Levinas and Derrida' in 2013 in Dublin. While the collection of essays here is far more than a 'conference proceedings' and a number of essays herein were not presented at that conference, the project nonetheless took its first steps at that event. We would like to thank the Irish Research Council for its funding and the UCD School of Philosophy for supporting that conference, in particular the then head of school Maria Baghramian.

In compiling this collection, we were faced with the difficult decision of how to order the essays. Any thematic division seemed to limit each individual essay by forcing it to be 'about' only one thing. We therefore decided to order them alphabetically by authors' surnames so that each essay can stand on its own and relate to each other essay in its own way. What all of the essays share, we believe, is a new way to approach the relation between each of the three thinkers.

The collection begins with a challenge to Levinas's claim that we must leave the 'climate' of Heidegger's philosophy to find an ethics. Ileana Borţun argues that Levinas overlooks the nature of responsibility already found within the Heideggerian structure of Being-with and Dasein-with. Joseph Cohen and Raphael Zagury-Orly investigate the relation between Derrida's thinking and the tradition of philosophy. Taking 'the limits of truth' as a guide word, Cohen and Zagury-Orly follow Derrida's departure from Heidegger and Levinas through the themes and times of truth, justice, and the impossible. Arthur Cools, in Chap. 3, approaches the relation between Levinas and Derrida from their shared mistrust of metaphorical language. However, 'skin' in the work of Levinas and 'gift' in that of Derrida, demonstrate the manner in which both thinkers invariably fall back into the metaphorical language they wish to shake off. Paul Ennis investigates the role of death in Heidegger and Derrida, framing his essay through the recent move away from phenomenology in thinkers such as Quentin Meillassoux and Ray Brassier. Ennis argues phenomenology must confront its inevitable defeat by a time which exceeds the human. Lisa Foran returns us to the theme of language in an essay that centres on the possibility of naming. Foran argues that unlike Derrida, Heidegger and Levinas remain trapped in the tradition they wish to escape insofar as they name difference itself.

How philosophy defines itself has been a philosophical pursuit throughout its history. Tziovanis Georgakis in his contribution describes this concern with the enclosure of philosophy as both a farce and a *deus ex machina*. The paradoxical but unavoidable relation between heteronomy and autonomy frames his investigation into this *deus ex machina* as it operates in the work of Heidegger and Derrida. Carlos Guttiérrez begins with the question of how to listen to the other person without destroying their absolute alterity. Tracing otherness from Heidegger to Levinas to Derrida, Guttiérrez offers Hans-Georg Gadamer's approach as a path between the extremities of the former thinkers; a path along which we might truly *listen* to the other. Sinéad Hogan takes up the work of all three of our thinkers interrogating their relationship through the prism of a graphic, which is to say an aesthetic, intervention. Hogan asks how the line between 'aesthetics' and 'critical thinking' becomes disrupted in the work of Heidegger and Levinas, via Derrida. Oisín Keohane describes the interrelation between Heidegger's *Machtlose* and Derrida's *impou-*

voir. François Raffoul explores the Heidegger/Levinas debate on the notion of responsibility. If Heidegger has taught us that Being is *transcendence* pure and simple, Raffoul then questions whether the Other can only be said to lie beyond Being.

The relation between the early Derrida and Heidegger is examined from the concept of time in Rajesh Sampath's contribution. Mauro Senatore traces Derrida's thought of the *usure*, suggesting that it is not only the interpretation of Levinas's metaphysics but also the 'metaphoricity of metaphor' at work in Derrida. Simon Skempton reconceptualises the notion of 'deconstructive personhood' along the lines of the Derridean theme of singularity; arguing that, despite their differences, Heidegger and Levinas share Derrida's concern with the impossibility of making personhood into a present and proper identity. Rozemund Uljée describes the closeness and distance between Heidegger and Derrida in their attempts to think difference in relation to the notion of revelation. Lawrence Vogel investigates the triangular relationship between Heidegger, Martin Buber, and Levinas regarding the notion of intersubjectivity. Vogel argues that each thinker identifies a potentiality he takes to be the defining mark of our humanity itself.

While no work on the relation between Heidegger, Levinas, and Derrida could claim to be complete, we hope that this collection of essays reveals the depth of the relation between them and their continued relevance in and for philosophy today.

Newcastle   Lisa Foran
The Netherlands   Rozemund Uljée
October 2015

Substitution and *Mit(da)sein*: An Existential Interpretation of the Responsibility for the Other

Ileana Borțun

Abstract This paper challenges Levinas's thesis that it is necessary to escape Heidegger's fundamental ontology in order to think ethically. It discusses how Levinas thinks the ethical relationship in *Otherwise than Being*, as "substitution," as "responsibility for the responsibility of the other," and it shows that one's responsibility for the other's responsibility can also be interpreted existentially, as authentic *Fürsorge*, as care for the other's care. The "substitution of one for the other" and the "care for the other" are indeed different, but not antithetical. Firstly, Dasein's authentic existentiell understanding of the other does not reduce him to "the same", because it does not "reduce" him to the apriori structures of Dasein. Secondly, the equiprimordiality of "Being-with" (*Mitsein*) and "Dasein-with" (*Mitdasein*) – in short, *Mitt(da)sein* – indicates the exposure of one to the other within the factical modes of Being-with-one-another and, therefore, the indebtedness of one to the other for one's potentiality-for-Being. Consequently, Dasein's assumed responsibility or authentic care for its potentiality-for-Being is not ego(t)istic, as Levinas contends, but entails caring for the other's Being, for his unique otherness.

Keywords Levinas • Substitution • Heidegger • Mitsein • Mitdasein • Responsibility • Care

1 Introduction

It is often considered that Levinas's powerful critique of Heidegger's fundamental ontology exposes the inherent limitations of this ontology with regard to ethics; its intrinsic inability to think the otherness of the other and the I as responsible for the other. According to Levinas, the hermeneutics of Dasein, despite its existential character, does not escape the traditional "'egoism' of ontology" (Levinas 1969, p. 46) which means both egotism and ethical egoism. In Heidegger's case, this "egoism" would be epitomized by the interpretation of Dasein's Being as *care* for (its own)

I. Borțun (✉)
The Romanian Society for Phenomenology, Bucharest, Romania
e-mail: ileana.bortun@phenomenology.ro

© Springer International Publishing Switzerland 2016
L. Foran, R. Uljée (eds.), *Heidegger, Levinas, Derrida: The Question of Difference*, Contributions To Phenomenology 86,
DOI 10.1007/978-3-319-39232-5_1

1

Being, given that Dasein, "in its very Being, has this Being as an issue" (Heidegger 1962, p. 104). In other words, Dasein, as existence, has to become itself and therefore always exists within an understanding of (its own) Being and it relates to every being by an understanding of that being's Being. Levinas considers that *understanding* the other means *knowing* him by subordinating his otherness to a general concept: "Being." Since "[t]hrough the suppression of the singular, through generalization, knowing is idealism" (Levinas 2011, p. 87), then Heidegger's ontology seems to be guilty of idealism; of reducing the other to the same, like any other ontology before it. For Levinas, "the same" designates both the sameness implied by the generality of "Being" and the undisturbed identity of the I, who by understanding the other never encounters the other, but just confirms itself in its self-enclosure. Thus, Dasein's existing *"for the sake of* itself" (Heidegger 1962, p. 364) appears to be incompatible with existing for the sake of the others.[1]

Although Levinas is not persuaded by Heidegger's insistence that Dasein's understanding is more originary than knowledge, his critique employs a fundamental implication of this fact: to understand (the other) is to act (toward the other). Levinas believes that by understanding the other, Dasein not only subordinates the other's alterity, as "specific difference," to a genus, but also subjects the other to its spontaneity, its powers. This opens the way for treating the other as if he were an object at one's disposal, "something" that one could even dispose of by murder.[2]

In response to this ontological oppression of the other, Levinas contests the traditional priority of ontology over ethics and tries to think the ethical relation non-ontologically through the calling into question of one's spontaneity by the presence of the other human (*l'Autrui*) as the "absolutely other" (*l'absolument Autre*) (Levinas 1969, p. 39). Irreducible to any common denominator, the other cannot be understood, the other is not a phenomenon. The ethical relation is non-reciprocal; it consists in finding oneself infinitely responsible for the other, addressed by the principle "you shall not commit murder" which is "the very signifyingness of the face" of the other (ibid., p. 262) – who "by his face [is]… the manifestation of the height in which God is revealed" (ibid., p. 79). This absolute otherness disrupts sameness; thus, the I gains its singularity: in existing for the other, the I is "no longer reduced to his place within a totality" (ibid., p. 246).

In this paper, I will challenge Levinas's view that it is *necessary* to escape Heidegger's phenomenological ontology in order to think ethically. The thesis that through understanding Dasein subordinates the other to a general concept, indicates that Levinas does not fully consider the *existential* character of Heideggerian ontology and its implications, and is therefore improper. I will argue that, if we look

---

[1] Levinas explicitly contrasts the responsibility for others with "the concern [i.e. *care* (*souci*)] 'that existence takes for its very existence'" (Levinas 2011, p. 93), with "the limited and egoist fate of him who is only for-himself" (ibid., p. 116).

[2] In a 1990 "Prefatory Note" to his *Reflections on the Philosophy of Hitlerism* (1934), Levinas affirms his conviction that "the source of the bloody barbarism of National Socialism … stems from the essential possibility of *elemental Evil* … which … is inscribed within the ontology of a being concerned with Being (*de l'être soucieux d'être*)… Such a possibility still threatens the subject correlative with Being …, that famous subject of transcendental idealism that before all else wishes to be free and thinks itself free" (Levinas 1990, p. 63).

beyond the non-relational aspect of Dasein's individualization, famously emphasized by Heidegger, we can see that fundamental ontology enables us to think the
ethical relation precisely as *responsibility* for the other's otherness: for *his own*
potentiality-for-Being, *his* individualization. Not only could the existential analytic
be the foundation for an ethical theory, but it is in itself ethical.[3] To exist authentically as *Da* sein, as Being-in-the-world, hence as always already Being-with other
Daseins; and to inhabit one's *ethos* or unique place; entails an originary ethical relation to oneself and *the others*. That is, it entails an ethical relation to each other in
his or her irreducible, albeit not absolute, otherness.

Starting from Derrida's Violence and Metaphysics (1964), I will begin by
questioning (in section 2) Levinas's tenet that it is possible to find oneself responsible for an other who, completely dissimilar, cannot be understood by analogy with
oneself. I will then discuss (in section 3) how Levinas, in answer to Derrida, thinks
the ethical relation in *Otherwise than Being* (1974) as "substitution of one for the
other" as "responsibility for the responsibility of the other". I will argue that this
does entail an understanding of what I and the other have in common (although this
understanding is not, for Levinas, existentially grounded): the pre-originary substitution by which I find myself responsible for the other's responsibility involves my
(existentiell) understanding of myself *and* the other as responsible beings. This
allows us to consider the "responsibility for the responsibility of the other" from an
existential perspective.

Surely, by substitution Levinas intends to avoid thinking responsibility starting
from one's understanding of the other as another I, because he wants to subvert the
egocentric understanding of the ethical agent: "The word *I* means *here I am*, answering for everything and for everyone" (Levinas 2011, p. 114). To be oneself means to
be always already responsible for the others. Nevertheless, considering Heidegger's
own destruction of the subject, this is similarly true of Dasein (although for different
reasons). As I will argue (in section 4), Levinas's thesis that Dasein reduces the
other to the same (besides ignoring that Heideggerian Being is not a genus) disre-
gards the fold between the ontological-existential interpretation and the ontic-
existentiell understanding. The latter does not thematize the other, does not "reduce"
him to the apriori structures of Dasein. Then I will show (in section 5) that the
responsibility for the other's responsibility can be interpreted existentially, as *care
for the other's care*, and that Dasein's responsibility is not completely opposed to
that advocated by Levinas.[4] The existential co-originarity (or equiprimordiality) of
"Being-with" (*Mitsein*) and "Dasein-with" (*Mitdasein*) – in short, *Mit(da)sein* –
indicates the heteronomy of Dasein's self; the *exposure of one to the other* within
the factical modes of Being-with-one-another (*Miteinandersein*), so that Dasein is
always already responsible also for the other Daseins, not merely for "itself."

---

[3] It is "ethical" in the pre-theoretical sense of the Greek *ethos*: "abode, dwelling place," used by
Heidegger (1993b, pp. 256, 258) when he characterizes the thought of Being as "the originary
ethics."

[4] Levinas's "substitution" and Heidegger's authentic "care for" the other or "solicitude" (*Fürsorge*)
are different, but not – as Marion (2011, pp. 57–59) argues – diametrically opposed.

2   The Other as Other Than Myself

In questioning the thesis of incompatibility between Heidegger's phenomenological ontology and ethics, it is fruitful to start from Derrida's argument regarding Levinas's insistence that the other is not a phenomenon. Derrida observes that my respect for the other's otherness is unthinkable without him *appearing* to me as *other than myself* (Derrida 2001, p. 151). Husserl's argument by analogy from the Fifth Cartesian Meditation does not reduce otherness to sameness: precisely because I cannot attain to the other "immediately and originally, silently, in communion with the other's own experience," the analogical appresentation of the other is "the opposite of victorious assimilation" of the other within the same (ibid., pp. 154–155).

Derrida's analysis suggests that analogy as such has an ethical significance, for it involves the recognition of the difference that prevents the reduction of similarity to sameness. From this perspective, Dasein's (authentic) understanding of the other's Being is indeed a recognition of otherness, if only because it discloses the other as another Being-toward-death. This understanding *lets* the other *be* as he truly is, as an other potentiality-for-Being, irreducible to myself precisely because I cannot die his death, that is, I cannot live his existence toward death, I cannot exist in his "place" (although we co-exist).[5]

However, since "other than myself" means here an alter *Dasein*, any "analogy" (authentic or not) between myself and the other should be interpreted existentially in connection with *Mitsein*. Dasein is primordially Being-with, and not a "primordial ego [that] constitutes the ego who is other for him" (Husserl 1960, p. 119).[6] Dasein does not constitute the "intersubjective" relation but is instead *constituted by it*: *Mitsein* is a constitutive aspect of Dasein's Being, indicating that each Dasein individualizes itself *through* and *within* the factical modes of *Miteinandersein* (existentially interpreted as *Mit(da)sein*). That is why Heidegger says that empathy becomes possible only on the basis of Being-with (1962, pp. 124–125). The primordiality of *Mitsein* means that the relation to the other *is not secondary* to the relation to oneself. To be sure, Levinas acknowledges that "for Heidegger intersubjectivity is a coexistence, a *we* prior to the I and the other"; but he considers it a "neutral intersubjectivity," where singularities are erased (Levinas 1969, p. 68). Nevertheless, this reading of *Mitsein* is one version of his improper interpretation of *Sein* as conceptual generality. Actually, singularities are blurred by the domination

---

[5] The understanding – or, for later Heidegger, thinking – of Being can be regarded as a recognition of otherness also because it is not a cognition, but a *letting be* of Being: Being is "the other of thought," because "one can have to let be only that which one is not" (Derrida 2001, p. 176). As I argue toward the end of this paper, that is why Dasein's authentic self-understanding, by which it lets itself be its potentiality-for-Being, is not actually a movement of the same.

[6] Heidegger specifically warns us off confusing Dasein "in each case mine" with an ego. Mineness (*Jemeinigkeit*) "belongs to any existent Dasein ... as the condition which makes authenticity and inauthenticity possible" (Heidegger 1962, p. [53]). So this "*ontologically* constitutive state" explains also Dasein's everyday and rather inauthentic self-understanding, on which the philosophy of subject actually rests (cf. ibid., pp. [114–115]).

of *das Man* in everyday Being-with-one-another, not by *Mitsein* as such, which –
equiprimordially with *Mitdasein* – designates the co-existence of beings who have
their Being to be, have to singularize themselves. Anxiety disentangles Dasein from
the indefinite "they" only to disclose its being always already *with* the other Daseins
and, as I will argue later, *exposed* to them and, therefore, *indebted* to them for its
individuality.

Derrida also argues that Levinas's ethics remains dependent on ontology because
its language is ontological (cf. Derrida 2001, pp. 136–146). We find a specific illustra-
tion of this in "Is Ontology Fundamental?", where Levinas writes that ethical thinking is all about

> finding the place where the human no longer concerns us from the perspective of the hori-
> zon of Being (*l'être*), that is to say, no longer offers itself to our powers. The being (*l'étant*)
> as such (and not as incarnation of universal Being) can only be in a relation where we speak
> to this being. The being is the human being and it is as a neighbor that a human being is
> accessible. (Levinas 1996b/1951, pp. 8/96; tr. mod.)

Thus formulated, Levinas's project remains within Heidegger's ontico-ontological
difference – given that for Heidegger being is *not* an "incarnation of universal
Being," because Being is *not* a genus but the *disclosure* of beings, and thus Dasein's
Being is, in each case, the Being of a certain human being.[7] In thinking the "[human]
being as such," the ontological is still entailed. As I will argue later, such an entail-
ment *does not* preclude the ethical relation: when Dasein is authentic, it speaks *to*
the other, not *about* the other, namely it does not thematize the other Dasein, it does
not "reduce" him to "Dasein."

3 The Substitution of One for the Other

In *Otherwise than Being*, Levinas responds to Derrida by developing the distinction
between *the Saying*, which is ethical as one's passive and direct exposure to the
other; and *the Said*, the ontological thematization that is ultimately inscribed in any
philosophical discourse (Levinas 2011, pp. 5–6).[8] In *writing about* the ethical relation, the Said is unavoidable. But Levinas fights the Said's tendency to annihilate
the Saying, by deconstructing it from within. "Substitution" is most illustrative of
this endeavor.

---

[7] Being "is no class or genus of beings; yet it pertains to every being. Its 'universality' is to be
sought higher up"; "Being is the *transcendens*," i.e. it is not to be found among beings; yet it is not
divorced from them. Most importantly, the transcendence of *Dasein's* Being "implies the possibility and the necessity of the most radical *individuation*" (Heidegger 1962, p. [38]). — Since Being
is not a "first being," Heidegger's ontology is not a "first philosophy." Accordingly, it is highly
problematic to conflate it with traditional ontology, as Levinas does. On this point, see for example
Derrida 2001, pp. 170–171, and Raffoul 2005, pp. 144–145.

[8] This distinction is meant "to surpass the ontological difference by ethics" (Marion 2005, p. 313):
the Saying is pre-originary to the Said, in whose amphibology Levinas (2011, p. 6) locates the
ontological difference.

The "substitution of one for the other" is meant to undermine subjectivity understood as autonomy and self-coincidence, to erode the self-domination and self-centeredness which, for Levinas, also characterize Dasein. He uses "substitution" – coming from the Latin *sub* ("under") and *statuere* ("to place") – to name the fact of finding oneself, most passively, *placed under* the weight of responsibility (ibid., p. 116). A responsibility before any freedom, "an exposure to the other … without holding back, exposure of exposed-ness, expression, saying" (ibid., p. 15).

Substitution is the very subjection of the subject to the other. Unlike the Dasein of Levinas's interpretation, this ethical subject is neither powerful nor voluntary; its individuality consists in its subjection to responsibility – not for himself, but for the other: "I exist through the other and for the other" (ibid., p. 114), and not through myself and for myself. I am responsible even for the other's responsibility for me:

> To be oneself, otherwise than being (*autrement qu'être*), to be dis-interested, is to bear the wretchedness and bankruptcy of the other, and even the responsibility that the other can have for me. To be oneself … is always to have one degree of responsibility more, the responsibility for the responsibility of the other. (ibid., p. 117)

Nevertheless, this responsibility for the other *human* (not for other alterities) involves, in Heideggerian terms, an *existentiell understanding* of the other: I should "know" a human from a jug, a lion or a tree. My finding myself, beyond my egoism, responsible even for the other's responsibility involves my (pre-ontological) understanding that, unlike things, animals or plants; humans are responsible, that both I and the other are responsible beings.

Obviously, Levinas avoids explaining this understanding *existentially*, because this would mean for him that I encounter the other by the mediation of a general concept, "Being". That I remain – and the other becomes – enclosed within the sphere of the same, of the ego(t)istic subject. For Levinas, my responsibility for the other is prior to my encounter with a certain other not thanks to our apriori structures (ibid., p. 86), but rather to my having been *created* as submitted to the other. Substitution is "the absolute passivity of being a creature" (ibid., p. 121), of having a soul, which is "the other in me" (ibid., pp. 69; 191, n. 3). I am *already* one-for-the-other, *before* existing for myself (i.e. before being Dasein). And "it is only thanks to God that, as a subject incomparable with the other, I am approached as an other by the others, that is, 'for myself'. 'Thanks to God' I am another for the others" (ibid., p. 158). Conversely, it is thanks to God that I can approach the other as an absolutely other. Thus, by substitution Levinas counter-responds to Derrida's argument that I can relate to the other only by analogy with myself, that his otherness cannot be absolute (Bernasconi 2002, p. 243). Levinas's answer is that the other is not other than myself, but is already within me, as my soul.

Nonetheless, it is not necessary to proceed otherwise than existentially in order to think one's responsibility for (the responsibility of) the other. I believe it is possible to interpret the ethical relation within Heidegger's existential analytic, namely as the authentic existentiell understanding of one's Being *and* the other's Being, made possible by *Mit(da)sein*. In order to argue this, I will first show why I think

Levinas's interpretation of fundamental ontology as a reduction of the other to the same is improper.

4 Levinas's Disregard for the Ontico–Ontological Fold

Most relevant in our context is that Levinas's critique employs precisely the dichotomies that Heidegger sets out to destruct: subject–object, immanence–exteriority, essence–existence.[9] Levinas reads *"The 'essence' of Dasein lies in its existence"* not as a *destruction* of essence through the interpretation of Dasein's Being as *existence*, as Heidegger (1962, p. [42]) intends it, but rather as a *renewal* of essence *as* existence which amplifies the ethical problems posed by essentialism. Levinas takes Heidegger's notion that understanding is more originary than knowledge as if it would entail transferring the characteristics of theoretical knowledge to the whole of existence. Thus, he considers Heidegger's hermeneutics of facticity to be only a *renewal* of traditional ontology, consisting "in that the knowledge of Being in general – fundamental ontology – presupposes the *factual situation* of the mind (*l'esprit*) that knows," so that now the understanding of Being "does not presuppose a merely theoretical attitude but the whole of human comportment. The whole human being is ontology" (Levinas 1996b, pp. 2–3). Hence the object is completely absorbed into the subject, the exteriority falls back into immanence, "the other" in "the same," and fundamental ontology appears to be a new, more dangerous idealism.[10]

Nevertheless, fundamental ontology *is not* "the knowledge of Being in general," by which Dasein, as knowing subject, would gain dominance over existence. This is so not only because the "generality" of Being *is not* the universality of a genus and the ontological understanding of Being *is not* a knowledge that reduces difference to a common genus. But also because it is not "the knowledge of Being in general" but rather *the existential analytic of Dasein* that is fundamental ontology, "from which alone all other ontologies can take their rise," including the ontology of Being "in general," *des Seins überhaupt* (Heidegger 1962, p. [13]). Factical Dasein is *the ontic foundation of ontology*, for it is the only being who lives within an understanding of Being. Dasein does not *have* this understanding as its property, but *is* understanding: the very way in which Dasein exists, i.e. relates to beings, exhibits a certain interpretation (*Auslegung*) of the understanding of those beings' Being, including its own. And the existential analytic is *fundamental ontology* because it is

---

[9] That Levinas does not fully acknowledge Heidegger's destruction of subjectivity is already detectable in his commentary *Martin Heidegger and Ontology* (1932), where he says that *Being and Time* analyzes "the subjectivity of the subject" (Levinas 1996a, pp. 18, 26, 28).

[10] For a discussion of Levinas's interpretation of Heideggerian ontology as idealism, see Lilly 2008, pp. 43ff. As Lilly puts it, this interpretation is "a fantasm that simplifies Heidegger's thought"; Levinas "does not just misread Heidegger, but vigorously suppresses basic elements of Heidegger's thought whose recognition would have challenged his misreading" (ibid., pp. 35–36).

an ontological interpretation (*Interpretation*) of the ontic-existentiell understanding of Being, analyzed as one constitutive aspect of Dasein's Being.

By saying "the whole human being is ontology," Levinas unjustly conflates the ontic with the ontological. Actually, they are conjoined in a *fold*, being neither completely separate, nor quite identical. The human being is always already not ontological, but *pre*-ontological. The ontic-existentiell self-understanding becomes ontological only when factical Dasein interprets itself *formally*, disclosing what is true of each individual Dasein, and when it also thematizes the ultimate condition of possibility for its self-understanding. Thus, in *Being and Time* the formal interpretation of Dasein's *Being* – as *existence*, as *Being-in-the-world*, eventually as *care* – is followed by the unveiling of the *meaning* of Dasein's Being: *temporality*. In Heidegger's usage, "meaning" (*Sinn*) is not *what* is understood, which is the Being (of a being), but rather the *horizon* where the understanding of (that being's) Being is possible (ibid., p. 151).[11]

Since the meaning becomes explicit only in ontological discourse (ibid., p. 324), the distinction between *Being* and the *meaning* of Being[12] is crucial in our context. This distinction indicates the fold between *the existentiell understanding*, which understands a being's Being without thematizing it; and *the existential interpretation*, which thematizes not only the Being but also its meaning, i.e. the condition of possibility of ontological thematization itself.

The disregard for the ontico–ontological fold deeply informs Levinas's thesis that Dasein's understanding reduces the other to the same, and it is identifiable in the following phrase, where Levinas implicitly equates Being (which is, for him, a general concept) with its meaning, the horizon: "Since Husserl the whole of phenomenology is the promotion of the idea of *horizon*, which for it plays a role equivalent to that of the *concept* in classical idealism; the existent (*l'étant*) emerges against a background that exceeds it, as the individual [emerges] in relation to the concept" (Levinas 1969/1971, pp. 44–45/35; tr. mod.). However, neither Being nor its meaning are "a background that exceeds" beings. Being does not stand "behind" beings: it is *their phenomenality*. And the meaning of Being does not stand "behind" Being: it is *its* meaning (cf. Heidegger 1962, pp. 35–36). The meaning "exceeds" just the existentiell understanding, but only in the sense that it is not apparent within it.

Levinas's critique can be now paraphrased as follows: by the authentic ontic-existentiell understanding of its Being, factical Dasein[13] appropriates the *generality* of Being (thus confirming itself in its sameness) and, by understanding the other Dasein's Being, *reduces* him to the sameness entailed by their common apriori structures: care/temporality. So only as Dasein, irrespective of being a creature, I am

---

[11] By determining *temporality* as what makes possible the interpretation of Dasein's Being as *care*, the existential analytic fulfils its foundational role, permitting "the interpretation of *time* as the possible horizon for any understanding whatsoever of Being" (ibid., p. [1]).

[12] Certainly, Dasein's Being is not separated from its meaning, which is the meaning *of this Being itself* (ibid., p. [325]); but they are not indistinguishable.

[13] We must say *factical* Dasein because *it* is the one involved in a concrete existentiell relation – authentic/ethical or not – with the other, and not Dasein "in general."

incapable of "seeing" the other's otherness because I am immersed into an egoistic care for my own authenticity, regarded as appropriation of generality.

Nevertheless, the ontological thematization, so much denounced by Levinas, *does not* pertain to the existentiell (self-)understanding of factical Dasein. That Dasein, "in its very Being, has this Being as an issue" does not mean that it necessarily has this Being as a *theme*; this happens only when it understands itself ontologically. Surely, Heidegger has to analyze the existentiell understanding in *formal-existential* terms, saying that Dasein understands itself authentically only when it has become transparent to itself in all the constitutive aspects of its Being as *care*, including its *Being-with* other Daseins (ibid., p. 146). But this does not mean that factical Dasein understands itself authentically only if it understands itself *precisely* as "Dasein," "Being-with" or "care"! Actually, Dasein *is* its authentic understanding of its Being(-with), it *is* its authentic possibilities only as long as it "does not grasp [them] thematically," but lets itself *be* these possibilities (ibid., p. [145]). The existentiell understanding is not knowledge; not even transcendental knowledge.

Consequently, by understanding the other Dasein authentically, I do not "reduce" his individuality to his existential structures. Certainly, these structures which we share (as conditions of possibility for our own distinct individualization) *are* involved – thanks to them, the other discloses himself to me as another *human* – but they are not thematized. When I *am* my authentic understanding of the other, I do not privilege any generality over our individualities, *I just let them be*. Moreover, as I will argue below, letting myself be my individual potentiality-for-Being *entails* letting the other be his individual potentiality-for-Being, because as *Mit(da)sein* I am also responsible for the other.

5   *Mit(da)sein* and the Responsibility of One for the Other

Similarly to Levinasian responsibility, Dasein's responsibility is not derived from certain decisions or actions.[14] Having no pre-existing essence, Dasein is *always already* responsible for becoming itself; it has inscribed in its Being the responsibility for this Being. By not assuming it, Dasein does not escape the burden of individualization; it just exists inauthentically, unethically. By understanding itself authentically, Dasein does not become suddenly responsible, but finds itself already "subjected" to its inescapable responsibility.

The assumption of this responsibility cannot signify an exclusive, egoistic concern for "oneself." Dasein is Being-in-the-world and thus not merely Being-its-Self (*Selbstsein*) but, co-originarily, Being-with (*Mitsein*) *and* Dasein-with (*Mitdasein*). Factical Dasein is authentic only when it understands itself, formally speaking, as

---

[14] Of course, one important difference is that while Dasein's responsibility is more fundamental than accountability, Levinas's substitution is the reversal of it (cf. Raffoul 2010, pp. 163–219; 242ff).

"Dasein," i.e. when *all* the aspects that constitute equiprimordially its Being-in-the-world are disclosed to itself, including "Being-with" others, who are "Dasein-with" for it. And if we look closer at *Mitdasein* – which is usually neglected by commentators, despite its co-originarity with *Mitsein* (ibid., p. 114) – we can see perhaps more clearly that when factical Dasein understands itself authentically, when it finds itself to be inescapably responsible for letting itself be the one it can truly become, it finds itself to be *likewise responsible* for others; for their unique otherness.

While Being-with refers to one's own Dasein, making explicit that even in solitude it is always already with others; Dasein-with "characterizes the Dasein of others" – for the one who is Being-with (ibid., p. [121]). *Mitdasein* accentuates that the others appear to me not as jugs, lions or trees, but as "Daseins"; beings who are bound to become themselves. But most important is the *bidirectionality* indicated by *Mitdasein*: although Dasein-with characterizes the others, it is a constitutive aspect of *my* Being. Hence, it describes not just how they appear *to me*, but how *I* appear to them: as another *Dasein*. So when I understand myself authentically, I understand that I am – formally speaking – both "Being-with" others, who are "Dasein-with" for me, *and "Dasein-with" for others*, who are "Being-with" me. When I "see" the other, I "know" that he also "sees" me: I "see" myself as another Dasein for the other.

The co-originarity between *Mitsein* and *Mitdasein* shows how radically Dasein differs from a self-sufficient ego: *Mit*(*da*)*sein* indicates that one's factical existence entails *the exposure of one to the other*.[15] Thrown into a world shared with other Daseins – beings that understand one another (authentically or not) – *my existence is intertwined with the others' existence*; my ownmost possibilities of Being are intertwined with theirs.[16] Although nobody else can die or live in my "place" (inhabit my *ethos*), my existence is not a "private fact".[17] It is in each case *mine*, yet *shared* with others. This is the paradox (not the contradiction) of Heidegger's destruction of the subject, which prevents the "existential 'solipsism'" to be a genuine solipsism. Dasein's anxiety in the face of its death "discloses it as '*solus ipse*'" by isolating it from the indefinite "they," not from co-existence itself. Anxiety interrupts only inauthentic forms of the exposure and brings Dasein "face to face with itself as Being-in-the-world" (ibid., p. 188), as *Mit*(*da*)*sein*. In the existential interpretation of Dasein's Being-in-the-world as *care*, the relationship to others remains a constitutive aspect, as *care for* the other. Care is a plural structure whose unity is ensured by the co-originarity of its parts, which means that caring for the other is neither

---

[15] That Dasein's existence should be seen as exposure is emphasized by Nancy (1999, p. 207), who rightly argues for the need to radicalize *Mitsein* in order to dispel the apparent solipsism of Dasein's individualization. My insistence on the co-originarity between *Mitsein* and *Mitdasein* is one attempt in this direction.

[16] This becomes clear when, for example, somebody important to me dies and I feel that a part of me has died too, namely those possibilities that I could have realized (only) in relation to that person (together with or inspired by her).

[17] The idea that existence is a "private fact" (Levinas 1987, p. 41) deeply informs Levinas's – ultimately, unsustainable – thesis that Dasein is a solipsistic subject (cf. ibid., p. 65).

separate from, nor secondary to caring for oneself (ibid., p. 193). Therefore, being responsible for myself is intertwined with being responsible for the other.

More precisely, *Mit(da)sein* indicates that *my self-understanding comprises not only my understanding of the other, but also the other's understanding of me*. Being disclosed to myself, authentically, not merely as "myself" but as an other for others means "seeing" that their existentiell understanding of my Being – implicit in how they have related and might relate toward me – is constitutive of my self-understanding. My ownmost possibilities are given by my constitutive past (*Gewesenheit*), configured within my having been with-one-another: with my parents, teachers and peers, with all those to whom I have ever related (including those I have read and read about). When my potentiality-for-Being becomes transparent to me, I understand that *I am inescapably indebted to the others* for it[18] and, because I am an other for them, that *each of them is likewise indebted to me*. I am (co)responsible for the other's Being, for his care for himself *and the others*. Thus, paraphrasing Levinas, I am responsible even for the responsibility that the other has for me.

My responsibility is prior to my "resoluteness," which only modulates it authentically:

> Dasein's resoluteness toward itself is what first makes it possible to let the others who are with it "be" in their ownmost potentiality-for-Being, and to co-disclose this potentiality in the care for the other which leaps forth and liberates. When Dasein is resolute, it can become the "conscience" of others. (ibid., p. [298]; tr. mod.)

"Resoluteness" involves the will but, contra Levinas, it cannot be reduced to voluntarism.[19] It is the authentic mode of Dasein's disclosedness, where Dasein is *called into question* by the uncanniness of its Being (ibid., p. 276) and *finds itself* as constantly Being-guilty (*Schuldigsein*), responsible for its Being (ibid., pp. 286ff). Conscience's call is something "neither planned … nor voluntarily performed… 'It' calls, against our expectations and even against our will" (ibid., p. 275). *Dasein's will is only responsive*: "wanting to have a conscience" (*das Gewissen-haben-wollen*) is only Dasein's *understanding* of this call toward its ownmost potentiality-for-Being, by which Dasein *lets* itself *be* that potentiality (ibid., p. 288). Dasein does not ground itself; Dasein only assumes the responsibility to which it, as *thrown* ground (ibid., p. 284), is already "subjected."

This assumption of responsibility is my authentic *response* to the fact – ontologically interpreted as *Mit(da)sein* – of being thrown *into a common world* and, therefore, responsible for myself *and for the other*, whether I want it or not.[20] Because *I cannot avoid affecting the other*, I cannot be myself without this response. Being

---

[18] I am indebted to them even privatively for my potentiality-for-Being: even when someone does not respect my individuality, I still can understand, however implicitly, how I should be treated.

[19] The translation of *Entschlossenheit* by "resoluteness" (in French, "résolution") is dictionary-wise correct, but hermeneutically misleading: it loses the kinship with *Erschlossenheit*, "disclosedness," which is not under Dasein's control, it "is not the deliberate action of a subject" (Heidegger 1993a, p. 192).

[20] My Dasein "has, in Being-with others, already become guilty toward them" (Heidegger 1962, p. [288]).

authentic exceeds the logic of reciprocity; it means caring authentically also for those who do not care authentically for me (and might never will).

Because the other is part of my past so that I am constantly indebted to him for my potentiality-for-Being, my self is always already constituted by otherness.[21] It is so also because the ontico-ontological difference, where Being is "other" for being, is active within Dasein's relationship with its (potentiality-for-) Being: "*In conscience, Dasein calls itself*"; but the call "comes *from* me and yet *from beyond me*" (Heidegger 1962, p. 275). It comes from my *potentiality-for-*Being, my *possible* self, "who" is uncanny (*unheimlich*) for my they-self, accustomed to beings; it is "like an *alien* voice" (ibid., p. 277).[22] This indicates an irremediable dissymmetry, a "temporal noncoincidence with oneself" (Dastur 2002, p. 94). My possible self and my authentic self are not simply "the same." Through an existentiell modification of the existential "they" (Heidegger 1962, p. 130) and a disentanglement of my they-self from its inauthentic concretization; I am authentic as long as I remain *oriented toward* my ownmost possibilities. As long as I exist, I can never exhaust these. This "other," my own potentiality-for-Being, will always be beyond me – also because I cannot master the past where it has been constituted. Therefore, by understanding the other in his potentiality-for-Being, I "see" him not as an alter ego, but as an alter *aliud*. Contrary to Levinas's contention, to authentically understand the other does not mean to dominate him, because what is understood exceeds my control.

6   Conclusions

Unlike in Levinas, within the existential interpretation of the responsibility for the other that I have proposed; the other is other than oneself. However, otherness is already within oneself, although this is here understood not through a pre-originary substitution, but within the ontico-ontological fold. On the one hand, I am my potentiality-for-Being, which is "other" for my they-self; on the other hand, this potentiality-for-Being has been constituted within my relationships with others, to whom I am indebted (if even only privatively) for my authentic possibilities.

My freedom is finite not only because of my thrownness into death, but also because *I cannot avoid being exposed to* (i.e. *understood by*) *the other Dasein, nor affecting him* (i.e. *understanding him*). This is the *ethical* limit to my freedom: I cannot be authentic without assuming this double exposure. Levinas is wrong when he states that Dasein's finite freedom, being "measured by powers," pertains to "the ideal of the satisfied man, to whom all that is possible is permissible" (Levinas 1998, pp. 139–140). When I am disclosed to myself authentically, I "see" not only

---

[21] For a wider discussion of the heteronomy of Dasein's self, see for example Schürmann 2003, pp. 532 ff.

[22] It is uncanny because it is *other* – not "an anthropological or ontic other," for it is not a being (Raffoul 2010, p. 252). It is my Being.

my "powers" but also my limits – the boundaries which individualize me. I understand that the other Dasein, with whose existence mine is intertwined, is a limit to my freedom: I cannot be myself irrespective of – or at the expense of – the other.[23]

As I said initially, the point of showing that the "responsibility for the responsibility of the other" can be interpreted existentially has been to challenge Levinas's thesis that the ethical relation cannot be thought within Heidegger's fundamental ontology. Certainly, the responsibility entailed by the originary exposure to one another and the responsibility understood as a pre-originary "substitution of one for the other" are based on different assumptions (given Heidegger's methodological atheism and the "presence" of God in Levinas's ethics). But they are not completely divergent. To be sure, authentic care for the other is not substitutive: it does not "leap in" for the other, trying to live his life in his "place" (as overprotective parents do with their child) Rather, authentic care "leaps ahead" (*vorausspringt*) of the other, helping him "to become transparent to himself *in* his care and to become *free for* it" (Heidegger 1962, p. 122). But this means only that my assumed involvement in the other's existence should not hide from him his own care (e.g. I should not obscure my child's responsibility for her existence by spoiling her); I would not respect the other's otherness by doing so. This does not mean I should care for some abstract possibilities and remain indifferent to, in Levinas's words, "the wretchedness and bankruptcy" of the other, to what threatens his Being-in-the-world itself (e.g. I have to shelter the persecuted fugitive). Moreover, my Dasein's responsibility for the other is, like the Levinasian one, "a responsibility increasing in the measure it is assumed" (Levinas 1969, p. 244), because my assumed involvement in the other's existence increases the intertwining of our existences and, therefore, my indebtedness to the other.

Nonetheless, the responsibility of one Dasein for another Dasein is less radical than substitution, being limited by the fact that my relationship to the other remains authentic – i.e. ethical – only as long as it does not become a subtle form of avoiding the responsibility for my Being. Because this responsibility *involves* the responsibility for the other, this restriction does not make it a hidden form of egoism (e.g. the possibility of self-sacrifice is not excluded), but prevents this originary responsibility for the other from becoming an oppression of one's Dasein (which Levinas's substitution might seem to be). This would be also an oppression of the other Dasein, because forgetting oneself by "leaping in" for the other would suffocate his individuality. The responsibility interpreted as care for the other's care is limited by the respect for his responsibility.

Thus, an authentic "substitution" of the voice of the other's conscience can mean only that I, through an ethical *hypokrisis*, assume this voice, but only so as to *let* it *be*, without trying to make it "mine." When I understand authentically the other's potentiality-for-Being, I only "stand under" it, for it is a shared burden. I have to speak this silent voice if the other is not experienced in hearing it (as it is a child) or

---

[23] By doing this I would also violate the individuality of those others whose existence is intertwined with his existence and thus, *however indirectly*, with mine.

has forgotten it; but only in order to support it – since I am always already "subjected" to it, by the very fact of understanding it.

References

Bernasconi, Robert. 2002. What is the question to which "substitution" is the answer? In *The Cambridge Companion to Levinas*, ed. Simon Critchley and Robert Bernasconi, 234–251. Cambridge: Cambridge University Press.

Dastur, Françoise. 2002. The call of conscience. The most intimate alterity. In *Heidegger and practical philosophy*, ed. François Raffoul and David Pettigrew, 87–97. Albany: State University of New York Press.

Derrida, Jacques. 2001. Violence and metaphysics: An essay on the thought of Emmanuel Levinas [1964]. In Jacques Derrida, *Writing and Difference* (trans: Alan Bass), 97–192. London: Routledge.

Heidegger, Martin. 1962. *Being and Time* (trans: John Macquarrie and Edward Robinson). Oxford: Basil Blackwell.

Heidegger, Martin. 1993a. The origin of the work of art [1935–6] (trans: Albert Hofstadter). In Martin Heidegger, *Basic Writings*, ed. Davis Farrell Krell, 139–212. New York: Harper Collins Publishers.

Heidegger, Martin. 1993b. Letter on "humanism" [1946] (trans: Frank A. Capuzzi and J. Glenn Gray). In Martin Heidegger, *Basic Writings*, ed. David Farrell Krell, 213–265. New York: Harper Collins Publishers.

Husserl, Edmund. 1960. *Cartesian Meditations* [1929-] (trans: Dorion Cairns). Dordrecht: Springer.

Levinas, Emmanuel. 1951. L'Ontologie est-elle fondamentale?. *Revue de Métaphysique et de Morale* 1 (janvier-mars):88–98.

Levinas, Emmanuel. 1969. *Totality and Infinity. An Essay on Exteriority* [1961] (trans: Alphonso Lingis). Pittsburgh: Duquesne University Press. Levinas, Emmanuel. 1971. *Totalité et Infini. Essai sur l'extériorité*. Paris: Livre de Poche

Levinas, Emmanuel. 1987. *Time and the Other* [1948] (trans: Richard A. Cohen). Pittsburgh: Duquesne University Press.

Levinas, Emmanuel. 1990. Reflections on the Philosophy of Hitlerism [1934] (trans: Seán Hand). *Critical Inquiry* 17(1):62–71.

Levinas, Emmanuel. 1996a. Martin Heidegger and Ontology [1932] (trans: by The Committee of Public Safety). *Diacritics* 26 (1):11–32.

Levinas, Emmanuel. 1996b. Is Ontology fundamental? (trans: Simon Critchley, Peter Atterton, and Graham Noctor). In Emmanuel Levinas, *Basic Philosophical Writings*, ed. Adriaan Peperzak, Simon Critchley, and Robert Bernasconi, 1–10. Bloomington: Indiana University Press.

Levinas, Emmanuel. 1998. From the one to the other: transcendence and time [1983] (trans. Michael B. Smith and Barbara Harshav). In Emmanuel Levinas, *Entre Nous: On Thinking-of-the-Other*, 133–153. New York: Columbia University Press.

Levinas, Emmanuel. 2011. *Otherwise than Being or Beyond Essence* [1974] (trans: Alphonso Lingis). Pittsburgh: Duquesne University Press.

Lilly, Reginald. 2008. Levinas's Heideggerian fantasm. In *French interpretations of Heidegger. An exceptional reception*, ed. David Pettigrew and François Raffoul, 35–58. Albany: State University of New York Press.

Marion, Jean-Luc. 2005. A note concerning the ontological indifference [1998]. In *Emmanuel Levinas. Critical assessments of leading philosophers*, Levinas, phenomenology and his critics, vol. I, ed. Katz Claire and Trout Clara, 312–325. London: Routledge.

Marion, Jean-Luc. 2011. *The Reason of the Gift* [2008] (trans: Stephen E. Lewis). Charlottesville: University of Virginia Press.

Nancy, Jean-Luc. 1999. *La Communauté désœuvrée* [1983/1986]. Paris: Christian Bourgois.

Raffoul, François. 2005. Being and the other: Ethics and ontology in Levinas and Heidegger [1999]. In *Addressing Levinas*, ed. Nelson Eric Sean, Kapust Antje, and Still Kent, 138–151. Evanston: Northwestern University Press.

Raffoul, François. 2010. *The origins of responsibility*. Bloomington: Indiana University Press.

Schürmann, Reiner. 2003. *Broken Hegemonies* [1996] (trans: Reginald Lilly). Bloomington: Indiana University Press.

The Future of Deconstruction: Beyond the Impossible

Joseph Cohen and Raphael Zagury-Orly

Abstract The "…limits of truth" – this passage, retrieved from Diderot's *Essay on the Life of Seneca*, opens Jacques Derrida's *Aporias*. With this expression, Derrida is not simply placing his reflection under the tutelage of a philosophical heritage, in this case that of Diderot's and Seneca's; but also pointing towards the unsettling, ambiguous and equivocal, nature of this tradition. The unsettling nature of this tradition means, as always for Derrida, the aporetic movement which incessantly punctuates any tradition. We shall see that, for Derrida, our own "Western" philosophical tradition– its concepts, motives, intentions and meanings – is always and already engaged in an aporetic movement, never simply resolving or accomplishing itself, never capable of limiting itself to what it manifests or presents itself as. It is thus persistently and incessantly supplementing its ownmost determinations. We must hence assert from the outset of this essay: Derrida does not, as does Hegel or even, to a certain extent, Heidegger, philosophize from a signified endpoint of metaphysical thought or history.

Keywords Deconstruction • Positivity • Impossible • Aporia • Truth • Justice

The "…limits of truth"[1] – this passage, retrieved from Diderot's *Essay on the Life of Seneca*, opens Jacques Derrida's *Aporias*. With this expression, Derrida is not simply placing his reflection under the tutelage of a philosophical heritage, in this case that of Diderot's and Seneca's; but also pointing towards the *unsettling*, ambiguous and equivocal, nature of this tradition. The unsettling nature of this tradition means, as always for Derrida, the *aporetic* movement which incessantly punctuates *any* tradition. We shall see that, for Derrida, *our* own "Western" philosophical tradition – its concepts, motives, intentions and meanings – is always and already engaged in an *aporetic* movement, never simply resolving or accomplishing itself,

---

[1] Derrida, *Aporias*, tr. T. Dutoit, Stanford, Stanford University Press 1993, p. 1.

J. Cohen (✉)
School of Philosophy, University College Dublin, Dublin, Ireland
e-mail: joseph.cohen@ucd.ie

R. Zagury-Orly
Bezalel Academy of Arts and Design, Jerusalem, Israel

© Springer International Publishing Switzerland 2016   17
L. Foran, R. Uljée (eds.), *Heidegger, Levinas, Derrida: The Question of Difference*, Contributions To Phenomenology 86,
DOI 10.1007/978-3-319-39232-5_2

never capable of limiting itself to what it manifests or presents itself as. It is thus persistently and incessantly *supplementing* its ownmost determinations. We must hence assert from the outset of this essay: Derrida does *not*, as does Hegel or even, to a certain extent, Heidegger, philosophize from a signified *endpoint* of metaphysical thought or history. Derrida does not philosophize out of exigency to think the utmost possibility of reappropriating the "truth of philosophy" in the form of an "absolute knowledge" that would culminate in a systematic grasp of its development. Nor does Derrida philosophize from the possibility of *overcoming* the "forgetfulness of the meaning of Being" (where that forgetting is the *fact* of metaphysics or onto-theology) in the gesture of a *thinking* where *sojourning* within the unthought and concealed source, or origin, of its event is gathered or unified. For Derrida, our philosophical tradition deploys itself through incessant multiplications of *aporias* whose "indecision" between the "negative" and the "positive", the "impossible" and the "possible" never ceases to play itself out; never comes to a point where a resolution, a realization, an accomplishment, an "end of philosophy" can be declared, affirmed or stipulated; or adopt the form of a substantial and stable ground fixing a *unifying logos* of its meaning.

Three introductory remarks on the "experience" of the *aporia*:

1. Philosophical ideas, positions, norms, systematic unifications, however dynamic and inclusive, are inherently *aporetic*. They never simply limit themselves to their ownmost determinations – whether these be theoretical, practical, or aesthetic. There is always and already *more* to them than their determinations. More than what is determined by them. Philosophical concepts are exposed to their *supplement* incessantly conveying them *otherwise* than according to what they primarily are deemed to signify. This incessant movement does not emerge from an interior or exterior source, foundation or reason. It occurs through a dislocated and un-located movement of *differing*.

2. The *"aporetization"* of philosophical concepts is not however to be thought as a directing motive or a foundational modality operating within the history of philosophy. It is not a grounding "thesis" for the deployment of the history of ideas. For it is never reducible to the fundamental institution of a Law from which the history of these ideas could establish or re-establish itself. The *aporia* cannot therefore be simply reduced to a logical paradox, antinomy, or resolvable problem.

3. The *"aporetization"* is *at once and at the same time* inherent and heterogeneous to the deployment of the philosophical tradition. Which means: the history of philosophy – and for Derrida this history is not appropriable under one single orientation or simple direction and intention, but multiplies its own historicity always beyond its ownmost identity – ceaselessly undetermines itself beyond and outside of itself. This point is of capital importance. For it marks that the indetermination of the history of philosophy is *at one and at the same time* undecidably both reappropriable – through, for example, the figures of the "sublime", "difference", the "unthought", the "concealed" – and irreappropriable – through, for example, the figures of *"différance"*, the "spectre", the "to come [*l'à-venir*]".

The history of philosophy is thereby, for Derrida, always replacing, differing and transposing its identification by incessantly carrying itself to other trans-formations of itself according to an uncontrollable, disjoined, irrepressible deployment of *supplements*. For "the supplement supplements. It adds only to replace. It intervenes or insinuates itself *in-the-place-of*; if it fills, it is as if one fills a void. If it represents and makes an image, it is by the anterior default of a presence. Compensatory and vicarious, the supplement is an adjunct, a subaltern instance which *takes-(the)-place*. As substitute, it is not simply added to the positivity of a presence, it produces no relief, its place is assigned in the structure by the mark of an emptiness. Somewhere, something can be filled up *of itself*, can accomplish itself, only by allowing itself to be filled through sign and proxy. The sign is always the supplement of the thing itself."[2] In this sense, the history of philosophy arises from its emptiness and thus never simply masks a hidden origin from which it can grasp or seize the determinations of its own develop-ment but rather, incessantly voiding itself, necessarily evolves beyond any fixity or fixed resolute position.

Thinking the history of philosophy thus calls for the incessant multiplication of its inherent *aporias* always and already transposing its motives, intentions, meanings *wholly otherwise* than how these give or present themselves in the deployment of their historicity. The "impossible" pervades and permeates the very possibility of the history of philosophical thinking: it is "impossible" to fix and consequently affirm a *logos* capable of constituting or unifying the foundation or ground of think-ing; impossible thus to mark a sole directing orientation for the history of philo-sophical thinking. This "*aporetization*" does not resume itself in a "metaphysics of presence", nor does it constitute itself as an "originary *arche*" sustaining the philo-sophical tradition. It "intervenes and insinuates"[3] itself *otherwise* than through a *destruction* of the onto-theological tradition,[4] a destruction that would have meant showing that it is possible to think the "truth" of the history of philosophy from the horizon of its unthought or forgotten origin.

What occurs within this "*aporetization*" if it is neither a foundation nor a *destruc-tion* of the foundational structures of thinking? The "*aporetization*" is the *supple-mentary undecidability* of any distinction in the history of philosophical thought, whether past, present or future. In this sense, deconstruction remains attentive to any fixed conceptual opposition and suspicious of the modes through which these are repeated from past distinctions or emanate from entirely novel determinations.

---

[2] Derrida, *Of Grammatology*, tr. G. Spivak, Baltimore, J. Hopkins University Press, 1976, p. 145.

[3] *Ibid.*

[4] This is why Derrida states in the opening lines of Chapter I in *Of Grammatology* : "…it inaugu-rates the destruction, not the demolition but the de-sedimentation, the deconstruction, of all the significations that have their source in that of the *Logos*. Particularly the signification of *truth*. All the metaphysical determinations of truth, and even the one beyond metaphysical onto-theology that Heidegger reminds us of, are more or less immediately inseparable from the instance of the *logos*, or of a reason thought within the lineage of the *logos*, in whatever sense it is understood…". (p. 20).

Indeed, deconstruction incessantly questions the self-sufficient reason, usage or practice, from which distinctions, oppositions, divisions stem.

This is why Derrida does not only read the history of philosophy according to the idea – generalizable to *most* philosophers – that this history develops through repeated reductions. The idea of *reduction*, for Derrida – beyond the story it carries of engaging an entirely novel beginning in the reframing of philosophical ideas – requires its *deconstruction*. That is, the idea of *reduction* requires that it be rethought and re-questioned in itself and in the further oppositions and distinctions it engages. For Derrida, although the *motif* of reduction rethinks and reformulates inherited philosophical boundaries and limits, it nonetheless furthers and extends established metaphysical oppositions and distinctions. And, in this manner, the *motif* of reduction always and already conveys the need to revolutionize, resolve, accomplish, re-appropriate the leading question in the history of philosophy by situating it within the horizon of an *end*, of an *end-point*; of a finality from which a "new" or "novel" beginning for thought can be undertaken.[5]

Confronting the *logos* of reduction with its innermost strategies, and most particularly with the teleological order it imposes on thinking, Derrida frees up *another modality* occurring throughout the deployment of our philosophical tradition: for it is incessantly affected by countless, unpredictable and unforeseen *aporias*. And the point must be clearly made: these *aporias* never simply constitute *presuppositional structures* from which the history of philosophical reductions, confusions or apparent presumptions (anthropological, metaphysical, political…) can be comprehended. Derrida reveals, within our philosophical tradition, its inherent *aporias* by showing how and why these constitute both unavoidable determinations *and at the same time* unforeseen indeterminations of thinking. Everything happens as though the tradition keeps exhausting itself through its own concretization, and, unpredictably projects and invents itself through undetermined occurrences.

Our opening quotation points towards the "limits of truth". The quote indicates firstly that there is a limit to truth, a limit of truth, that truth *has* a limit, a limit which ought not to be surpassed, a "threshold of tolerance", so to say. Furthermore, that in philosophy one *ought* never to push truth to the limit, and – as Derrida recalls by completing Diderot's quotation – that it is a *fault*, "too often generalized", to let oneself be carried away *beyond* the "limits of truth". To allow oneself to be swept away *beyond* the limits of truth is to commit, not only a philosophical error, but also a grave and, in truth, unforgivable *trespass*.

This unforgivable *trespass* however already orients this quotation towards *another* meaning. A meaning which reveals another side of truth about the truth, another side to truth: that truth itself *is* limited, finite, restrained and contained within its borders, forcing then the question: *what could it mean to stand at the limits of truth?* This question opens to the double, undecided and aporetic position of being at once *within* truth *and* already as close as one can be to the *other* of truth. The *other* of truth here does not mean falsehood; it is never simply opposed to truth. The *other* of truth insinuates an *other* than the classical opposition between truth

---

[5] Derrida, *Of Grammatology, op. cit.*, p. 4 *sq.*

and falsity which yielded countless philosophical oppositions and distinctions: identity and difference, the Same and the Other, the exception and the rule, and the proper and the improper.

The French expression "*se tenir à la limite de la vérité*" is in fact open to both these possibilities of reading. It is precisely *both* of them that Derrida will deploy and expound at the same time, and thus *supplement* with yet a further possibility stressing the "*affirmative*",[6] let us say the *positive*, beyond Diderot's warning.

Affirmative is Derrida's word in *Aporias*. *Positive* is ours, although it too was used in *Of Grammatology*.[7] We wish to claim that this *positivity* is at the heart of deconstruction. And furthermore, we wish to add, deconstruction plays itself out precisely within this "positivity" which does not resemble in any manner whatsoever what we usually hear in this word. To state it outright: this *positivity* and/or "affirmativity" is, to paraphrase Levinas, a "*difficult*" *positivity* which must first be entirely dissociated from Hegel's concept of "positivity" as elaborated in his early theological writings. There, "positivity" means the rule of a heteronomous and foreign Law subjugating one in a complete abdication of one's autonomous will, and thus signifies the most radical submission to an exteriority where one cannot see, think or interiorize, and which remains a formal and abstract negation. In contrast, the *positivity* at work in deconstruction never simply subjugates the present, that which presents itself, to an *Aufhebung* whereby its negative would be relieved of its negativity and become the positive form of a truth comprehending its limits and capable of accomplishing itself in a "good conscience". Rather, the *positivity* of deconstruction will always and already have to *confront* and *endure*[8] the negative, and thus never reserve for it a particular role by giving the assurance and the certitude of a truth capable of resuming, asserting and grasping, its essence. The idea of *positivity* we here intend is invoked by a certain manner of *exposing* the negative whereby this operation, through its impracticability, designates an affirmative "engagement". It is here that deconstruction touches upon an idea of justice: through an irresolvable negativity there is an engagement with both the *refusal* of all forms or strategies of justification and the *unsatiated or unappeased desire* therein for a surplus or supplement of justice.

That which marks this *supplementary positivity* is found in the very opening pages of *Aporias*: "It remains, in these two cases, that a certain border crossing does not seem impossible…"[9] To speak of the "limits of truth" is also to disclose an opening to a "certain border crossing" *beyond* "the limits of truth". In effect, the philosophical concept of truth in the history of onto-theology has always sought to perfect itself by *surpassing* and *appropriating* any limitation which imposed itself upon it. This means that a certain relation between truth, presence, and the movement of appropriation and depropriation (in Heidegger, for example) organizes and constitutes the history of truth. In this sense, the history of truth has always been a history

---

[6] Derrida, *Aporias, op. cit.*, p. 19.

[7] Derrida, *Of Grammatology, op. cit.*, p. 4.

[8] Derrida, *Aporias, op. cit.*, p. 78.

[9] *Ibid.*, pp. 1–2.

of limits, of surpassing limits, of appropriating and overcoming boundaries, fron-tiers, oppositional limitations, conflicts, separations, crises, etc. Philosophy has always sought to deploy truth through a further ground capable of completing it, a deeper and more profound foundation from which truth could present itself as justi-fied or determined truth. The speculative idealist tradition (Hegel, most particularly) is clearly marked by this *desire* inscribed within the very notion of truth to develop itself *beyond* the theoretical limitations restricting it to the cognitive act of the sub-ject. One need only think of the Hegelian critique of Kant where Hegel seeks to surpass the idea of truth as "adequation" of the subject's cognitive capabilities and the object of possible experience by subsuming it within the absolute comprehen-sion of Spirit.

In this sense, claims Derrida in these opening passages of *Aporias*, to venture *beyond* the "limits of truth" in order to ground and found truth itself has always been the very project inherent in metaphysical inquiry and the history of truth. For Derrida however, this deployment, this development, this reconciliation between Truth and the totality of being in Spirit, far from having expressed the idea of truth, or more precisely *by having* expressed its very essence, prompts and provokes the *supplementary* question, itself the sub-title of *Glas*: "*what remains of absolute knowledge?*"[10] This question conceals other questions, in which one can already sense something of the modality of "deconstruction": *how ought we to orient think-ing, if we understand that thinking is never simply circumscribable by the possibility of comprehending and determining itself in the appropriation of truth?* Or again: *towards which "heading" is thinking to be summoned when it does not simply cul-minate in the movement where truth recognizes its ownmost essence as that which expresses "everything that is"* (Hegel)?

These last questions are aimed at Hegel's speculative reappropriation of absolute truth. They open towards the *other in* Hegel *beyond* Hegel through marking the irreappropriable remnants of Hegel's hetero-tautological speculative dialectic:

> "Everything that is, all time, precomprehends itself, strictly, in the circle of Absolute Knowledge, which always comes back to the circle, presupposes its beginning, and only reaches that beginning at the end. Trying to *think* (but this word already holds back in the circle) the remain(s) of time (but time already engages in the circle) that would not be, that would not come under a present, under a mode of being or presence, and that consequently would fall outside the circle of Absolute Knowledge, would not fall from it as *its* negative, as a negative *sound*, all ready to take up again the tangent in order to remain stuck to the circle and let itself be drawn back in by it. The remain(s), it must be added, would not fall from it at all…"[11]

But we could here formulate, in the same vein of deconstructive suspicion, different questions towards Heidegger. Of course, the first of these need to be posed in the terms set out by *Sein und Zeit*: *towards which futurity is Dasein summoned when, standing in both truth and un-truth and at the heart of this decisive duality, he remains determined to respond in attunement to the destiny of Being?* The second

---

[10] Derrida, *Glas*, tr. J.P. Leavy and R. Rand, Lincoln, University of Nebraska Press, 1987.
[11] *Ibid.*, p. 226.

question can also be advanced in relation to the later Heidegger: *toward which "height" or "depth" is thinking called when it responds only and solely to the truth of Being – that is, to the determinate "play" between concealment and unconcealment (A-letheia) of Being itself?* And, the third question: *towards which "turn" is thinking called when it is entirely determined by the determinate movement of a Kehre – however undetermined this movement may pretend to be – which fixes clearly and distinctly what Heidegger situates as both the "end of philosophy" and the "beginning of thinking"?*

These questions mark a certain opening towards the *unreapropriable* in thinking. Derrida situates thinking within a rapport with the *unreapropriable* and therefore marks that *thinking occurs undecidably as both unreapropriable and reappropriable.* This means first that for Derrida the *unreapropriable*, under the name of the "other", the "singular", the "event", etc., has always been the *affair* of philosophy, the dimension through which and by which philosophical appropriation deployed its very possibility. Clearly said, Derrida never claimed to access or approach a form or a content more unreapropriable than those thought by our philosophical tradition – an unreapropriable more unreapropriable than any other unreapropriable, to employ a phrasing familiar to Blanchot. For Derrida, rather, the claim would be the following: if there is such a thing as an unreapropriable, it always and already, at the same time and simultaneously, *translates* and does *not translate itself* in its *appropriation.* That is, the unreapropriable and the appropriable *undecidedly* substitute one for the other, themselves incessantly *differing* to the point where there is no order capable of grasping the movement of their distinction, difference, opposition. For Derrida, the unreapropriable does not constitute the originary event of the appropriable. And from this point of view the appropriable cannot constitute the *memorialization* of the unreapropriable. Both are undecidably and incessantly "replayed", "reformulated", "reactivated", each time in a singular manner.

In this sense, and we must emphasize it here, "deconstruction", contrary to how it has often been interpreted, is not a simple quest for a space *beyond* the determination of truth as if this space would constitute an objective place outside of truth. Derrida's thought is not a step outside the history of metaphysics. He would immediately question the pretention and legitimacy of such a step. Neither is Derrida's thought, however, a step within the history of metaphysics. "Deconstruction" is all at once a step *outside* and a step *within*, a step and a non-step – let us say here the *undecidability* of any possibility of arming oneself with the assurance of imposing on thought a resolute order: a "play" of the step within and of its refusal to situate itself entirely within. Rather than marking a space or a sphere which would stand outside truth or simply beyond the history of truth in the process of the history of Being, "deconstruction" insists on a *spacing* as an inherent "*aporetization*" within the essence of this history, of its concepts, of its languages. Every position from which directive norms or orders of determination are determined – even when these do not assert themselves as norms, orders or judgments properly said – would occur through their inherent *disjunction*. Which means: each and every position always and already *determines* and *undetermines* itself through the *same* movement of "deconstruction", of *undeconstructible auto-deconstruction*. We could also say:

every deconstruction is an *auto*-deconstruction and each *auto*-deconstruction is, as such, undeconstructible.

Derrida incessantly puts into question the structure of *presupposition*. Indeed "deconstruction" thinks *otherwise* – and this word is not chosen lightly for it means to mark that "*aporetization*" neither operates *against* nor *with* a presuppositional "logic". Derrida questions all the classical motives our philosophical tradition has constructed for this very "logic" – conscience, thinking, responsibility, sameness, foundation, reason etc. – *and* questions, at the same time, those informing their *reversal*: unconsciousness, unthought, Being, otherness, "visage". In this sense, "deconstruction" is not simply – a claim heard all too often since 1967 – a gesture which would consist in stepping beyond metaphysics identified as presence, logocentrism or ethnocentrism. Derrida states it bluntly in 1967, on the very first page of *Of Grammatology*. Deconstruction is not reducible to the simple desire to transgress the "limits of truth" in the effort to "do away" with truth. Rather, deconstruction opens a certain "*wake*" of truth and a certain "*safeguard*" of its "limits".

But let us proceed very carefully with these words – *wake* and *safeguard* – which carry an undoubtable Heideggerian weight.

This "*wake*" and this "*safeguard*" operate according to an entirely other modality than that which seeks to explicate the "Truth of Being" as "donation". For Derrida, it is not about glimpsing a more undetermined event than Heidegger's *Ereignis*. Rather, what Derrida marks is an entirely other modality operating within the very structure of donation – entirely other than that which seeks to gain a *glimpse* towards the source of what is given, of the retained or concealed, kept and safeguarded resource of donation. As if Derrida was here posing the question: why would we not also see, in this return to the *spacing* which gives presence, a type of determination *other* than the determined realm of entities?

We are already departing here from the Heideggerian lexicon and analytic of these words. In truth, we are departing from the modality that seeks to isolate and differentiate the improper and the proper, the unconcealed and the concealed. In this sense, deconstruction commands a "*safeguard*" of truth, its limits, its process, its presence, keeping it to a *wholly other possibility* than the determination of truth, or than the conditions of possibility capable of determining truth. *We shall see that for Derrida this possibility is the impossible.* That is the *at least* double, undecided and undecidable, movement of the *indeterminable determining itself* and at the same time *the determinable undertermining itself.* This at least double movement inhabits, according to Derrida, each and every concept we can think. We will return to this "ambiguous and bizarre logic", as Derrida calls it. But suffice it to say for now that, for Derrida, this "safeguard" of truth never assures a *dividend* or secures a *gain* for truth – that is, will never guarantee anything of truth or for truth. It does not assure a *presence* of truth or a presentation of what *is* truth. Rather: it *projects* any "determination" or "actualization" of truth into its *impossible,* as if to *think truth* is to incessantly rivet truth to the exhaustion or the emptying out of its possible determinations.

The question of truth needs to be wholly re-formulated. Its reformulation will now be: according to which Law is truth "guarded" and "safeguarded" from *empty-*

ing itself out in its determination? Of wearing itself out in its very possibility? The question here is: why does truth require another Law for its possibility? For, all traditional modalities of the Law engage a type of "enframing" in which what is so conditioned is thereby also consumed, worn out, negated.

This is a truly *edgy* question. Perhaps, it inaugurates an entirely novel *drama* in the history of philosophy – a drama which Nietzsche, more than Heidegger, approached without engaging with it entirely. This drama replays the entire question of *access* to truth. It reformulates the question of *access* to that which constitutes concepts *per se* in our philosophical tradition.

What Derrida is pointing at is that the justificatory movement of truth, its possibility, – through its own historical deployment – destroys itself, and thus that nothing is left of truth in its determination as truth and in its presentification *as such*. And hence, Derrida risks the following: truth *differs* outside its determination, *replays* itself incessantly, *breaches* its own modality to the point where it discloses itself as always *haunted* by a *wholly other than truth occurring within the determination of truth*. The determination of truth is other to itself each time it deploys its possibility, each time it affirms itself. For Derrida, this radical impossibility of fixing or naming truth leaves it *without* origin, foundation or presupposition for its own determination. In this sense, deconstruction seeks to accompany as far as possible the deep philosophical motives of origin, foundation and presupposition by developing their inherent *aporetic movement* that is, to the point where they cease to organize themselves in accordance with their own logic. Origin, foundation and presupposition always and already supplement themselves *beyond* themselves to the point where they are not thinkable as origin, foundation and/or presupposition. Their *auto-deconstructive* movement opens to an incessant reformulation of their possible meaning – possible to the point where they could begin to produce countless other irrecuperable and irreappropriable performatives. Deconstruction forces these performatives to respond to an unpredictable *play* within themselves – an unpredictable play of *indeterminations*.

This *play* is perhaps what we could already call here the *positivity of deconstruction*. A *certain positivity of indeterminations, of incessant play inherent to every concept of our tradition* which would open the space, the spacing, the extension for these concepts to always and already come otherwise than through their own presentation. We are here touching what Derrida sometimes called the *without*, let us say: the *positivity of the without*. As if the inherent deconstruction of truth opened, not only an exhaustion of the determination of truth in its own determination, but within truth and yet beyond truth, within truth *without* truth, a certain idea of *justice* irreducible to truth. A *certain positivity* signalling towards that which *could arrive otherwise* than legitimized by the frontiers and the contextualization, the development and the deployment of truth.

What could this *positivity* mean? Why and how does it engage with justice? And how does it maintain a relation to truth in its relation to justice? Towards which future, but also towards which past and which present, could it project thinking? And towards which horizon – if one can still speak here of horizon – could it lead man, woman, God, animal? What could be signified by a *thinking* which would not be solely comprehended through the determination of truth, but by the *wholly other than truth in truth*?

This *positivity* is marked in Derrida's writing by the phrase found in 'Force of Law,' a proposition Derrida borrows from Levinas' *Totality and Infinity*. The phrase reads as follows: "*Truth supposes Justice*". To which one must add another phrase Derrida subscribes to, in his words, "without reservation" (announcing the *indeconstructibility* of justice): "justice – the relation to the other".

What do these propositions mean? How are we to understand and think this incessant movement of auto-deconstruction when it does not close itself off in a unilaterality, a sealed system but rather disseminates constantly what it produces? How are we to think this movement which both accompanies and differs from any thought *per se* or system of thought: be it critique, dialectic, onto-phenomenological, hermeneutic, etc.? How are we to understand "deconstruction" when it does not bring about the scene of a promise, of a *telos*, and does not convey anything like a *turn*, nor does it carry the hope or the "Good News" of a *turn*, nor does it even claim any grasp of that which we refer to and cannot avoid referring to in any discourse or action (be it political, moral, scientific, artistic, etc.) How to understand a truth *supposed* by justice when we understand that justice is not here establishing or instituting, does not incarnate itself in a presence or a principle of justification, and that this supposition is not comprehended in any historical frame whatsoever? Derrida suspects that the language of the *turn* remains affected by a massive structure of presupposition (of course, not a foundational presupposition, but nonetheless a determined structure orchestrating the modality of the *turn* itself, one which is determined by the strictly double relation between the veiled origin of presence and its unveiled presentification). This determined structure maintains itself from *Being and Time* on; it is radicalized throughout Heidegger's writings even when a seemingly undetermined movement appears to be working and informing its very deployment. For Derrida, and although he accompanies Heidegger's path of thinking, the entire idea of the *turn* – in order for it to remain meaningful, in order for it to address us, in order for us to be responsible for it – rests and counts on, remains determined by the idea of *donation*. That is, the idea that donation maintains itself through holding onto and preserving two poles – two poles which are kept within the event and the gift of Being, and of which we are called to think: the proper and the improper/ the *lethe* and the *a-lethe*. And took Derrida to pose the question: perhaps thinking occurs *otherwise* than according to the predominance of donation? Perhaps Derrida urges to thinking *without* origin, next to and within the desire of origin, the opening of the unforeseen dissemination of *presences*. In his words, in *Given Time*: "Is there any other definition of desire?"[12] A desire other than the "desire to accede to the property of the proper"[13]? As if this discourse was simultaneously driven by the possibility of opening that which conditions thinking and that which un-conditions it: another definition of the desire to think.

---

[12] Derrida, *Given Time: The Counterfeit Money*, tr. P. Kamuf, Chicago and London, University of Chicago Press 1992, p. 22.

[13] *Ibid.*

This ought not to mean that justice would serve as a novel and re-discovered foundation for truth. Justice is not, for Derrida, the *condition of possibility* of truth. In this sense, Derrida does not simply *turn on its head* the classical conception of "truth as foundation of justice" and arrive at the formulation of "justice as foundation for truth". Rather – to quote here from Derrida' in some of the most beautiful and powerful pages on Levinas in *Adieu*[14] – this proposition *alters* and *defies* the "logic of supposition and conditionality", inasmuch as it exhausts the possibility of stipulating a ground or a foundation. It marks that justice *haunts* truth without justice composing or constituting a foundation of truth and at the same time without truth ever being capable of seizing or grasping justice within itself. For Derrida, hence, what is engaged by this proposition, *"Truth supposes Justice"*, is a certain *de-foundation* of truth exposing it to the *spectrality* of justice: that is, to its undeconstructible indetermination. It is thus an entirely other manner of affecting truth – otherwise than according to the "logic of supposition". Justice, for Derrida, will be thought as a *spectral indetermination* – the *spectre* is both that which never shows itself and yet returns (le *revenant*) to haunt the place of stable and fixed determinations of truth as well as the innumerable definitions and variations of and on truth. Truth *occurs* through this *spectral indetermination* but never finds a condition of possibility or actuality. The impossibility of truth determining itself as such supposes the *indeterminability* of justice. Justice marks that truth *never* determines itself as such in its ownmost determination; truth always appears in the impossibility of its determination.

This is precisely why truth is always and already *auto-deconstructible*, why truth *deconstructs itself*. Truth as it appears is always and already deconstructing itself into an impossible determination of itself. In this sense, truth occurs, presents itself, appears, but as already and always deconstructed, that is where its possible determination marks the impossibility of its determination, the impossibility of presenting itself as that which it asserts itself to be. Truth occurs, presents itself always and already as *aporetic*. However, this *aporia* in the very "essence of truth" does not mean that there is *no possible truth* or no *possibility for truth*. Rather, it means that the very possibility of truth is exhausted in its determination, in its presence, in its presenting itself and thus that if the possibility of truth is *preserved* it can only be so by the *impossibility* of truth grounding itself in a fixed determination of its presence. This means: truth proceeds as *aporia*. It does not determine itself from a ground or a foundation, hidden or manifest, it rather lies in the incessant movement of its own *"aporetization"*. Truth, in this sense for Derrida, does not lie in a hidden structure waiting to be revealed by an act of interpretation or a modality of comprehension. Truth, always and already exhausting itself in its own determination, in its own presentation – *and such would be the sentinel and safeguard of its possibility* – is always *to come*. It proceeds from an indeterminable justice – that is it incessantly aporetizes itself. This is why Derrida always reasserts the *otherness of truth in the expression of truth*. This otherness opens towards a *differing* where what is deter-

---

[14] Derrida, *Adieu – to Emmanuel Levinas*, tr. P.-A Brault and M. Naas, Stanford, Stanford University Press, 1997.

mined as truth, what is labelled as truth, is always and already *other* than truth, it is always and already the impossibility of any determination of truth.

It is precisely this *"différance"* which must be thought, according to Derrida: truth is that which arrives as always *other* than what effectively has arrived, does arrive or could arrive.

This *"différance"* at the *heart* of "deconstruction" marks that it, "deconstruction", is not bound by truth. For "deconstruction" occurs where the order of truth is already and always at the mercy of *an other* than the actuality and the possibility of truth. In this sense, "deconstruction" seeks to unleash a regime where the "gift" of truth remains *without* its givenness, a truth given *without* it being given through its determination or actualization.

Derrida deploys this incessant "deconstructibility" of truth by stating that truth is always exposed to the *indeconstructibility of justice*. This "indeconstructibility of justice" is the core meaning of the phrase "Truth supposes Justice". Certainly this "indeconstructibility" of justice appeared in Derrida's writing as a surprise; in many regards it produced profound astonishment. It appears in "Force of Law: The 'Mystical Foundation of Authority'"[15] – a conference Derrida held at the Cardozo School of Law at the Yeshiva University in New York – where the directing question was to "define" "deconstruction" through its possible relation, if any, to *justice*. Derrida answered this task by the surprising claim according to which "deconstruction" was always and already occurring through and as the "indeconstructibility of justice". And that justice was, then, for the incessant work of "deconstruction", *indeconstructible*.

What is meant by this *indeconstructibility of justice*? How are we to think this indeconstructibility of justice where, for Derrida, everything *deconstructs itself*?

It needs to be said from the outset that *justice is always of the other*. Justice is always desiring the other within the same. Desiring the undetermination of truth within the determination of truth. What does this claim entail? It marks that justice as indeconstructible never exhaust itself in truth, never simply returns to itself in any or all determinations of truth and thus remains radically untranslatable as truth. Why? Because justice is not, for Derrida, outside, opposite or distinct from truth, but rather is indeconstructible within truth, incessantly haunting truth, forcing truth to its irreapropriability. Justice incessantly engages truth in the movement of its auto-deconstruction and makes it impossible that truth could ever appropriate or reappropriate its ownmost auto-deconstruction.

This is why for Derrida justice is riveted to an incessantly "differing time". Justice as indeconstructible works in the past, future and present – that is, insists on the impossibility for the auto-deconstruction of truth to terminate itself, to accomplish and realize itself entirely. Insists on the impossibility for truth to resolve and content itself in a limit. In "deconstruction", contrarily to the history of metaphysics in its prioritization of truth, the auto-deconstruction of truth can never limit itself. Why? For it is, always and already, impossible for truth to comprehend itself as

---

[15] Derrida, "Force of Law: The 'Mystical Foundation of Authority'", in *Deconstruction and the Possibility of Justice*, (Eds. D. Cornell, M. Rosenfield and D. G. Carlson, London, Routledge 1992.

justice. And inversely it is impossible for justice to limit itself to truth. Impossible, that is, for truth – despite the history of metaphysics – not to engage in an auto-deconstruct of itself and thereby open to the fragile possibility of being exposed to the *trace* of justice. This fragile possibility within truth of tracing an indeconstructible justice rebels against all limits to truth, all limitations imposed on truth, as well as all limits or limitations imposed on truth by truth…

References

Derrida 1976. *Of Grammatology*. Trans. G. Spivak. Baltimore: J. Hopkins University Press.

Derrida. 1987. *Glas*. Trans. J.P. Leavy and R. Rand. Lincoln: University of Nebraska Press.

Derrida. 1992a. *Given Time: Counterfeit Money*. Trans. P. Kamuf. Chicago: Chicago University Press.

Derrida. 1992b. Force of law: The 'Mystical Foundation of Authority'. In *Deconstruction and the possibility of justice*, ed. D. Cornell, M. Rosenfield, and D.G. Carlson. London: Routledge.

Derrida. 1993 *Aporias*. Trans. T. Dutoit. Stanford: Stanford University Press.

Derrida. 1997. *Adieu – to Emmanuel Levinas*. Trans. P.-A Brault and M. Naas. Stanford: Stanford University Press.

The Gift and the Skin: Derrida and Levinas on Language, Metaphor and Subjectivity

Arthur Cools

Abstract In this article, I discuss the ambiguous role of metaphor in the philosophies of Emmanuel Levinas and Jacques Derrida. In line with Heidegger's criticism of metaphor as a means of metaphysical thinking, both relate language to an otherness that exceeds any ontological clarification. However, both reintroduce basic metaphors in order to be able to address the question of subjectivity: the skin in Levinas' analysis of substitution in *Otherwise than Being*, the gift in Derrida's writings, in particluar his readings of Plato's *pharmakon*. In focusing on these two metaphors, I have a double intention: to show that they are indeed 'basic' and that they reveal the different orientation of both philosophies in an irreducible way. My main argument in order to achieve this goal is rather paradoxical: it consists in arguing that the appearance of the metaphor of the skin in Levinas' philosophy and that of the gift in Derrida's are dependent upon the way each of them conceives the non-metaphorical relationship of language to otherness, that I call "otherness by excess" in the case of Levinas and "otherness by default" in the case of Derrida.

Keywords Metaphor • Subjectivity • Metaphysics • Language • Substitution

In this article, I will address the persistent differend between Emmanuel Levinas and Jacques Derrida. I will approach it by focusing on the concept of language. Language is definitely a central issue in both philosophies. However, they do not speak the same language. In the differend between the two, the distinction between written and spoken language *seems* to be essential. From a Derridian point of view, Levinas' philosophy is an example of logocentrism: it defines language as discourse spoken to the other person. According to Levinas' view, Derrida's differential language of writing entails a materialism which neutralizes meaning in an endless chain of signifiers. While this opposition is not entirely wrong, it is perhaps too simplistically stated to clarify what is at stake in their differend. In fact, this way of presenting their differend avoids two main questions, the answers to which determine the meaning of the opposition mentioned: How is language related to an

A. Cools (✉)
Centre for European Philosophy, University of Antwerp, Antwerp, Belgium
e-mail: arthur.cools@uantwerpen.be

© Springer International Publishing Switzerland 2016   31
L. Foran, R. Uljée (eds.), *Heidegger, Levinas, Derrida: The Question of Difference*, Contributions To Phenomenology 86,
DOI 10.1007/978-3-319-39232-5_3

irreducible otherness (how can it be)? And, how is subjectivity dependent on a linguistic relationship (how does it appear from it)? Considering these two questions, I will show that both Levinas and Derrida are caught in a similar paradox: while the use of metaphor becomes inevitable in addressing the second question, the first question is at odds with any metaphorical understanding of language.

One may wonder why we introduce the notion of metaphor in order to elucidate the insistent differend between the two, as both Derrida and Levinas are critical with regard to the use of metaphor, which cannot encapsulate their respective understanding of language. In the first section below, I will examine this critical stance towards metaphorical language and briefly summarize the influence of Heidegger's criticism of metaphor as a means of metaphysical thinking. It is important to recall this criticism because it opens the possibility of another relationship between language and otherness (unlike that of metaphor). This non-metaphorical relationship is crucial to explain the differend between Levinas and Derrida. I will call the otherness to which language is related 'otherness by default' in the case of Derrida and 'otherness by excess' in the case of Levinas. In the second section of the article I will argue that both philosophies inevitably reintroduce a metaphorical understanding of language because they are confronted with the difficulty of how to consider language as a relationship from which subjectivity appears. I will focus on two basic metaphors: the skin, which plays a major role in the metaphorical operation in Levinas' analysis of subjectivity in *Otherwise than Being*; and the gift, which is mentioned in many different ways in Derrida's texts but introduces in particular a metaphorical displacement, as is shown, for example, in his reading of Plato's *pharmakon* in 'Plato's Pharmacy' and of Kierkegaard's interpretation of Abraham's sacrifice in *The Gift of Death*.

1   Language Beyond Its Metaphysical Determination

Derrida's and Levinas' approaches to language have a common ground. Both point out that it is not sufficient to define language within the limits of a metaphysical understanding. For both, language is never just a means to articulate the essences or the properties of essences captured by the activity of thinking. Language first opens a relationship that precedes the conceptual clarification of thought. Moreover, both reject the hermeneutic understanding of this opening, as articulated by Martin Heidegger in *Being and Time*, who grounds language in the original disclosedness (*Erschlossenheit*) of *Dasein* and relates any propositional expression to the original understanding of world (Heidegger 1996, §44). The opening to which Levinas and Derrida refer precedes the understanding of world, as well as the comprehension of my own relationship to being. For both, the relationship opened by language entails an otherness that exceeds any ontological clarification.

Whether defined as 'discourse' as is the case in *Totality and Infinity* or as 'Saying' (*Dire*) in *Otherwise than Being*, according to Levinas language is the opening of a relationship to an otherness which does not yet belong to the world and which does not disappear in this relationship, but remains 'non-touchable' and 'absolute' in the sense of 'separated' (Levinas 1969, p. 172). The expression of the face of the other person is necessary in order to articulate the sense of the opening of language and the manifestation of its otherness. Derrida, however, approaches the otherness to which language is related in terms of writing (*écriture*). Writing considered as 'the origin of language' (Derrida 1976, p. 44) is the far-reaching consequence arising from the linguistic renewal found in Ferdinand de Saussure's *Cours de linguistique générale*. It implies the subverting idea that it is not sufficient to describe the opening of language within the limits of metaphysical concepts, such as logos, reason, meaning, presence, consciousness, but that it is necessary to reverse the relationship of dependence between these notions and writing. From this perspective, the written text is not the deficient modus of attesting to the truth of metaphysical concepts, but, on the contrary, the metaphysical understanding of language appears to be the effect of a production of significations from a chain and displacement of signifiers, the differential relations between which are uncontrollable.

Let us examine more precisely how otherness is at stake in these two different approaches to language. It might be that the difference between the two implies a different criticism of the metaphysical determination of language. The later Heidegger offers a clear starting point from which to assess this difference. In a famous passage from *The Principle of Reason*, Heidegger considers metaphor to be 'the norm' (*das Maß*) of the metaphysical determination of language. He seems to refer to the Platonic tradition when he recalls that the transfer of meaning, characteristic of metaphor, presupposes the distinction between the sensible and the non-sensible. This distinction defines, according to Heidegger, 'a basic trait of what is called metaphysics and which normatively determines Western thinking' (Heidegger 1991, p. 48). It also determines the traditional understanding of language. Heidegger thus calls metaphor 'the norm for our conception of the essence of language' (Ibid.). In other words, as the linguistic transference from the sensible to the non-sensible, metaphor provides the norm for the metaphysical determination of language.

In this respect, Heidegger's reflection on metaphor reveals that the search for a language beyond its metaphysical determination implies a criticism of the metaphorical understanding of language. While we will find a similar criticism in Levinas' and Derrida's approaches to language, Heidegger helps us to understand how otherness comes into play and, more precisely, how language, beyond its metaphysical determination, relates to an irreducible otherness. In his approach to the essence of language in his *Brief über den Humanismus*, Heidegger uses the expression 'the house of being'. This expression intends to think language originally, namely 'from its correspondence *to* Being and indeed as this correspondence' (Heidegger 2011, p. 161). Therefore, it seems mistaken to interpret the expression 'the house of being' merely as a metaphor. Nevertheless, the expression obviously entails a transfer of meaning between something familiar to human beings, the house in which they live, and something unfamiliar, the essence of language. This way of transferring meaning is clearly metaphorical according to Aristotle's general definition of metaphors in his *Poetics*: 'metaphor consists in giving the thing a name that belongs to something else' (1457a30-b10, Aristotle 1984, p. 2332). In his commentary on this expression in 'The Retreat of Metaphor', Derrida remarks that the direction of this transference is in fact the reverse of that which Aristotle attributes to metaphors (Derrida 2007, pp. 69–70). In Aristotle's view, metaphors enable us to learn something new: they transpose a property of a being we are familiar with, to a being to which we have not yet applied this property. In Heidegger's use of 'the house of being', however, the direction of transfer is reversed: it 'does not disclose being in the light of the familiarity of a house, but rather robs the house of its familiarity and homeliness' (Van der Heiden 2013, p. 231). The expression 'the house of being' does not intend to make us appropriate the sense of being by a dwelling with which we are familiar, but on the contrary to uproot our experience of dwelling and being at home by revealing the strangeness – the un-homeliness (*das Unheimliche*) – of the original sense of being.

This interpretation shows how the experience of otherness is at stake in the search for language beyond its metaphysical determination. In Heidegger's view, the use of metaphor conceals the original understanding of language similarly to the way metaphysics does with regard to the understanding of being. On this basis, the task to 'overcome' (*überwinden*) metaphysics implies undoing this concealment, to dismiss the metaphorical understanding of language and to reveal the strangeness of being that withdraws from any metaphysical determination. The meaning of otherness cannot be described in the same way in Levinas' approach to language. His criticism of metaphor is not limited to the metaphysical distinction between the sensible and the intelligible, but is directed against the naturalizing aspects of the metaphorical transference, which he detects in the history of Western philosophy and especially in Heidegger's predilection for formulas such as (up)rootedness as a way of dwelling, the light of being, or nature speaking through the voice of man. Metaphorical language is an expression of what Levinas calls ontological thinking, the main feature of which he defines in terms of the logic of participation: 'Participation is a way of referring to the other: it is to have and unfold one's own being without at any point losing contact with the other' (Levinas 1969, p. 61). Participation therefore involves the omnipresence of a totality: it implies that the meaning of any single being is dependent on the whole in which it takes part. This characteristic makes metaphorical language reductive in a fundamental way.

One can distinguish the following criticisms. The metaphorical transfer of meaning defines a common trait that is essential for every single part of the whole. In this respect, it is unable to account for each single being in relationship to its own being, but only capable of determining it in function of its relationship to the whole – the common ground in which it takes part. Moreover, this common ground, to which metaphors refer in order to create a correlation; is itself something mute and limitless, which Levinas calls the 'elemental' (Ibid., pp. 130–2). Every single being is immersed in it and cannot detach itself from it. This immersion entails the danger of a naturalization. Since the metaphorical transference does not exclude reciprocity between the different parts of the transfer, the mute and unlimited ground concerns and submerges the essence of each single being in an equally arbitrary way, as it is expressed by it. As a result, what is considered as a humanization of the natural being (for example, in expressions such as 'the stream of consciousness', 'the light of being' or '*homo homini lupus*') can be equally considered as a naturalization of the human being.

The meaning of the face, as analyzed by Levinas, is clearly at odds with these features of metaphorical language. First and foremost, it expresses the idea of separation and as such it breaks with the logic of participation. The face relates me to an otherness – the otherness of the other – without the possibility of reducing it to the same and without the possibility of synchronizing it with the same by immersion in a third (by integrating it into a whole). Moreover, the face opens the possibility of language – discourse beginning with the act of responding to the other – without binding its otherness into the reciprocity of a correlation and beyond any movement of immersion in the elemental. Finally, the face disentangles the double bind of the naturalization of human relationships because it elevates me in a personal, human way by calling me to respond, and by directing my response to the otherness of the other person. As a result, the otherness of the face is at once absolute, separated and detached from the relationship in which it becomes present, and yet meaningful in an immediate, non-figural way because it touches me and penetrates me without allowing me to undo or to escape its penetration, and without me being sufficiently equipped to receive it. In other words, in Levinas' view, it is not sufficient to say that the otherness of the face is concealed and that it withdraws from any ontological determination, as Heidegger does with regard to the strangeness of being, rather it is necessary to say that the meaning of the face insistently breaks through its concealment and persecutes me without any possibility of appeasement. It persistently disturbs the ontological order, exceeding it in an excessive way, that is, by resisting its reductive logic and disrupting its closure. For this reason, I call it an otherness by excess: it is beyond any norm that is able to create an equivalence; it invades, disturbs and intervenes in the order of the same as a persistent disruption.

Derrida's criticism of the metaphysical determination of language takes a different direction. It does not concern metaphorical language as such, but the concept of metaphor, that is, the discourse that attempts to establish a clear distinction between metaphorical language and non-metaphorical language. This discourse is characteristic of metaphysics, which grounds its own logos in the opposition between concept and metaphor and which, moreover, subordinates the equivocality of the latter to the transparency of the former. Derrida thus also subscribes to the Heideggerian claim that the concept of metaphor is only given within the limits of metaphysics. However, in his broader meta-reflection, Derrida points to what he calls 'the condition for the impossibility' (Derrida 1982, p. 219) of developing an adequate concept of metaphor. In this perspective, his criticism also includes a critical stance with regard to Levinas' attempt to define and dismiss metaphorical language.

In fact, Derrida's criticism shows at once the impossibility of escaping and the impossibility of controlling the metaphorical use of language. Traditionally, philosophical discourse distinguishes between effective metaphors (vivid metaphors) and erased metaphors (death metaphors). This distinction is established on the basis of the concept of the erosive use of metaphors, which become accepted in common language as expressions of ideas. Philosophical discourse thus recognizes the metaphorical displacements in common language and defines at once as its proper task to retreat from the use of vivid metaphors. According to Derrida, the notion of use and the concept of erosion, however, are not sufficient to establish the distinction mentioned. Philosophical discourse is not able to define a restrictive economy of metaphorical transfers. The whole project of developing an adequate concept of metaphor is itself based upon 'a blind spot or central deafness' (Ibid., p. 228). The concept of metaphor is necessarily a philosophical product and belongs therefore to the inside of philosophical discourse. However, it requires the possibility of an external position with regard to all metaphorical transfers of the language on which this same discourse is dependent.

Derrida's criticism of the concept of metaphor discovers what he calls the metaphoricity of language that precedes the distinction between metaphor and concept. It implies that the concept of metaphor and the metaphysical determination of language are not able to exhaust or fix the transfers and displacements of language. It implies moreover that we can never gain access to language as language, either within or beyond its metaphysical determination. For Derrida, the search for the original understanding of the essence of language is based upon the illusion that it is possible to retreat from the metaphorical use of language. This search for the origin or the essence or the proper use of language is itself an effect of the metaphysical understanding of language. Metaphoricity, as Derrida introduces it, cannot be described using the same oppositions behind the distinction between concept and metaphor, for example: literal/figural, proper/improper, sensible/intelligible, vivid/death, original/derivative.

The strangeness that this metaphoricity evokes undermines any constitution of meaning, including the meaning or experience of otherness beyond the metaphysical determination of being. The displacements and transfers of the metaphoricity of language are not limited to the movement of reversing the metaphorical transfer from the familiar to the uncanny, as Heidegger understands it when he dismisses a metaphorical understanding of the expression 'the house of being'. They precede the distinction between familiar/uncanny. They do not reveal, beyond any use of metaphor, a primordial and immediate meaning of otherness that is absolute and detached from the relationship in which it appears, but that nevertheless breaks through its concealment, as Levinas thematizes it in the relationship to the face of the other. They also precede this relationship and the distinction between the same and the other which accompanies it. They are neutral with regard to any claim or relationship that pretends to determine their meaning. It is indeed not possible to submit or to reduce them to the determination of any intention to express meaning. However, inversely, there is no way of producing meaning without already dealing with the uncontrollable displacements of language. No approach to language is possible without the duplications of a transfer. In this respect, the metaphoricity of language implies as much the impossibility of a radical otherness as the impossibility of a radical transparency of language. With regard to the metaphoricity of language, I am inevitably in a position of (re-)using and (re-)valorizing the chain of signifiers, I am inevitably caught in an incessant and uncertain process of negotiation. For that reason, the strangeness to which this metaphoricity of language relates beyond its metaphysical determination can be called an otherness by default.

2   Basic Metaphors and the Condition of Subjectivity

The previous section has revealed an important difference between Derrida and Levinas which stems from their different criticisms of the metaphorical understanding of language. Levinas points to a radical otherness beyond any use of metaphor, which not only exceeds the ontological logic of participation in an irreducible way but also intrudes into it and disturbs it by breaking through its closure. Derrida discovers beyond the metaphorical use of language the metaphoricity of language which continuously destabilizes and subverts the basic assumptions of any ontological understanding. Therefore, the meaning of 'otherness' and the condition of its appearance are dissimilar in Levinas' and Derrida's reflections on language. Despite this difference, both face a similar problem. Both consider language to open a relationship but it is not yet clear how this relationship is possible. The problem that Levinas has to address can be summarized by the question: How is a relationship with a radical otherness possible without being immediately annihilated by this otherness? The problem for Derrida concerns the distinction between meaninglessness and meaningfulness: without this distinction it is difficult to see how language is able to create a sense-giving relationship. How can such a relationship appear on the basis of the metaphoricity of language?

Both questions in fact concern the problem of how subjectivity is capable of expressing itself in the relationship to otherness. My answer will be that both Levinas and Derrida have to introduce basic metaphors in order to be able to account for this problem. In what follows, I will therefore briefly discuss the metaphor of the skin in Levinas' account of subjectivity in *Otherwise than Being* and the metaphor of the gift in Derrida's readings of Western figures of subjectivity, such as in his reading of Plato in 'Plato's Pharmacy' (Derrida 1981) and of Kierkegaard in *The Gift of Death* (Derrida 2008).

In his account of subjectivity in *Otherwise than Being*, Levinas introduces the expression 'too tight for its skin' (*mal dans sa peau*) as a metaphor used to express the condition of the identity of the self as being-for-the-other: 'In responsibility, as one assigned or elected from the outside, assigned as irreplaceable, the subject is accused in its skin, too tight for its skin. Cutting across every relation' (Levinas 1981, p. 106). The metaphorical use of the skin is not limited to the expression '*mal dans sa peau*' – which means 'being uneasy in relation to oneself'. The reverse is the case: the metaphorical meaning of this expression stems from the comparison with the skin, which expresses the relation of selfhood as such: 'The ego … is in itself like one is in one's skin, that is, already tight, ill at ease in one's own skin' [*déjà à l'étroit, mal dans sa peau*] (Ibid., p. 108). In other words, the comparison with the skin expresses the experience of an irreducible otherness within the condition of subjectivity: 'To revert to oneself is not to establish oneself at home, even if stripped of all one's acquisitions. It is to be like a stranger, hunted down even in one's home, contested in one's own identity and one's own poverty, which, like a skin still enclosing the self, would set it up in an inwardness, already settled on itself, already a substance' (Ibid., p. 92).

It is tempting to dismiss a strictly metaphorical understanding of this expression in the same way that Heidegger does with the expression of 'the house of being'. Is Levinas not reversing the process of metaphorization by introducing a radical otherness within the borders of selfhood? While this interpretation is not incorrect, it fails to account for the metaphorical operation that Levinas reintroduces in order to articulate the condition of subjectivity in relation to the otherness of the other, which exceeds all categories of the same.

Levinas's notes on metaphor, which remained unpublished during his lifetime, enable us to shed light on this metaphorical operation. In these notes, Levinas calls metaphor 'the essence of language' (Levinas 2009, p. 229)[1] and considers all signification to be metaphorical. He is well aware of the problem that this causes for his concept of radical otherness and he attempts to re-define the metaphorical transfer of language in relation to the meaning of transcendence. In his interpretation of the metaphorical transfer, he attempts to relate the logic of participation to an infinite movement that exceeds this logic and which refers to a transcendence: 'it is impossible to expel the metaphor and the exceeding and the passage to the infinite' (Ibid., p. 242). He rejects, therefore, the notion of resemblance, as it is insufficient to articulate the metaphorical operation: 'as long as we explicitly consider resemblance, we are not in contact with the essence of metaphor: the movement of a transfer and the amplification are lost because of a thought immersed in resemblance like a static essence' (Ibid., p. 237). The metaphorical displacement of meaning leads beyond the recognition of a sameness with a given sense. Levinas describes the metaphorical transfer in terms of a movement of exceeding; of a surplus of meaning: 'Metaphor – what the word signifies beyond its denotation' (Ibid., p. 232). As a result, the function of metaphor is not to unveil, but to elevate. 'Every signification – as signification – is metaphorical, it leads to the heights'. The movement of metaphorical displacement does not end in a final term which embraces the total sense of the movement, but is infinite: 'the movement leading to the heights is without end'. Levinas calls this irreducible movement to the heights, 'the ground of human spirituality'.

It appears from these notes that Levinas' understanding of the metaphorical operation is intrinsically oriented by the reference to the otherness of the human face. Levinas describes the metaphorical operation on the basis of a metonymic relationship, a relationship of proximity (from skin to skin) without implying a reference to a third (understood as a whole). In *Otherwise than Being*, the skin already appears in the account of the meaning of the face. In fact, it is the skin which introduces this meaning into the order of the visible. It bridges the gap between the visible and the invisible that the notion of the face created in Levinas' philosophy, the gap between the plastic form and the infinite. As such, Levinas calls the skin a 'modification' of the face: 'a skin that is always a modification of a face, a face that is weighed down by a skin' (Levinas 1981, p. 85). However, this modification does not mean that the skin synthesizes the opposites, nor that it presents the outer (visible) surface (or envelope) behind which the (invisible) face shelters. The skin does

---

[1] Translations of this text are mine.

not undo the separation and it does not reduce the face to its plastic form. The skin reveals in the visible what withdraws from the visible; it relates the experience of the other to what exceeds the visible. As such, the skin is the condition of possibility of the appearance of exorbitance. It brings what Levinas calls the trace of '*illeity*', which escapes any presentation and withdraws from any visible appearance, in relation to the possibility of an approach that also exposes the face: 'A face approached, a contact with a skin – a face weighed down by a skin, and a skin in which, even in obscenity, the altered face breaths' (Ibid., p. 89). The disclosure of the face is the vulnerable exposure of the skin. In this regard, it is interesting to note that Levinas already seems to use the skin as a metaphor for the trace in the expression 'skin with wrinkles' (*peau à rides*): 'It is poverty, skin with wrinkles, which are a trace of itself' (Ibid., p. 88).

From the skin of the other's face to the skin of the condition of selfhood, the same features appear: (1) poverty as the modality of the appearance of an otherness that is exorbitant and irreducible to the visible, (2) exposure 'to wounds and outrages' that not only concerns the disclosure of the face but also constitutes the identity of selfhood, and (3) the specific 'materiality' of the skin, which Levinas calls a 'passivity, more passive still than the passivity of effects' (Ibid., p. 108), because of its 'susceptibility', 'vulnerability' and 'exposedness to wounds'. However, from the skin of the other's face to the skin of the condition of selfhood, there is also displacement of meaning and separation: with regard to selfhood, the skin is also a disclosure of inwardness. This displacement is not secondary, but the opening of the relationship to the otherness of the other and as such the source of all metaphorical understanding. Given this double movement of similarity and displacement, it is clear that Levinas introduces the skin as a basic metaphor in order to express the condition of subjectivity in its relation to an otherness which does not disappear in this relationship and from which subjectivity receives its meaning. In doing so, he invites us to reconsider the classical interpretation of the metaphorical process and to no longer understand it in reference to a pre-given sense of a whole (or a third), but in terms of the face to face relationship of proximity.

The question of how subjectivity arises from and is dependent on the metaphoricity of language is a central issue in Derrida's writings. An answer to this question requires going against the grain of a deconstructive reading, that is, not following the contingent and ambiguous dissemination of displacements and transfers of signifiers, but examining the traces and choices through which a logic is developed and a definite orientation is inscribed within the metaphoricity of language. From the metaphoricity of language, which continuously undermines this possibility; how can a relationship in which it is possible to determine its meaning and in which subjectivity is able to deal with it, arise?

In order to answer this question from a Derridian perspective, I will focus on the metaphorical transfers evoked by the notion of the gift (*don, présent, cadeau*) in his writings. As is well known since Marcel Mauss' *Essai sur le don*, the gift belongs to the same economic semantic field as the concepts of use and consumption (*usage* and *usure*), which have, as we saw in the previous section, a central role in Derrida's approach to language. The gift expresses a certain value of the given: without the surplus value of the given, it is not possible to speak of a gift. The gift is, moreover, an event *par excellence*: it exists because of the act of giving. It implies a displacement from the giver to the receiver. As such, it opens an economic logic because it raises the question of the proper use and meaning of the gift and it partakes in a process of transfer. However, unlike the notion of use, the gift implies an address (*envoi*). While use can be based upon habit, a transfer of reciprocity in which the employees are not specific, the gift allows the relationship between giver and receiver to appear in the economic semantic field. The address of the gift says something about the giver and the receiver. Whatever the intentions of the giver, whatever the impact of their presence on the value of the given, the gift is directed to the receiver. It puts the receiver in the position of an addressee and implies therefore a sense of an obligation (to answer, to respond, to do something with it). The receiver is asked to decide whether or not to accept the gift, they have the opportunity to reject it or ignore it, and as such a choice is made.

The notion of the gift thus enables Derrida to establish a relationship between the metaphoricity of language (the uncontrollable dissemination of transfers and displacements) on the one hand, and the instance (and the instant) of a choice, on the other, which creates a distinction between giver/receiver, inside/outside, proper/improper, self/other. Derrida has commented on all these issues on several occasions, but I would like to refer to two main passages which in my view are crucial to demonstrating the significance of the notion of the gift and the efficacy of its metaphorical displacement in Derrida's readings. The notion of the gift has a fundamental role in Derrida's interpretation of two basic stories having an enormous impact on European culture: the biblical story of the sacrifice of Abraham and the story of the origin of writing in Plato's *Phaedrus*. The role of the gift is fundamental in both texts, not only because these stories would not have been possible without the opening scene of a gift (the gift of Isaac in the case of Abraham and the gift of writing in the story about Thoth in the case of Plato), but also because both stories are at the origin of a determinate concept of subjectivity in Western philosophy understood in terms of responsibility. Derrida's readings reveal astonishing similarities between the two stories beyond their manifest different meanings, similarities which shed an interesting light on the metaphorical process provoked by the notion of the gift.

First of all, the gift itself entails an irreducible ambiguity. Its positive and negative consequences are inseparable. In the case of the gift of writing, this ambiguity is expressed by the notion of *pharmakos*, which means both 'remedy' and 'poison'. Writing as an instrument to conserve ideas and events is presented and recommended by Thoth as a remedy against oblivion and the deficiencies of memory. However, writing is for that same reason considered and rejected, according to the myth that Socrates retells, as poisonous to the faculty of remembering and of recalling to mind the vivid presence of the idea. Derrida carefully analyses the equivocal recurrences of the notion of *pharmakos* in Plato's text and demonstrates how Plato's rejection of writing and his understanding of logos turn around this ambiguity and its translation (Derrida 1981, p. 75 f.). In the case of the gift of Isaac, the ambiguity is given with the name of Isaac: the first son of Abraham, given to him as a sign of the covenant with his personal and unique God, is the sole being that Abraham can give in turn to God in order to prove his faithfulness. Isaac is the unique sign of the presence of that union, but the presence of the sign might become an impediment to Abraham's faithfulness and love of God. In his comments on Kierkegaard's interpretation of Abraham, Derrida brings to the fore this double bind of betrayal and faithfulness in Abraham's response to the call of God to sacrifice his son (Derrida 2008, pp. 69–70).

In order to deal with this ambiguity, both stories inscribe the address of the gift within the basic structure of the relationship between father and son. In the story of Abraham's sacrifice, this relationship is obvious. It is the core element of the narrative, without which the ordeal on the mount Moriah and the entire question of the human sacrifice to God does not make sense. However, the relationship between father and son not only concerns the relationship between Abraham and his son Isaac, but also that between Abraham and his personal God. Like a father, this God – who kept his promise in allowing Sarah to give birth to her first son despite her old age – is soliciting Abraham's love in challenging his faithfulness. Both God and Abraham are therefore in the position of giving and receiving: the gift to Abraham with the birth of his first son, the gift to God with the sacrifice of Isaac. In the story of the *Phaedrus*, the relationship between father and son is introduced in order to distinguish the logos, the vivid presence of speech, from the artifact of the written text. The origin and the power of logos is assigned to the position of the father (cf. Derrida 1981, p. 78). Without his presence and without his assistance, logos is unable to affirm itself and that is precisely what happens in written signs, which for that reason are considered 'orphans'. In the myth of Thoth, the king of Egypt is assigned to the position of the father. Guaranteeing the vivid presence of logos, he is in the position of giving and receiving. The gift of writing is presented to him in order for him to evaluate it. The rejection of this gift is the affirmation of another gift: his presence and assistance to the vivid power of speech.

In his reading of both texts, Derrida shows in detail how the inscription of the gift within the father-son relationship is decisive with regard to the metaphoricity of language. According to his interpretation, this relationship is 'the hearth of all metaphoricity' (Ibid., p. 81), for it determines the answer given to the address of the gift (and thus the choice that has been made): it opens a field of ascriptions (powers, dependencies and loyalties), it installs a hierarchy between positions (priority of the position of the father, who has the power to decide; dependency of the son with regard to the father's power) and it introduces an oppositional structure in order to define essential distinctions such as responsible/irresponsible, proper/improper, life/death, interiority/exteriority (all of these oppositions can be easily retraced in the two stories). As such, the father-son relationship is able to stabilize the indeterminate ambiguities and deferrals of the gift, to distribute the responsibilities of the positions of the giver and the receiver and to delineate in this regard basic figures of subjectivity.

However, in articulating this process of decision-making and its consequences, Derrida also reveals a logic of substitution at its core: the lamb which substitutes for Isaac at the very moment of the sacrifice, the written text which substitutes for the event of speech. Substitution implies here three conflicting assumptions: (1) the substitute (the lamb, the written text) is secondary with regard to the substituted (the son, the logos), (2) substitution reverses the relationship of dependency (the relationship of Abraham to his son Isaac is dependent on the lamb, the power of logos is dependent on the written text), (3) this reversal is negated and repressed by subjectivity defined in terms of a father-son relationship. In this regard, Derrida points to a blind spot in any concept of subjectivity, which undermines the oppositional structure on which this concept is based.

3   Final Remarks

One can rightly doubt whether it is possible to capture the sense of an entire philosophical oeuvre with one basic metaphor. Yet, it is possible to consider it as a significant indication of a philosophical orientation. We argued in the previous reflections that it is possible to approach the differend between Levinas and Derrida by pointing to the metaphor of the skin in Levinas' account of subjectivity and to the economy of the gift in Derrida's writings. On this basis, it appears that the differences between them concern both the understanding of metaphorical transfer and the condition of subjectivity. The gift in Derrida's writing is not a metaphor in the same way as the skin is in *Otherwise than Being*. Implying the event of an address from giver to receiver, it intervenes in the uncontrollable circuit of signifiers and opens the condition of a metaphorical understanding of language. As such, the gift has a basic significance in Derrida's readings because it bridges the gap between the undefinable metaphoricity of language and a language that is able to distinguish between the meaningful and the meaningless. While the gift is not sufficient to stabilize this relationship or to replace the former by the latter, subjectivity is the name of this substitution. It arises from the ascriptions, priorities and oppositions that intend to deal with the address of the gift and determine its meaning. However, subjectivity is not able to erase the traces of its dependency on the gift.

In this way, Derrida has the means to criticize and undermine any philosophy of subjectivity that negates or forgets this dependency. He continuously demonstrates by careful readings the contingent transfers and displacements of essential oppositions and hierarchies. In particular, the philosophy of Levinas, which presents itself explicitly as a defense of subjectivity, is a preferred target of this reading strategy. It is indeed possible to point to basic ascriptions (for example, selfhood assigned by the other), priorities (for example, the uniqueness of the other who addresses me from the heights) and oppositions (for example, the self and the other) which structure Levinas' philosophy. Yet, in emphasizing the metaphor of the skin, our approach enabled us to shed another light on Derrida's readings of Levinas. The metaphorical displacement in Levinas' account of subjectivity is not based upon a metaphysical understanding of a pre-given sense of logos, but upon a relationship of proximity with an otherness that exceeds any determination. In using expressions such as 'too tight for its skin' (*mal dans sa peau*), Levinas also defines subjectivity as 'substitution' (Levinas 1981, p. xlii, cf. chapter IV). However, this substitution is precisely not the emergence of a closure of meaning or that of a powerful subjectivity. On the contrary, it is anarchic and disruptive, and it assigns above all a bodily position, beyond any determination of language as a vivid presence of speech. In short, the whole case of the differend might be summarized by this single phrase: 'subjectivity is the name of a substitution'.

References

Aristotle. 1984. *The Complete Works of Aristotle*. Trans. J. Barnes. Princeton: Princeton University Press.
Derrida, Jacques. 1976. *Of Grammatology*. Trans. G. Chakravorty Spivak. Baltimore: John Hopkins University Press.
Derrida, Jacques. 1981. Plato's pharmacy. In *Dissemination*. Trans. B. Johnson. Chicago: University of Chicago Press.
Derrida, Jacques. 1982. White mythology: Metaphor in the text of philosophy. In *Margins of philosophy*, ed. A. Bass, 207–271. Chicago: University of Chicago Press.
Derrida, Jacques. 2007. The retrait of metaphor. In *Psyche: inventions of the other*, ed. P. Kamuf, 48–80. Stanford: Stanford University Press.
Derrida, Jacques. 2008. *The Gift of Death & Literature in Secret*. Trans. D. Wills. Chicago: Chicago University Press.
Heidegger, Martin. 1991. *The Principle of Reason*. Trans. R. Lilly. Bloomington: Indiana University Press.
Heidegger, Martin. 1996. *Being and Time*. Trans. J. Stambaugh. New York: State University of New York Press.
Heidegger, Martin. 2011. Letter on humanism. In *Basic Writings*. Trans. F. A. Capuzzi and J. G. Greay, 147–181. London: Routledge.
Levinas, Emmanuel. 1969. *Totality and Infinity. An Essay on Exteriority*. Trans. A. Lingis. Pittsburg: Duquesne University Press.
Levinas, Emmanuel. 1981. *Otherwise than Being or Beyond Essence*. Trans. A. Lingis. The Hague: Martinus Nijhoff.
Levinas, Emmanuel. 2009. Notes sur la métaphore. In *Œuvres 1. Carnets de captivité suivi de Écrits sur la captivité et Notes philosophiques divers*, ed. Rodolphe Calin and Catherine de Chalier, 227–242. Paris: Grasset & Fasquelle/IMEC Editeur.
Van der Heiden, Gert-Jan. 2013. Heidegger thinking (without) metaphors: on 'The House of Being' and 'Words, as Flowers'. In *Metaphors in modern and contemporary philosophy*, eds. Arthur Cools, Walter Van Herck, Koenraad Verrycken, 227–241. Brussels: University of Antwerp Press.

No Longer Being-There: Phenomenology and Death

Paul J. Ennis

Abstract In contemporary Continental philosophy there has been a recent trend toward realism and a rejection of what Quentin Meillassoux names correlationism. However, one of the most significant responses to Meillassoux's position has come from the contemporary Derridean Martin Hägglund and it brings us indirectly to what this author contends lies at the heart of the phenomenological conception of death. Meillassoux is critical of the correlationist position because it cannot think the time before being, especially as discussed in the natural sciences. To be concise Meillassoux is concerned with whether it is possible to think this time without rendering them through a correlationist, or in a lighter phrase, anti-realist, lens. In *After Finitude* one example provided of how powerful correlationism is, comes through the excision of mind-independent primary (or mathematical) qualities in the post-Kantian tradition as thinkable in-themselves – a position Meillassoux claims has come to be seen as naïve (realism). What then, for instance, to make of statements about the time before being, indexed by 'arche-fossils' referring to 'the existence of an ancestral reality or event'? The answer Meillassoux notes is usually given as intersubjectivity. This may not, at first, seem contentious.

Keywords Correlationism • Death • Speculative realism • Heidegger • Meillassoux • Brassier • Subjectivity

1 Introduction: The Questioner

In contemporary Continental philosophy there has been a recent trend toward realism and a rejection of what Quentin Meillassoux names correlationism or 'the idea according to which we only ever have access to the correlation between thinking and being, and never to either term considered apart from the other.'[1] However, one

---

[1] Quentin Meillassoux, *After Finitude: An Essay on the Necessity of Contingency*, trans. Ray Brassier (London: Continuum, 2008), 5.

P.J. Ennis (✉)
School of Business, University College Dublin, Dublin, Ireland
e-mail: paul.ennis@ucd.ie

© Springer International Publishing Switzerland 2016   45
L. Foran, R. Uljée (eds.), *Heidegger, Levinas, Derrida: The Question of Difference*, Contributions To Phenomenology 86,
DOI 10.1007/978-3-319-39232-5_4

of the most significant responses to Meillassoux's position has come from the contemporary Derridean Martin Hägglund and it brings us indirectly to what this author
contends lies at the heart of the phenomenological conception of death.[2] Meillassoux
is critical of the correlationist position because it cannot think the time *before* being,
especially as discussed in the natural sciences, and asks:

> How are we to grasp the *meaning* of scientific statements bearing explicitly upon a mani-
> festation of the world that is posited as anterior to the emergence of thought and even of
> life – *posited, that is, as anterior to every form of human relation to the world?*[3]

To be concise, Meillassoux is concerned with whether it is possible to think this
time without rendering it through a correlationist, or in a lighter phrase, anti-realist,
lens. In *After Finitude* one example provided of how powerful correlationism is
comes through the excision of mind-independent primary (or mathematical) qualities in the post-Kantian tradition as thinkable in-themselves – a position Meillassoux
claims has come to be seen as naïve (realism).[4] What then, for instance, to make of
statements about the time before being, indexed by 'arche-fossils' referring to 'the
existence of an ancestral reality or event?'[5] The answer Meillassoux notes is usually
given as intersubjectivity: 'From this point on, *intersubjectivity*, the consensus of a
community, supplants the *adequation* between the representations of a solitary subject and the thing itself…'[6] This may not, at first, seem contentious.

Nonetheless, one aspect of Meillassoux's project is to reveal how intersubjectivity entails an anti-realist '*retrojection of the past on the basis of the present*' where
we re-read ancestral time from the standpoint of the now and thus invert the linear
time of science.[7] However, we must note that Meillassoux insists the rhetorical
approach in the opening pages of *After Finitude* is intended as an *aporia*, but this
has not stopped many thinkers from attempting to counter his critique.[8] The contemporary Derridean Martin Hägglund notes that when it comes to the issue of 'how
ancestral time recorded itself' Meillassoux 'is strangely silent.'[9] Furthermore, in
relation to mathematics, calculation in relation to ancestral time depends 'on the
material support of arche-fossils, which *presuppose* the trace structure of time.'[10] It
is not the case that one is attempting to undermine the natural sciences but, more
significantly, that a rigorous philosophical consideration of the ancestral realm
requires that one accept the operations, and therefore the intrusion, of thinking into

---

[2] In Martin Hägglund, 'The Challenge of Radical Atheism: A Response,' *CR: The New Centennial Review* 9, no. 1 (2009): 242.

[3] Meillassoux, *After Finitude: An Essay on the Necessity of Contingency*: 9–10. His italics.

[4] Ibid., 2.

[5] Ibid., 10.

[6] Ibid., 4. His italics.

[7] Ibid., 16. His italics.

[8] Quentin Meillassoux, *Time without becoming*, trans. Anna Longo (United Kingdom: Mimesis International, 2014), 19.

[9] Hägglund, 'The Challenge of Radical Atheism: A Response,' 242.

[10] Ibid. His italics.

our engagements with it and this include recognizing that the time before being as only understood because of the traces left behind. It does not matter whether we agree with Žižek that 'consciousness developed as an unintended by-product that acquired a kind of second-degree survivalist function...'[11] The point is that we cannot but see everything from our vantage point as conscious, thinking entities. In discussing articulation, trace, or time at all one immediately evokes the one enmeshed within thinking and being – the questioner.

Meillassoux, as Gratton claims, has an implicit set of targets in mind, namely: 'French and German phenomenology (Husserl, Sartre, Merleau-Ponty, etc.) and post-phenomenology (Lacan, Derrida, Deleuze, Foucault, etc.).'[12] Despite this, Derrida stressed that the charge of anti-realism, or what is more commonly known now as correlationism, is a canard and that deconstruction constitutes a 'transcendental realism' that always comes 'forward in the name of the real' and he even posited that considered as such 'nothing is more realist than deconstruction.'[13] This argument that deconstruction is a hyper-intensive realism is also put forward by Caputo in his defense of Derrida against the anti-realist charge:

> Derrida is certainly dedicated to dealing with what is real, with what there is (*il y a*), but he is not satisfied to say that the real is the simply present, so he always has an eye on what is real beyond the real, on the real that is not yet real, on what is coming, on the *peut-être* and the *s'il y en a*. Derrida displaces the simple primacy of the sensible-real in two ways, first, by seeing to it that the sensible-real too is the effect of the trace, and secondly, by seeing to it that the real is always haunted by the specters of the *arrivants* and the *revenants*. That is why I have described deconstruction as a hyper-realism.[14]

How, then, can Derrida, Caputo, and Hägglund read phenomenology as realist in spite of Meillassoux's critique, whether it is merely meant as an *aporia* or not?[15] What will be put forward is how this "more realist than realism" position is implicitly tied up with the question of finitude and how death remains for us an impossible limit. As Derrida reminds us death cannot be experienced and, in a manner, to be properly realist is to respect the limits of finitude.[16] This a standpoint that also lurks in the work of Levinas for whom alterity, the Other, and the resistance we encounter in relation to the real, all act as motivational prompts to an ethics reliant on precisely the impossibility of encountering them directly.[17] Is this not, perhaps, more a

---

[11] Slavoj Žižek and Glyn Daly, *Conversations with Žižek* (Cambridge: Polity Press, 2004), 59.

[12] Peter Gratton, 'After the Subject: Meillassoux's Ontology of "What May Be",' *Pli: The Warwick Journal of Philosophy* 20 (2009): 60.

[13] Jacques Derrida, *Paper Machine*, trans. Rachel Bowlby (Stanford, CA: Stanford University Press, 2005), 96.

[14] John D. Caputo, 'The Return of Anti-Religion: From Radical Atheism to Radical Theology,' *Journal for Cultural and Religious Theory* 11, no. 2 (2011): 50.

[15] Meillassoux will later make his escape from correlationism using precisely death as a means of weakening it. See Meillassoux, *After Finitude: An Essay on the Necessity of Contingency*: 59.

[16] Jacques Derrida, *Aporias*, trans. Thomas Dutoit (Stanford, CA: Stanford University Press, 1993), 21–23.

[17] See, for instance, Emmanuel Levinas, *Totality and Infinity: An Essay on Exteriority*, trans. Alphonso Lingis (Pittsburgh: Duquesne University Press, 2005). Unfortunately for reasons of

"rhetoric of realism" as Sparrow has argued?[18] To understand the function of death in the phenomenological tradition, with regard to its relation to the natural sciences and the broader question of realism, one must first go to the source material: the work of Martin Heidegger and the demarcation he introduces between the time of the natural sciences and temporality, with its implicit commitment to the limits of finitude, experienced by the "subject," specifically the transcendental-ontological subject.

2   From Transcendental Science to the History of Ontology

To grasp the significance of death in phenomenology we need to go back to the transition from transcendental science to the insertion of history into the phenomenological tradition by Martin Heidegger.[19] In §3 of *Being and Time* Heidegger is content to compare his task to Kant's Critical project in the *Critique of Pure Reason*.[20] The first indication that Heidegger's arguments are formally transcendental occurs in the recursive tactic dispensed against the regional sciences in the opening arguments of *Being and Time*. In §3 three important claims are made in relation to the sciences specifically. The first is that a regional science emerges from an interrogation with a set of '"fundamental concepts."'[21] The second is that such concepts determine the direction of a scientific discipline and the final claim is that these concepts determine the questions that structure that discipline.[22] Heidegger proceeds to define the regional sciences as '…the totality of fundamentally coherent true propositions.'[23] It is a collection of true propositions, but Heidegger is keen to

---

economy the stress in this article will be on Martin Heidegger at the expense of both Derrida and Levinas for reasons that will become clear soon.

[18] See Tom Sparrow, *The End of Phenomenology: Metaphysics and the New Realism* (Edinburgh: Edinburgh University Press, 2014), 69–82.

[19] A similar move is made, of course, by Husserl, but since our focus is death it will be here bracketed. See Edmund Husserl, *The Crisis of European Sciences and Transcendental Phenomenology*, trans. David Carr (Evanston: Northwestern University Press, 1970).

[20] Martin Heidegger, *Being and Time*, trans. Joan Stambaugh (Albany: State University of New York Press, 1996). See also Immanuel Kant, *Critique of Pure Reason*, trans. Paul Guyer and Allen W. Wood (Cambridge: Cambridge University Press, 2007). The significant background texts that influenced Heidegger's emphasis on the ontological question are, beginning with the phenomenological perspective, the following: Edmund Husserl, *Logische Untersuchungen. Erster Teil: Prolegomena zur Reinen Logik* (Tübingen: Max Niemeyer Verlag, 1993).; Edmund Husserl, *Logische Untersuchungen. Zweiter Teil: Untersuchungen zur Phänomenologie und Theorie der Erkenntnis* (Tübingen: Max Niemeyer Verlag, 1993). From the traditional ontological perspective, also see: Franz Brentano, *Von der mannigfachen Bedeutung des Seienden nach Aristoteles* (Freiburg: Herder, 1862).; Carl Braig, *Vom Sein: Abriß der Ontologie* (Freiburg: Herder, 1896). This emphasis retains intellectual primacy throughout Heidegger's career.

[21] Heidegger, *Being and Time*: 7.

[22] Ibid., 7–8.

[23] Ibid., 9.

distinguish the questioner from the results of their inquiry. Hence, Heidegger fully accepts that the regional sciences have an important function, but to mark the distinction between them and transcendental science we gain the ontic sciences that have as their content beings, but crucially we discover that peculiar to the 'ontical foundation' of the questioner, denoted as Dasein, is its orientation toward the ontological question.[24] This is the case because Dasein alone can think the 'ontological difference' between being [*Sein, das Sein*] and beings [*das Seiende*].[25]

Although Heidegger affirms the question of the meaning of being will remain a '*transcendental science*', there is a clear translation from transcendental subject, as Heidegger had inherited it from the transcendental tradition; to Dasein *qua* ontological entity, distinct in its knowledge of being. And, as we will see, this is not necessarily always a positive insight.[26] Heidegger arrives at his insight by leaning, but nonetheless *expanding* on the transcendental method.[27] The ontological difference is defined in *The Basic Problems of Phenomenology* as an '*ontological-transcendental differentiation.*'[28] The missing link in the Kantian method is the phenomenological reduction that goes one step further than the Kantian analysis of the uses of pure reason and infiltrates the region of pure consciousness made possible through a bracketing of the general positing of the natural attitude, as Husserl had argued[29]: 'We call this basic component of phenomenological method – the leading back or re-duction of investigative vision from a naively apprehended being to being – phenomenological reduction.'[30] Heidegger compliments the reduction with 'phenomenological construction' that is linked tightly with phenomenological destruction as put to use in *Being and Time* to offset the traditional tendencies of ontology.[31] *Being and Time* is, then, an attempt to extract, by various means, an orientation for addressing the question of the meaning of being by examining the presuppositions concerning the question that have appeared throughout the philo-

---

[24] Martin Heidegger, *The Basic Problems of Phenomenology*, trans. Albert Hofstadter (Bloomington: Indiana University Press, 1982), 19.

[25] Ibid., 17.

[26] Ibid. His italics.

[27] Ibid., 28. Lilian Alweiss makes a similar claim: 'Moreover, for Heidegger the legitimating ground does not lie in reason; it is *not* subjective, but inheres in the things *themselves*, which are *not* at our disposal. Nonetheless, Heidegger is advocating a transcendental philosophy, even if it is one that is prised from subjectivity and intelligibility. It is a transcendental philosophy that can be understood only negatively insofar as the transcendental conditions do *not* belong to the horizon of Dasein but manifest themselves only on the reverse side of its horizon.' In Lilian Alweiss, 'Leaving Metaphysics to Itself,' *International Journal of Philosophical Studies* 15, no. 3 (2007): 358. Her italics.

[28] Heidegger, *The Basic Problems of Phenomenology*: 20. His italics.

[29] See Edmund Husserl, *Cartesian Meditations: An Introduction to Phenomenology*, trans. Dorion Cairns (The Hague: Martinus Nijhoff Publishers, 1960), 21.

[30] Heidegger, *The Basic Problems of Phenomenology*: 21. His italics.

[31] Ibid., 23.; Heidegger, *Being and Time*: 21.

sophical tradition.[32] With these considerations in mind it is easier to grasp Heidegger's tentative and cautious definition of phenomenological method as only ever a 'concept of method.'[33]

This is an attempt to shift the emphasis in relation to many traditional philosophical problems. For instance, to Heidegger questions such as those found between realists and anti-realists are useful only in so much as they shed light on the ontological question and, in fact, Heidegger generally avoids standing on either side of the standard realist and anti-realist debates, as Patricia Glazebrook notes:

> ...Heidegger is a realist who nonetheless holds antirealist assumptions, and...this position is neither garbled nor self-contradictory. Rather, it exchanges the either/or of realism/anti-realism for a both/and. His realist commitment to the transcendent actuality of nature goes hand in hand with the thesis that human understanding is projective, and its corollary that the idea of a reality independent of understanding is unintelligible.[34]

The same can be said of his stance on truth since, for Heidegger, truth is not gained but experienced as disclosure.[35] In its ontological sense truth is actually quite common since it is disclosure as such and, granting this, needs to be seen as situated historically, but to understand *why* it is helpful to contrast Heidegger's position with that of the neo-Kantianism of his times.[36] Heidegger characterizes the neo-Kantians as resisting all attempts at historizing the Kantian standpoint including the modest historiographical reading.[37] Heidegger criticized such resistance as naïve because it

---

[32] This mirrors the Husserlian attack on presuppositions, preconceptions, and prejudices. Extending from his earliest work on arithmetic and number Husserl demonstrates, principally in his first *Logische Untersuchungen*, that there are three prejudices of psychologism that lead it to consider logic as a series of conditioned psychological operations. See Husserl, *Logische Untersuchungen. Erster Teil*: *Prolegomena zur Reinen Logik*: §41–49 and §43–9. Alweiss remarks: 'For Husserl... the threat of psychologism can only be overcome successfully if we are able to show "how we can grasp thoughts and recognise them to be true" without reducing them to mental processes, despite the fact that they are intended.' In Lilian Alweiss, 'Between Internalism and Externalism: Husserl's Account of Intentionality,' *Inquiry* 52, no. 1 (2009): 57. Husserl undermined psychologism using a comparison between pure and mathematical logic, and did so by distinguishing between the psychologised instances of arithmetical or logical operations from their idealized determinate basis. See Edmund Husserl, *Philosophie der Arithmetik*: *Psychologische und Logische Untersuchungen*, *I* (Haag: Martinus Nijhoff, 1970).

[33] Heidegger, *Being and Time*: 24. His italics.

[34] Trish Glazebrook, 'Heidegger and Scientific Realism,' *Continental Philosophy Review* 34 (2001): 362.

[35] Hence for Heidegger '*Da-sein is its disclosedness.*' Heidegger, *Being and Time*: 125. His italics.

[36] The neo-Kantian school was divided into two sets. The Marburg school is notable for three thinkers: Hermann Cohen (1842–1918), Ernst Cassirer (1874–1945) and Paul Natorp (1854–1924). There was also the Baden or Southwest school known for Heinrich Rickert (1863–1936) and Wilhelm Windelband (1848–1915). For an excellent overview of Heidegger's relationship to neo-Kantianism see Charles R. Bambach, *Heidegger, Dilthey, and the Crisis of Historicism* (Ithaca: Cornell University Press, 1995). In relation to Dilthey and neo-Kantianism, see Ilse Bulhof, *Wilhelm Dilthey*: *A Hermeneutic Approach to the Study of History and Culture* (The Hague: Martinus Nijhoff Publishers, 1980).

[37] This period of intellectual tension is covered extensively in the following articles: John E. Jalbert, 'Husserl's Position between Dilthey and the Windelband-Rickert School of Neo-Kantianism,'

does not recognize that the philosophical tradition is comprised of intersecting inflections and the effect these inflections have on one's philosophical position.[38] Attention must, then, be paid to the 'history of ontology' or one is liable to fall into the trap of unacknowledged presuppositions the entire phenomenological tradition is designed to filter out.[39] This is the reasoning behind the equation, in *Being and Time*, of phenomenological method with hermeneutical method: 'Phenomenology of Da-sein is *hermeneutics* in the original signification of that word, which designates the work of interpretation.'[40] We cannot take a view from nowhere with a free-floating transcendental subject operating as if it were not entangled in a tradition replete with ontological assumptions that must be uncovered and deconstructed.

3   History and the Questioner

This relates us back to Heidegger's phenomenological point concerning the recursion that can be applied to all epistemological stances – who asks the question? In this general sense Heidegger insists on focusing on the persistent problem of the questioner as much as the question and now, armed with the hermeneutical method, one can also examine from what *time* the question is asked. There is a wealth of situations preceding each Dasein. This tells us that there must be a phenomenology appropriate to the "time" a Dasein is "thrown" into.[41] The expansion of phenomenological method toward the question concerning the meaning of being is, thereby, also its opening toward temporality.[42] The ontological question is only possible because of this temporalization of the questioner and Heidegger makes this explicit when he tells us:

> …time is Dasein. Dasein is my specificity, and this can be specificity in what is futural by running ahead to a certain yet indeterminate past. Dasein always is in a manner of its possible temporal being. Dasein is time, time is temporal. Dasein is not time, but temporality.[43]

Heidegger's counter-position to static accounts of philosophy is that any sufficient account of our situation must recognize that Dasein is conditioned in temporal terms and it therefore becomes important to consider the phenomenon of Dasein's 'facticity.'[44] What does the phenomenon of facticity indicate about the region we

---

Journal of the History of Philosophy 26, no. 2 (1988): 279–96.; Rudolf A. Makkreel, 'Wilhelm Dilthey and the Neo-Kantians: The Distinction of the Geisteswissenschaften and the Kulturwissenschaften,' *Journal of the History of Philosophy* 7, no. 4 (1969): 423–40.

[38] Heidegger, *Being and Time*: 17–19.

[39] Ibid., 20.

[40] Ibid., 37.

[41] Ibid., 127.

[42] Ibid., 15.

[43] In Martin Heidegger, *The Concept of Time*, trans. William McNeill (Oxford: Blackwell Publishing, 1992), 20E.

[44] Heidegger, *Being and Time*: 52.

find ourselves in? Thrownness indicates a certain contingency to each Dasein's existence such that 'Dasein exists factically.'[45] Each Dasein, along with others, brings to the table their own temporal surplus where ontic events outside the truth of being are rendered, through disclosure, into ontological events taking place within a wider history of ontology or what will later be expressed through the term *Ereignis*, although we will not be overly concerned with what occurs post-*Kehre*.[46]

Each Dasein is also beholden to a form of 'mineness' that can only be their own due to the specific contingency of personal 'birth and death.'[47] There is one clear response to this issue: one falls into an inauthentic existence of 'everyday indifference' in order not to dwell on such matters.[48] Nonetheless certain moods intrude upon inauthentic existence, but most significantly '*Angst*' (or anxiety) crucially refuses to let us be completely free of awareness of one's finitude.[49] Angst discloses inauthentic existence as a method of '*fleeing*' from the thought of death.[50] It also, in turn, reveals how death, conceived *ontologically* is not a mere 'perishing,' but registers to each Dasein their own specificity and potential for authentic existence.[51] Heidegger is stressing, in essence, that the distinction between mere perishing as an empirical entity is to be differentiated from death in its ontological sense. This hints at what this author considers the implicit commitment of Heidegger to the *transcendental* core of "correlationism."[52] Heidegger informs us that we are distinct as the (transcendental) entities that have a relation to being, but what goes unanswered is the moment of transformation from, as Meillassoux puts it, '*non-being into being*.'[53] Here there is an elevation of "human" death (Dasein) over the deaths of other entities and an indifference to the time prior to the emergence of Dasein. For Heidegger

---

[45] Ibid., 167.

[46] Roth provides a useful account of the etymological connotations one finds in the word *Ereignis* as it is used by Heidegger: '*Ereignis* is related to *eigen*, meaning "own and "proper" with clear connotations of *eigentum* meaning "property" or "a possession." *Ereignis* is also related to *ereigen* meaning "to prove" or "to show" in the sense of a demonstration…And lastly, it is related to *eignen*, meaning "suitable" or "appropriate" where appropriate may be understood both as "proper" and as "to acquire." Along with all these connotations, *Ereignis* must also be thought as "event" and it is usually translated as "event of appropriation" so as to reflect some of these relationships. In the event of *Ereignis*, entities are brought forth into their own, becoming what they are.' In Michael Roth, *The Poetics of Resistance: Heidegger's Line* (Evanston, IL: Northwestern University Press, 1996), 38. See Martin Heidegger, *Contributions to Philosophy (From Enowning)*, trans. Parvis Emad and Kenneth Maly (Bloomington, IN: Indiana University Press, 1999). Heidegger is even content to say that: 'Be-ing is the en-owning of truth.' In Martin Heidegger, *Mindfulness* (London: Continuum International Publishing Group, 2006), 82.

[47] Heidegger, *Being and Time*: 49; 215.

[48] Ibid., 41.

[49] Ibid., 172.

[50] Ibid., 223.

[51] Ibid.

[52] See Paul J. Ennis, 'The Transcendental Core of Correlationism,' *Cosmos and History* 7, no. 1 (2011).

[53] Meillassoux, *After Finitude: An Essay on the Necessity of Contingency*: 21. His italics.

being has priority, but is this epistemically justified? Or can one even say that a transcendentally-inspired ontology is, in fact, ontologically prior in explanatory terms?

The split is between time and temporality, according to the transcendentalist, is a clear one. The empirical refers to the content of the natural sciences where bodies merely perish, but the transcendental subject is something different since it is the 'set of *conditions*' marking out ourselves as of a different order from base matter.[54] Meillassoux's response to the transcendental position begins by accepting that the transcendental subject exists in a different sense from other entities, but he insists that the dependency of the transcendental subject on its empirical instantiation remains important since it allows the transcendental subject to occur and have a '*point of view*.'[55] Meillassoux reminds us that in as much as temporal time 'temporalizes' it is also true that the time of science has its own function in temporalizing 'the emergence of living bodies' and must be seen as a condition, in turn, '*for the taking place of the transcendental*.'[56] Heidegger can be critiqued on this score in his failure to integrate the time of science with the temporality of transcendental science. We can see both failures operative in Heidegger's approach to truth and especially his remarks on natural laws since it is here that one is supposed to find clear-cut examples of immutable truths. Heidegger claimed that before the articulation of Newton's laws it is impossible to state whether they were true or false:

> The fact that before Newton his laws were neither true nor false cannot mean that the beings which they point out in a discovering way did not previously exist. The laws became true through Newton, through them beings in themselves became accessible for Da-sein.[57]

This does not mean that prior to their articulation Newton's laws were not operative. Rather, it means that once they were articulated it then became possible to think about their epistemic validity. What became possible was the actualization and disclosure of their truth and this corresponds to their maximal ontological sense according to Heidegger's schematic. This is the specific logic of the correlationist position, to borrow Meillassoux's term once more, where in order to gain the wealth of 'transcendental experience,' as Husserl put it, we must deflate the empirical and inflate the ontological.[58]

Heidegger, one might contend, ends up in the position of being as restrictively transcendentalist as his mentor since his history of ontology, despite its various epochal shifts, retains the kernel of the Husserlian claim that: 'Cognition is, after all, only human cognition, bound up with human intellectual forms, and unfit...to

---

[54] Ibid., 23. His italics.

[55] Ibid., 24. His italics.

[56] Ibid., 25.

[57] Heidegger, *Being and Time*: 208.

[58] Husserl, *Cartesian Meditations: An Introduction to Phenomenology*: 27.

reach the things in themselves.'[59] Like Husserl, the importance of always 'starting from the ego,' or, in Heidegger's case Dasein, insulates phenomenological inquiry from the empirical.[60] This is not to suggest that, like his mentor, Heidegger remains tethered to the old phenomenological problem of 'transcendental solipsism,' but that phenomenology's dissociation from the natural sciences, a transcendental condition, will be consequential.[61] For instance, Heidegger's gaze remains restrictive to our temporality whether we mean by this the focus on the Greek beginning (past), the critique of the metaphysics *qua* technics (present), or the '*saving power*' to come (future).[62] There is nothing inherently problematic about these as themes since, in a manner, Heidegger is motivated, albeit it is not often explicit, by human freedom.[63] Yet toward the end of his life a definite quietism sets in, where, alongside thinkers to come, salvation may come only in the form of a God.[64] Where this brings contemporary phenomenology, via the ethical evolution of phenomenology in Levinas and Derrida, is a pious turn to ambiguity, as when Caputo explicitly states '…one has faith just because one does not know.'[65] Or if one rejects the theological option one can opt for the naturalizing one that, as Sparrow notes, 'is surely paradoxical given insofar as phenomenology is originally constituted a suspension of the natural attitude.'[66] Although it may seem that we have strayed from the topic of death my contention is that neither "post-phenomenology" matters.

---

[59] Edmund Husserl, *The Idea of Phenomenology*, trans. William Alston and George Nakhnikian (Dordrecht: Kluwer, 1980), 17.

[60] Husserl, *The Crisis of European Sciences and Transcendental Phenomenology*: 185.

[61] Husserl, *Cartesian Meditations: An Introduction to Phenomenology*: 89.

[62] Any number of post-turn texts could be cited, but all of these themes are evident in his rightly famous piece Martin Heidegger, 'The Question Concerning Technology,' in *The Question Concerning Technology and Other Essays* (New York: Harper and Row 1977).

[63] Heidegger does explicitly engage the problem of the essence of human freedom, in relation to Schelling, since his 1930 Freiburg lecture *Von Wesen der menschlichen Freiheit*. See Martin Heidegger, *Von Wesen der menschlichen Freiheit. Einleitung in die Philosophie* (Frankfurt am Main: Vittorio Klostermann, 1982). Despite this Haar warns us that: '*Ereignis*, as much as being, even as *Gestell*, retains a "freedom" infinitely superior to that of man. Man can merely *await Ereignis* that, like the Turning, is already and is not yet, as *Gestell* is only the prelude. *Ereignis* is therefore the name given by way of anticipation to a possible "identification" between man and being, beyond metaphysics. In awaiting a new commencement, a new History, *Ereignis* in Heidegger's last writings disposes over man to the same extent and with the same total sovereignty as does being…' In Michel Haar, *Heidegger and the Essence of Man*, trans. William McNeill (Albany: State University of New York Press, 1993), 67. His italics.

[64] See Martin Heidegger, 'Only a God Can Save Us: Der Spiegel's Interview (September 23, 1966),' in *Martin Heidegger: Philosophical and Political Writings*, ed. Manfred Stassen (New York: Continuum, 2003), 24–48.

[65] In John D. Caputo, 'In Praise of Ambiguity,' in *Ambiguity in the Western Mind*, ed. Craig J. N. de Paulo, Patrick Messina, and Marc Stier (New York: Peter Lang, 2005), 31.

[66] Sparrow, *The End of Phenomenology: Metaphysics and the New Realism*: 11.

4 Terrestrial Death and Cosmological Extinction

We have seen that, due to its transcendental heritage (acknowledged or explicit), phenomenology is acutely prone to restriction. Its distaste for the empirical, even in its supposed naturalising moments, places it at odds with more open-ended philosophical positions. For instance, if we take Wilfrid Sellars' synoptic vision of philosophy as the attempt 'to understand how things in the broadest possible sense of the term hang together in the broadest possible sense of the term' the limitations become clear.[67] Sellars insisted that, considered in ontological terms, 'science is the measure of all things, of what is, that it is, and of what is not, that it is not,' but this need not mean one falls into reductionism.[68] Nor should it be considered shocking unless one find themselves, according to Meillassoux's take, unwilling to accept the literalness, and this does not undermine their revisability, of scientific statements.[69] In fact, what motivates phenomenology to react to "reductive" scientism need not be an issue at all. Sellars, for instance, retained a place for our self-understanding as human (the manifest image) through the necessity of normativity or the nexus of understanding required to make sense of scientific statements.[70] Sellars notes that '…in characterizing an episode or a state as that of *knowing*, we are not giving an empirical description of that episode or state; we are placing it in the logical space of reasons.'[71] However, there is an inverse to this. If we grant to the natural sciences our normative ear we discover some unsettling truths that stand outside our earthy concerns. In particular, a cosmological eye can render one's death radically insignificant.

Although meant as a ruse of provocation there is a profound truth about death contained in Lyotard's remark that '…in 4.5 billion years there will arrive the demise of your phenomenology and your utopian politics, and there'll be no one there to toll the death knell or hear it.'[72] Ray Brassier, building upon Lyotard, directly attacks the terrestrial myopia operative in continental philosophy.[73] Brassier argues that what occurs in the tradition's distancing from cosmological time is an attempt to retain for philosophy relevance and this is achieved by treating the "subject" as distinct in relation to its awareness of death, but as Lyotard remarks: '…solar death implies an irreparably exclusive disjunction between death and thought: if there's

---

[67] Wilfred Sellars, *Science, Perception and Reality* (Atascadero: Ridgeview Publishing Company, 1991), 1.

[68] Ibid., 173.

[69] See Meillassoux, *After Finitude: An Essay on the Necessity of Contingency*: 13.

[70] Sellars, *Science, Perception and Reality*: 18.

[71] Wilfred Sellars, *Empiricism and the Philosophy of Mind* (Cambridge, MA: Harvard University Press, 1997), 76.

[72] Jean-François Lyotard, *The Inhuman: Reflections on Time*, trans. Geoffrey Bennington and Rachel Bowlby (Stanford, CA: Stanford University Press, 1991), 9.

[73] Ray Brassier, *Nihil Unbound: Enlightenment and Extinction* (London: Palgrave Macmillan, 2007).

death, then there's no thought.'[74] This is a temptation we find even in the work of Meillassoux, a figure who may on first reading be conceived as unconcerned with the human, when he makes the case for the ultimate significance of essential mourning in a manner that mirrors Derrida's emphasis on the work of mourning.[75] However, when we place ourselves under the logical progression of cosmological time, and situate temporality within it, then terrestrial time and its dependency on the Sun, begins to look akin to an 'elaborately circuitous detour from stellar death.'[76] If we know, or are willing to accept the cosmological claims to this end, that the death of the Sun is inevitable it becomes possible to see how 'the sun is *dying* precisely to the same extent as human existence is bounded by *extinction*.'[77] From this perspective the fact that we are bound to the Sun ensures that our extinction is guaranteed.

Brassier pre-empts the retort, deemed 'vitalist eschatology,'[78] that we will always adapt, perhaps by escaping the planet, but this is to forget that even if we managed to perform such an operation nothing survives the heat-death of the Universe as that will be a time when there will be not only nowhere to go, but "nowhere."[79] This is what Brassier calls 'the transcendental scope of extinction' where we come to recognize we are 'a perishable thing in the world like any other.'[80] Re-reading, according to Brassier's logic of cosmological inevitability in relation to heat-death, Lyotard's provocation that 'everything's dead already,' the line is clear: the Universe succeeds in time toward a long-march of demise (one that included more time without us than with us).[81] There is no doubting this is a harsh lesson to take, especially for phenomenologically-inspired postmodern theology, but Brassier is insistent that 'philosophy should be more than a sop to the pathetic twinge of human self-esteem.'[82] There is perhaps closer affinity with the attempt to naturalize phenomenology since the transcendental scope of extinction, levelling us down ontologically to perishable entities, lets us see consciousness externally and as an object minus ontologically inflated notions such as transcendental subject or Dasein.[83] This is why 'the disenchantment of the world deserves to be celebrated as an achievement of intellectual maturity, not bewailed as a debilitating impoverishment' since it drives home the point that there is nothing special about us allowing for a more

---

[74] Lyotard, *The Inhuman: Reflections on Time*: 11.

[75] See Quentin Meillassoux, 'Spectral Dilemma,' in *Collapse IV: Concept Horror*, ed. Robin Mackay (Falmouth: Urbanomic, 2008), 261–75. See also Jacques Derrida, *The Work of Mourning*, trans. Pascale-Anne Brault and Michael Naas (Chicago, IL: University of Chicago Press, 2001).

[76] Brassier, *Nihil Unbound: Enlightenment and Extinction*: 223.

[77] Ibid., 224. His italics.

[78] Ibid., 227.

[79] Ibid., 228.

[80] Ibid., 229.

[81] Lyotard, *The Inhuman: Reflections on Time*: 9.

[82] Brassier, *Nihil Unbound: Enlightenment and Extinction*: xi.

[83] Ibid., 229.

muted, but realistic account of our own nature.[84] In the end there will only "be" no longer being-there.

References

Alweiss, Lilian. 2007. Leaving metaphysics to itself. *International Journal of Philosophical Studies* 15(3): 349–365.

Alweiss, Lilian. 2009. Between internalism and externalism: Husserl's account of intentionality. *Inquiry* 52(1): 53–78.

Bambach, Charles R. 1995. *Heidegger, Dilthey, and the crisis of historicism*. Ithaca: Cornell University Press.

Braig, Carl. 1896. *Vom Sein: Abriß der Ontologie*. Freiburg: Herder.

Brassier, Ray. 2007. *Nihil unbound: enlightenment and extinction*. London: Palgrave Macmillan.

Brentano, Franz. 1862. *Von der mannigfachen Bedeutung des Seienden nach Aristoteles*. Freiburg: Herder.

Bulhof, Ilse. 1980. *Wilhelm Dilthey: a hermeneutic approach to the study of history and culture*. The Hague: Martinus Nijhoff Publishers.

Bulhof, Ilse. 2011. The return of anti-religion: from radical atheism to radical theology. *Journal for Cultural and Religious Theory* 11(2): 32–124.

Caputo, John D. 2005. In praise of ambiguity. In *Ambiguity in the western mind*, ed. Craig J.N. de Paulo, Patrick Messina, and Marc Stier, 15–34. New York: Peter Lang.

Derrida, Jacques. 1993. *Aporias*. Trans. Thomas Dutoit. Stanford: Stanford University Press.

Derrida, Jacques. 2001. *The Work of Mourning*. Trans. Pascale-Anne Brault and Michael Naas. Chicago: University of Chicago Press.

Derrida, Jacques. 2005. *Paper Machine*. Trans. Rachel Bowlby. Stanford: Stanford University Press.

Ennis, Paul J. 2011. The transcendental core of correlationism. *Cosmos and History* 7(1): 37–48.

Glazebrook, Trish. 2001. Heidegger and scientific realism. *Continental Philosophy Review* 34: 361–401.

Gratton, Peter. 2009. After the subject: Meillassoux's ontology of "What May Be". *Pli: The Warwick Journal of Philosophy* 20: 55–80.

Haar, Michel. 1993. *Heidegger and the Essence of Man*. Trans. William McNeill. Albany: State University of New York Press.

Hägglund, Martin. 2009. The challenge of radical atheism: a response. *CR: The New Centennial Review* 9(1): 227–252.

Heidegger, Martin. 1977. The question concerning technology. In *The question concerning technology and other essays*, 3–35. New York: Harper and Row.

Heidegger, Martin. 1982a. *The Basic Problems of Phenomenology*. Trans. Albert Hofstadter. Bloomington: Indiana University Press.

Heidegger, Martin. 1982b. *Von Wesen der menschlichen Freiheit. Einleitung in die Philosophie*. Frankfurt am Main: Vittorio Klostermann.

Heidegger, Martin. 1992. *The Concept of Time*. Trans. William McNeill. Oxford: Blackwell Publishing.

Heidegger, Martin. 1996. *Being and Time*. Trans. Joan Stambaugh. Albany: State University of New York Press.

Heidegger, Martin. 1999. *Contributions to Philosophy (From Enowning)*. Trans. Parvis Emad and Kenneth Maly. Bloomington: Indiana University Press.

---

[84] Ibid., xi.

Heidegger, Martin. 2003. Only a God can save us: Der Spiegel's Interview (September 23, 1966). In *Martin Heidegger: philosophical and political writings*, ed. Manfred Stassen, 24–48. New York: Continuum.

Heidegger, Martin. 2006. *Mindfulness*. London: Continuum International Publishing Group.

Husserl, Edmund. 1960. *Cartesian Meditations: An Introduction to Phenomenology*. Trans. Dorion Cairns. The Hague: Martinus Nijhoff Publishers.

Husserl, Edmund. 1970a. *The Crisis of European Sciences and Transcendental Phenomenology*. Trans. David Carr. Evanston: Northwestern University Press.

Husserl, Edmund. 1970b. *Philosophie der Arithmetik: Psychologische und Logische Untersuchungen, I*. Haag: Martinus Nijhoff.

Husserl, Edmund. 1980. *The Idea of Phenomenology*. Trans. William Alston and George Nakhnikian. Dordrecht: Kluwer.

Husserl, Edmund. 1993a. *Logische Untersuchungen. Erster Teil: Prolegomena zur Reinen Logik*. Tübingen: Max Niemeyer Verlag.

Husserl, Edmund. 1993b. *Logische Untersuchungen. Zweiter Teil: Untersuchungen zur Phänomenologie und Theorie der Erkenntnis*. Tübingen: Max Niemeyer Verlag.

John, E. 1988. Husserl's position between Dilthey and the Windelband-Rickert school of Neo-Kantianism. *Journal of the History of Philosophy* 26(2): 279–296.

Kant, Immanuel. 2007. *Critique of Pure Reason*. Trans. Paul Guyer and Allen W. Wood. Cambridge: Cambridge University Press.

Levinas, Emmanuel. 2005. *Totality and Infinity: An Essay on Exteriority*. Trans. Alphonso Lingis. Pittsburgh: Duquesne University Press.

Lyotard, Jean-François. 1991. *The Inhuman: Reflections on Time*. Trans. Geoffrey Bennington and Rachel Bowlby. Stanford: Stanford University Press.

Makkreel, Rudolf A. 1969. Wilhelm Dilthey and the Neo-Kantians: The distinction of the Geisteswissenschaften and the Kulturwissenschaften. *Journal of the History of Philosophy* 7(4): 423–440.

Meillassoux, Quentin. 2008a. Spectral Dilemma. In *Collapse IV: Concept horror*, ed. Robin Mackay, 261–275. Falmouth: Urbanomic.

Meillassoux, Quentin. 2008b. *After Finitude: An Essay on the Necessity of Contingency*. Trans. Ray Brassier. London: Continuum.

Meillassoux, Quentin. 2014. *Time without becoming*. Trans. Anna Longo. London: Mimesis International.

Roth, Michael. 1996. *The poetics of resistance: Heidegger's line*. Evanston: Northwestern University Press.

Sellars, Wilfred. 1991. *Science, perception and reality*. Atascadero: Ridgeview Publishing Company.

Sellars, Wilfred. 1997. *Empiricism and the philosophy of mind*. Cambridge, MA: Harvard University Press.

Sparrow, Tom. 2014. *The end of phenomenology: Metaphysics and the new realism*. Edinburgh: Edinburgh University Press.

Žižek, Slavoj, and Glyn Daly. 2004. *Conversations with Žižek*. Cambridge: Polity Press.

The Untranslatable to Come: From Saying to Unsayable

Lisa Foran

Abstract The word 'saying' is used in English to translate both *die Sage* in the work of Martin Heidegger, and *le dire* in that of Emmanuel Levinas. In this chapter I sketch the manner in which these two 'sayings' converge and diverge around the place of language. Broadly speaking, I argue that in their treatment of this word Heidegger and Levinas remain within the tradition of metaphysics insofar as the term 'saying' names. It names precisely a difference within the space of which the human subject dwells. For Heidegger; the space of the ontological difference both named yet concealed in the essence of language (Saying) or, for Levinas; the space of the ethical difference named as the primary signification of the one's responsibility for the Other (saying). The naming of such a difference establishes limits which circumscribe a space or place for the subject and reduces that difference to something translatable. For Derrida, beyond such a difference between the one and the other, or between Being and being, is another difference. A difference that remains radically impossible. It is approached through numerous terms such as différance, supplement, trace, and so on in Derrida's work. But this very multiplicity of terms itself reveals the radical impossibility of it being named *as such*. Here, having outlined the accounts of Heidegger and Levinas, I conclude by approaching this radically untranslatable/unnameable/unsayable in Derrida through the word *Khōra*.

Keywords Heidegger • Levinas • Derrida • Translation • Language • Impossible • *Khōra*

L. Foran (✉)
Philosophical Studies, Newcastle University, Newcastle Upon Tyne, UK
e-mail: lisa.foran@ncl.ac.uk

© Springer International Publishing Switzerland 2016
L. Foran, R. Uljée (eds.), *Heidegger, Levinas, Derrida: The Question of Difference*, Contributions To Phenomenology 86,
DOI 10.1007/978-3-319-39232-5_5

1   Introduction

The word 'saying' is used in English to translate both *die Sage* in the work of Martin Heidegger, and *le dire* in that of Emmanuel Levinas.[1] In this chapter I sketch the manner in which these two 'sayings' converge and diverge around the place of language. Broadly speaking, I argue that in their treatment of this word Heidegger and Levinas remain within the tradition of metaphysics insofar as the term 'saying' names. It names precisely a difference within the space of which the human subject dwells. For Heidegger; the space of the ontological difference both named yet concealed in the essence of language (Saying) or, for Levinas; the space of the ethical difference named as the primary signification of the one's responsibility for the Other (saying). The naming of such a difference establishes limits which circumscribe a space or place for the subject and reduces that difference to something translatable. For Derrida, beyond such a difference between the one and the other, or between Being and being, is another difference. A difference that remains radically impossible. It is approached through numerous terms such as différance, supplement, trace, and so on in Derrida's work. But this very multiplicity of terms itself reveals the radical impossibility of it being named *as such*. Here, having outlined the accounts of Heidegger and Levinas, I conclude by approaching this radically untranslatable/unnameable/unsayable in Derrida through the word *Khōra*.

2   Heidegger's Saying

Language and its relation to Being occupies Heidegger's thinking from the time of his *Habilitationsschrift* on Duns Scotus in 1915. During the 1930s and 1940s language takes on a more and more central role, so that by the 1950s language is a principal focus in and of itself.[2] Heidegger's question in these later works is what is "the manner in which language has being"[3]? Heidegger proposes the phrase "the Being of language: the language of Being [*Das Wesen des Sprache*: *Die Sprache des Wesens*]"[4] as a "guide word" or possible response to this question. While this phrase

---

[1] 'Saying' with a capital 'S' will be used to denote Heidegger's *die Sage*, whereas 'saying' will be used for Levinas's *le dire*.

[2] Martin Heidegger, *Unterwegs Zur Sprache* [GA12] (Frankfurt am Main: Vittorio Klostermann, 1985). Trans. by Peter D. Hertz, *On the Way to Language*. New York: Harper & Row, 1971) [hereafter UZS] pp. 88–9/trans. p. 7.

[3] UZS p. 238/trans. p. 119.

[4] UZS p. 170/trans. p. 76 Translator Peter Hertz notes that *Wesen* would ordinarily be translated as 'essence' or 'essential nature' but that the context here "seems to demand the translation 'being'" (UZS n. trans. p. 76). However this is in some ways unsurprising. As Werner Marx points out, Heidegger quite deliberately translates *Eon/on* (Being) and *ousia* (essence) by the same word, namely *Anwesen* (presenting/presenting process); using *Anwesenden* (those present) to translate *eonta/onta* (beings). These translations seek to subvert the history of the words being and essence which, for Heidegger, have become 'empty' or mere 'general concepts' in philosophy. See: Werner

is not an assertion which can be proven as 'true' or 'false' in terms of 'correctness',[5] each side or part of the phrase can be examined to discover its meaning. Heidegger claims that the first part of the phrase, the 'Being of language', is to be understood as: "*Saying as Showing [Das Wesende der Sprache ist die Sage als die Zeige]*."[6] Saying, then, is a *logos apophantikos*. Language has the kind of Being that makes, or at least allows, things to appear; the Being of language *shows*. Saying, however, is not the same as speaking but is rather the condition of the possibility of speech, or 'language'.[7] Language speaks by showing or by letting appear all that is present.[8] What grants the present its presence, however, is Saying which is not inseparable from Being itself. For Heidegger, the relation between word and thing, between language and what is, has been expressed in a single word: *logos*, which "speaks simultaneously as the *name* for Being and for Saying."[9] It is not the case that Saying adds linguistic expression to phenomena which have *already* appeared; rather Heidegger insists that they appear only inasmuch as they are in Saying. Heidegger offers the following description:

> Saying [*Die Sage*] sets all present beings free into their given presence, and brings what is absent into its absence. Saying pervades and structures the openness of that clearing [*Lichtung*] which every appearance must seek out and every disappearance must leave behind, and in which every present or absent being must show, say, announce itself. Saying is the gathering that joins all appearance of the in itself manifold showing which everywhere lets all that is shown abide within itself.[10]

In these sentences 'Saying' could well be replaced by 'Being'. As with Being, Saying is not a being and, as with Being, Saying is without ground.[11] Saying therefore '*is*' Being; provided we bear in mind Heidegger's account of identity. As is so often the case in Heidegger's work, translation operates as a method for thinking the as yet unthought in the history of metaphysics. 'Identical' in Latin is *idem*, a translation of the Greek *auto*, an expression which means, Heidegger notes, 'the same'.[12] Yet the principle of identity, 'A = A', does not simply say 'every A is the same' but crucially that 'every A is the same *with* itself'. The 'with' is fundamental; it evidences identity as born of mediation. What is 'the same' is always 'the same *as*', or 'the same *with*', something else. Identity as 'sameness' thus implies relation

---

Marx, *Heidegger and the Tradition*. Trans. by Theodore Kisiel & Murray Greene (Evanston: Northwestern University Press, 1971) pp. 131–2.

[5] UZS p. 170/trans. p. 77 A claim of course in line with Heidegger's reformulation of 'truth' as *alētheia* rather than as *adequatio*.

[6] UZS p. 242/trans. p. 123.

[7] UZS p. 241/trans. p. 122.

[8] UZS p. 243/trans. p. 124.

[9] UZS p. 174/trans. p. 80 (my emphasis).

[10] UZS p. 246/trans. p. 126.

[11] UZS p. 244/trans. p. 125.

[12] Martin Heidegger, 'Identität und Differenz'. In *Identität und Differenz* [GA 11] (Frankfurt am Main: Vittorio Klostermann, 2006). pp. 27–80. Trans. by Joan Stambaugh, *Identity and Difference*. (New York: Harper & Row, 1969) [hereafter ID] p. 33/trans. p. 23.

"mediation, a connection, a synthesis: the unification into a unity."[13] Thus, 'Saying = Being' must be thought of as Saying is the 'same' *with* Being; they are gathered together in a mediated unity.

'The Being of language', then, refers to the manner in which Being and Saying (which are the same) unconceal or show that which is presently present. This first part of Heidegger's phrase deals with the *essence* or 'whatness' of language. On the other hand, in the second part of the phrase, 'the language of Being', 'Being' is to be understood verbally as 'being present' or 'being absent'. 'To be' here is understood by Heidegger as that which persists in its presence in that it "moves and makes way for all things"; language is what is "proper to what moves all things".[14] This understanding of the 'language of being' as that which sets in motion, corresponds to Heidegger's career long concern with the term *logos*. Being as truth gives beings their Being while withdrawing itself. In this withdrawal it provides the expanse in which beings gather and it preserves beings there in their present. The withdrawal of Being is the truth (*alētheia*) of Being insofar as this withdrawal is part of its essence. Being names the presencing of what is present, in the sense of a gathering which 'clears and shelters', and this in turn is designated for Heidegger by the word *logos*. "The [*logos*] ([*legein*], to gather or assemble) is experienced through [*alētheia*], the sheltering which reveals things."[15] *Logos* which clears and therefore shows that which is present is, however, also a groundless play. It is the mistaken understanding of *logos* as ground already in the works of Plato and Aristotle that leads to the onto-theo-logical constitution of metaphysics.[16] Heidegger's insistence is rather that Being must be thought of as *logos* – a 'groundless play' which sets all things in motion. But *logos* of course is also 'discourse', 'the word', 'utterance' – the language of Being as Saying as "that which moves all things."[17]

While Saying is not speaking, it nonetheless is made manifest as such, so what exactly does speaking entail for Heidegger? In *Sein und Zeit* keeping silent and listening are accorded a particular weight in the discussion of language. In that earlier work listening is the means through which an authentic Being-with becomes "transparent" to Dasein. In Heidegger's later work speaking as the manifestation of Saying also entails a listening, but the belonging-together it reveals is not the Being-with of Dasein. Rather, listening now reveals the manner in which the belonging together of man and Being is 'given' by *Ereignis*. Heidegger argues that in the listening which accompanies our speaking we listen to Saying itself. It is Saying that gives the gift of language and so it is only through listening to Saying that we have language at all.[18] Furthermore, this listening is possible only on the basis of a belonging-with:

---

[13] ID p. 34/trans. p. 25.

[14] UZS p. 190/trans. p. 95.

[15] Martin Heidegger, 'Der Spruch des Anaximander'. In *Holzwege* [GA 5] (Frankfurt am Main: Vittorio Klostermann, 1977). pp. 321–73. Trans. by David Farrell Krell & Frank A. Capuzzi, 'The Anaximander Fragment' in Martin Heidegger, *Early Greek Thinking*. New York: Harper & Row, 1975. pp. 13–58. [hereafter SA] p. 352/trans. p. 39.

[16] Werner Marx, *op.cit.* p. 156.

[17] UZS p. 191/trans. p. 95.

[18] UZS p. 243/trans. p. 123–4.

"[w]e hear Saying only because we belong within it. Saying grants the hearing, and thus the speaking, of language solely to those who belong within it."[19] This 'belonging with Saying' (which is the same *with* the 'belonging with Being') comes into its own only through the *Ereignis* – the mutually appropriating event of man and being coming together in their active nature "extended as a gift, one to the other."[20]

It is only in *Ereignis* that the full essence of Saying as showing can reach language, "language always speaks according to the mode in which the Appropriation [*Ereignis*] as such reveals itself or withdraws."[21] If, to come into its essence man must speak by way of listening to Saying, then equally Saying must be voiced by man. Their mutual co-belonging revealed only through *Ereignis* is summarised by Heidegger: "Saying is in need of being voiced in the word. But man is capable of speaking only insofar as he, belonging to Saying, listens to Saying, so that in resaying it he may be able to say a word."[22]

It would be tempting to think of this 'resaying' simply as a translation of Saying into man's said. However, this would perhaps be too rash. Heidegger describes Saying as a 'silent voice' by *way* of which we speak and to think of it as something *said* to man would be to misunderstand Heidegger's account. It is more, for Heidegger, that Saying as Being is what allows something (a being), its present in Being. In speaking, then, we unconceal that which has already been unconcealed by Being (Saying) itself. Nonetheless, what is it that we 'resay' in a word? What is the nature of the word?

Heidegger's reading of Stefan George's 'The Word'[23] provides some insight. The poem tells of the poet's relation with language. Initially the poet sought the word for something from the goddess of language who would bestow a word on each thing the poet brought to her shore. However, on one occasion the poet brings a prize "so rich and frail" for which the goddess has no word and immediately the 'prize' escapes. The last lines of George's poem read "[w]here word breaks off no thing may be."[24] For Heidegger the 'word' here in the poem gives a thing (a being) its Being. The word like Saying, indeed like Being itself, is not a being but rather the gift that gives Being – *es gibt Sein*: "the word itself gives […] the word gives Being."[25] If the word gives but in the poem the word is denied to the poet, this should not lead us to think that the 'prize' simply vanishes. Rather, it escapes him insofar as the "the word is denied. The denial is a holding back."[26] This does not mean that the prize is 'gone' but rather that it has sunk into concealment and this

---

[19] UZS p. 244/trans. p. 124.
[20] ID pp. 41–2/trans. p. 33.
[21] UZS p. 251/trans. p. 131.
[22] UZS p. 254/trans. p. 134 Heidegger uses 'man' and 'he'; I try to avoid these terms by using 'its' where possible.
[23] First published in 1919 and later published as part of the collection *Das Neue Reich*, in 1928 (see UZS p. 152/trans. p. 60).
[24] UZS p. 152/trans. p. 60*ff.*
[25] UZS p. 182/trans. pp. 87–8.
[26] UZS p. 183/trans. p. 88.

concealment itself reveals something to the poet. It reveals, in a way that cannot *yet* be said, "the intuited secret of the word, which in denying itself brings near to us its withheld nature."[27] The denial of the word here is at one with the withdrawal of Being. In the withdrawal of Being man is given over to thinking Being inasmuch as he is given his Being. Equally with the denial of the word, man (or the poet) is given to think the relation between Saying and Being as presencing. The denial itself is already a gift. What is interesting here, and particularly in terms of our concerns surrounding the possibility of naming, is how Heidegger understands this withdrawal or concealment as "the mysterious nearness of the far-tarrying power of the word."[28]

This 'mysteriousness' is the manner by which Heidegger refers to the unsaid, unthought or unspoken. The question now is whether this unsaid is simply unsaid as yet or radically unsayable. "The same word [*logos*], however, the word for Saying is also the word for Being, that is, for the presencing of beings."[29] While *logos* sets all things in motion and manifests as language, language itself can be a dangerous possession. Language, particularly in the form of rigid terminology, can entrap thinking. The *Gestell*, for example, reveals beings only in terms of their use; it reveals beings as 'standing-reserve' rather than in their own essence. Heidegger himself becomes increasingly suspect of terminology, claiming that he drops words such as 'hermeneutic', 'phenomenology' and so on in order to "abandon [his] thinking to namelessness".[30] As a result of this mistrust of rigid formulaic language Heidegger notes that Saying itself remains always 'beyond language' that "Saying will not let itself be captured in any statement."[31] The mysteriousness that Heidegger accords the 'word' above is precisely this ambiguous Saying: "[t]he treasure which never graced the poet's land is the word for the being of language."[32]

Saying, then, for Heidegger names (albeit ambiguously) Being – that which gives beings their Being and simultaneously withdraws itself thereby opening the space of difference in which man dwells. Saying as the essence of language may well have been forgotten in the history of metaphysics. Saying may also be difficult to grasp in language as a system of signs, insofar as that language has been marked by this metaphysical history. However, Saying is not unnameable as such, but is rather "beyond the reach of speaking" in the same way that Being is beyond the reach of thinking. That is, beyond the reach of speaking or thinking *thus far*. The task of thinking is to think the concealing/unconcealing movement of Being *in motion*; to think "the presence of the twofold, Being and beings – but this twofold understood in respect for thinking them."[33] Equally, one might claim, Saying must be thought as that which gives language in its own withdrawal. This thinking of

---

[27] *Ibid.*

[28] UZS p. 184/trans. p. 89.

[29] UZS p. 224/trans. p. 155.

[30] UZS p. 114/trans. p. 29.

[31] UZS p. 255/trans. p. 134.

[32] UZS p. 223/trans. p. 154.

[33] UZS p. 112/trans. pp. 26–7.

Saying or Being would appear at least to be on the horizon – and therefore possible, sayable, nameable – with Heidegger's own work. As Werner Marx points out, "Heidegger is convinced that the 'turn' from the oblivion of Being, from the withdrawal of creative Being, to the world essence has already 'e-vented' itself".[34]

3 Levinas's Saying

For Derrida, in naming, identifying and thereby limiting difference, Heidegger's thinking results in "a presumption of unity" gathered beneath and within the sole 'sending of Being'.[35] In this 'gathering' of philosophy, Derrida claims, something remains excluded. For Levinas, what is excluded is a thinking of radical alterity that could not be subsumed into the Same. In short, we might say that if for Heidegger philosophy forgot the ontological difference, then for Levinas philosophy – including Heidegger – forgot the ethical difference of the Other person (*Autrui*). Philosophy, claims Levinas, reduces everything to "the constitution of being" so that the approach of the Other becomes their manifestation in being and their immediate loss of alterity.[36] Levinas's question then to Heidegger, and indeed to the philosophical tradition is "Does a significance of signification exist which would not be equivalent to the transmutation of the Other into the Same?"[37] This question leads Levinas to posit various 'counterpoints' to the tradition of philosophy, or at least philosophy's description of the subject.

One of the overwhelming characteristics of this Levinasian contrapuntal subject is its sensibility (prior or separate to its intelligibility). The 1935 *De l'Évasion*, [*On Escape*], for example, describes the sentient aspect of life (in contradistinction to an intentional life) with accounts of nausea and shame. These physical experiences hurl us into an absolute present and reveal the desire to escape oppressive anonymous being (the *il y a*). Similarly, the 1947 *De l'existence à l'existant* [*Existence and Existants*] employs accounts of bodily states such as fatigue and insomnia, to reveal the gap between the bodily 'self' and the intentional 'I'. By the time of the more systematic *Totalité et infini* [*Totality and Infinity*] in 1961, Levinas goes so far as to state: "Sensibility constitutes the very egoism of the I, *which is sentient and not something sensed* [...] sensation breaks up every system".[38] Before any intentional

---

[34] Werner Marx, *op.cit.*, p. 240.

[35] Jacques Derrida *Points de suspension, Entretiens* (Paris: Éditions Galilée, 1992). Trans. by Peggy Kamuf & others, *Points… Interviews, 1974–1994* (Stanford: Stanford University Press, 1995) [hereafter Points] pp. 139–40/trans. p. 131.

[36] Emmanuel Levinas 'La trace de l'autre'. In *En découvrant l'existence avec Husserl et Heidegger* (Paris: Vrin, 1994). pp. 187–202. [hereafter TdA] p. 188.

[37] TdA p. 190 (my translation).

[38] Emmanuel Levinas, *Totalité et infini* (Paris: Le Livre de de Poche, 2011). Trans. by Alphonso Lingis, *Totality and Infinity*. Pennsylvania: Duquesne University Press, 1969. [hereafter TI] p. 53/ trans. p. 59 (Italics at source).

act, we are a body responding to our exposure to the world and specifically to our exposure to the other person – the Other. Prior to intentionality, argues Levinas, is sensibility.

This Levinasian subject is described as a consciousness with "no name, no situation", a consciousness without and before identity.[39] Subjectivity here is an *u-topos*, an exiled Abraham as opposed to the homeward bound Odysseus. This other kind of subjectivity interrupts the order of being, interrupts the subject's being-for-itself so that it is for-the-other. This being-for-the-other, that is, one's infinite responsibility for the other person; is the primary signification for Levinas. The question is no longer 'what is the meaning of being?', but 'what does my being mean for the other?' This notion of the subject as beyond a systemization (including that of a system of 'morality') is central for Levinasian ethics, or what Derrida describes as an 'ethics of ethics'.[40] Ethics cannot consist in reducing the singularity of a subject by simply inserting particular beings into an abstract ethical system. Ethics is rather *the* particularity of my existence in the face of the Other: ethics is 'first philosophy'. In this sense, for Levinas it is not that Heidegger failed to provide 'an ethics' as such, but rather that Heidegger in describing human existence failed to account for the manner in which that existence itself is, from the beginning, ethical.

The 1974 work *Autrement qu'être, ou au-delà de l'essence* [*Otherwise than Being or Beyond Essence*], takes this contrapuntal subject even further by now describing it as 'hostage' to the other. The 'otherwise than being' refers to that which comes before the ontological order, systematization and calculability. That is, the subject's infinite responsibility for the Other over and beyond the subject's concern for its own or proper being. Meaning is this infinite responsibility. What Levinas terms *saying* (*le dire*) in *Otherwise than Being* is the 'foreword of languages' [*avant-propos des langues*] and it leaves its trace in the *said*. Saying here, the foreword or preface of languages, is the primary signification of the one *for* the other which makes possible and leaves its trace in language understood as a system of signs – the said (*le dit*).[41]

"Saying signifies otherwise than as an apparitor [*appariteur*] presenting essence and entities."[42] This of course is in contradistinction to the Heideggerian 'Saying' examined above. It is worth highlighting Levinas's choice of words here – saying is not just an 'apparitor'. Coming from the Latin *apparere* ['to appear'] an apparitor was a Roman public servant attending an authoritative figure of Roman law. Levinas's claim here is that Saying is not the facilitator of an ontological (or political)

[39] Emmanuel Levinas *Éthique comme philosophie première*. (Paris: Éditions Payot & Rivages, 1998). Trans. By Seán Hand & Michael Temple, 'Ethics as First Philosophy' In Seán Hand (ed.) *The Levinas Reader*, Oxford: Blackwell, 1989. pp. 75–87. [hereafter EPP] p. 88/trans. p. 81.

[40] Jacques Derrida, *L'écriture et la différence*. (Paris: Les Éditions du Seuil, 1967). Trans. by Alan Bass, *Writing and Difference*. (London & New York: Routledge, 2001). [hereafter ED] p. 164/ trans. p. 138.

[41] Emmanuel Levinas, *Autrement qu'être ou au-delà de l'essence*. (Paris: Le Livre de Poche, 2010). Trans. by Alphonso Lingis, *Otherwise than Being or Beyond Essence* (The Hague: Martinus Nijhoff, 1981). [hereafter AQE] p. 17/trans. pp. 5–6.

[42] AQE p. 78/tans p. 46.

order but the ethical non-origin of such a structure. Language may well be 'the house of Being', but saying is not, in Heideggerian terms 'the essence or Being of language'. Rather saying is what disrupts and opens language to the non-place of signification; to the *otherwise* than being. As such, the Levinasian saying is *other to* 'that which makes appear'. That is, other to the authority of essence and, as we will shall see, other to the law of recuperable time.

Saying is not simply the giving of signs but rather the ambiguous transformation of the subject into a sign itself.[43] In this 'becoming-sign' of the subject, argues Levinas, is an exposure to trauma, a sensible vulnerability. The subject is its sensibility; exposed to the Other in a pure passivity: "an exposure to expressing and thus to Saying, and thus to Giving."[44] What is given here is the self, given in passivity and sacrificed without intention. The subject is both the giving and the gift that is given. A gift that cannot even be acknowledged as such, a gift that demands the *ingratitude* of the Other since: "Gratitude would be precisely the *return* of the movement to its origin."[45] The subject is the null-site between being and otherwise than being, the knot and the unravelling of that knot between the two. While on the one hand the immanence of being makes of the subject an intentional ego who can think, conceptualize and abstract through language; the otherwise than being is revealed in the subject's sensibility as the primary signification of responsibility. Whereas essence as interest, as the *il y a*, does not allow for interruption or exception, it fills in all the gaps so to speak; the other of being is a non place, is the exception to the immanence of being and it signifies subjectivity.[46] Subjectivity is not pure interest in its own perseverance but is marked and indeed constituted by the encounter with the Other which transforms the being, the interest, of the subject into being-for-another – responsibility. Sensibility, the subject's exposure to wounding and pain,[47] is the manner by which the subject is affected by the Other. Pain can never be re-presented, we can remember *that* we felt pain but we cannot feel it again, and it is this non-re-presentable quality of sensibility that reveals the diachronic time of the Other.

Central to the analysis of responsibility is the question of temporality and the manner in which it indicates the pre-original saying as the absolute responsibility for the Other. The problem, as Levinas states it, is how can subjectivity be thus extracted from essence, from being, without this extraction *lasting* or *taking place* in being? What is the time of the *utopos* of otherwise than being? What is the time of saying? The temporalization of time for Levinas is on the one hand a recuperation of everything through retention, memory and history whereby nothing is lost and everything is presented and represented in the 'scelerosization' of everything into substance. And yet, on the other hand, the temporalization of time must necessarily also include 'a lapse of time', the instant 'out of phase with itself', without which no time could *pass* at all. As Levinas describes it: "a lapse of time that does

---

[43] AQE p. 83/trans. p. 49.
[44] AQE p. 85/trans. p. 50.
[45] TdA, p. 191 (my translation).
[46] AQE p. 21 /trans. p. 8.
[47] See AQE pp. 111–155 /trans. pp. 69–78.

not return, a diachrony refractory to all synchronization."[48] The recuperating temporalizing of time also signals the irrecuperable lapse of time, a past which cannot be re-presented; a pre-original past. As with saying, that 'pre-original language' which was yet signalled in language and in the said (though subordinated by it); so the pre-original past is signalled in the recuperating temporalization of time. The beyond of language or of time will always be *outside* of being, beyond the materiality of ontology.

The temporalization of time which indicates the difference between being and otherwise than being, must, for Levinas, be conceived of as saying itself. Saying 'is' the temporalization of time.[49] In *Sein und Zeit*, Heidegger argues that Dasein itself temporalizes and that this is 'original time' which is proximally and for the most part lost in the everydayness of 'the they'. The later Heidegger sees time as a gift, a gift from the *Ereignis – es gibt Sein, es gibt Zeit*. Time and Being for Heidegger (both early and late) are intimately entwined and, given our account of Saying (*die Sage*) above; we can see how Saying, time, and Being are all part of this gift. For Levinas too the temporalization of time is inextricably linked with saying (and thus language), but here saying is responsibility for the Other *outside* of Heidegger's 'Same' or Being. Therefore, my responsibility for the Other takes place in the non-recuperable temporalization of time which is saying revealed in language. Saying (*le dire*) is precisely that which cannot be grasped since by its very nature it is beyond the ontological plane. Saying here is rooted in subjectivity, that non-lieu between being and otherwise than being, the knot that both links without encompassing and closes without closing-off the relation between the two. Subjectivity passively enacts and inhabits the denegation of this relation. "Subjectivity is precisely the knot and the closure – the knot or the closure – of essence and essence's other."[50]

How are we to understand this pre-original saying or pre-original past? "The time of the *said* and of *essence* there lets the pre-original be heard".[51] Signification, for Levinas, is found in the *an-archē* of the beyond being in the immediacy of the face-to-face relation of subject and Other. This pre-originary anarchical relation, however, is always already interrupted. The face-to-face relation of the otherwise than being is disrupted by the third party, understood as the principle of human society and origin itself. The pre-original, as Fabio Ciaramelli has argued, is not some 'older' or more originary origin, but rather that which interrupts the origin of the ontological order.[52] We can see here a play of double interruption taking place. On the one hand, there is the interruption of the origin of the ontological by the pre-originary, conceived as signification. And on the other hand, there is the interruption

[48] AQE p. 23 /trans. p. 9.

[49] AQE p. 23 /trans. p. 9.

[50] AQE p. 23 /trans. (modified) p. 10.

[51] AQE pp. 24–5 /trans. pp. 10–11.

[52] Fabio Ciaramelli 'The Riddle of the Pre-original' in Adrian T. Peperzak (ed.) *Ethics as First Philosophy: The Significance of Emmanual Levinas for Philosophy, Literature and Religion* (Routledge, New York & London: 1995) pp. 87–94. p. 88.

of the pre-originary, the signification of the face-to-face relation, by the origin of the ontological.

Subjectivity, then, as that non-lieu between being and being's other, is founded (with all the difficulties of using the term 'founded' in relation to a non-place) in its responsibility for the Other. This raises the question of reciprocity. It may seem that Levinas is making the subject dependent on the Other. If both the subject and the Other are located, or perhaps better *dis*located in this between space or non-lieu, then to what extent are the subject and Other on the same plane? In answer to these questions we must bear in mind Levinas's warning to "stay within the situation of extreme diachrony" and that the beyond being "contests the unconditional privilege of the question: where?"[53] To speak of the subject and the Other as being on the same plane is to reinstate ontology; to see the subject as 'dependent' on the Other would be to reinstate a material economy of exchange. The beyond being is not subject to such an economy since this kind of calculating thinking only returns us to a thinking of synchrony and system, rather than a thinking of diachrony and interruption.

Saying for Levinas, is prior to being, or perhaps not even 'prior', which would suggest a linear temporalization, saying is rather *outside* of being. Whereas being is 'play without responsibility', saying refers to the inversion of being's interest. Saying is the responsibility for, and the substitution of, one for the other beyond the immanence of being. However, saying must manifest in some way in the said. My infinite responsibility for the other must translate itself to the finite ontological plane if I am to enact it – for only a god could act in the infinite. Saying therefore, as responsibility prior to being, manifests itself in *a* language, whereby it is subordinated to the ontological order, that is, to the said. The task of philosophy for Levinas, is "an incessant unsaying of the said"[54] to free the primary signification of the otherwise than being, to remember the subject's responsibility for the Other. The infinite responsibility of the one for the Other as saying is translated in its manifestation into the said. This 'said', language as systems of signs, overtakes and betrays the inherent ambiguity of saying: "the subordination of the saying to the said, to the linguistic system and to ontology, is the price that manifestation demands. In language as said, everything translates itself before us – be that at the price of a betrayal."[55] But this betrayal and the possibility of reducing it through an unsaying, also reveals the manner in which Levinas fails to escape the tradition he interrogates; the manner in which he, in some sense, remains committed to a metaphysics of presence: "betrayal at the price of which everything manifests itself, *even the unsayable*".[56] Even the unsayable becomes said; the beyond being named, my responsibility defined.

---

[53] AQE p. 21/trans. p. 8.

[54] AQE p. 278/trans. p. 181 This notion of an 'unsaying' was already introduced in the preface to TI (p. 16 /tans. p. 30).

[55] AQE pp. 17–18/trans. (modified) p. 6.

[56] AQE p. 19 /trans. (modified) p. 7 my emphasis.

4 Conclusion: Derrida's *Khōra*

The focus thus far has been on the role of language in Heidegger and Levinas; specifically on that which makes language possible. For Heidegger that is Saying (*die Sage*) – the essence of language and in fact Being itself. For Heidegger, Saying gifts itself to man insofar as man, Being and Saying are gathered together in the *Ereignis*. For Levinas, saying (*le dire*) is the primary signification – the infinite responsibility of the one for the other, the otherwise than being. In both cases that which philosophy has forgotten – Being or Alterity – in some sense has now been remembered. Saying, for both thinkers remains enigmatic, equivocal and difficult to grasp. It is covered over by the sedimented language of metaphysics and as such demands either a resaying (Heidegger) or an unsaying (Levinas) so that its significance is not lost once again. Breathing life into saying's meaning, reanimating the body of the word with the soul of *the* signification, is the very task of philosophy. This signification, in both thinkers, centres on a thinking of difference – ontological or ethical. It is of course this thinking of difference that inscribes itself in Derrida's work. The difference with Derrida is to be found in the possibility of naming what that difference is. What remains as yet unthought in the work of Heidegger and Levinas, for Derrida, concerns the question of determination; the manner in which any determination, limitation or definition remains haunted by what it excludes. The saying of Heidegger and Levinas refers to a place – either the clearing of Being in which man dwells; or the non-lieu of subjectivity, the otherwise than being where man is held hostage for the other. For Derrida these named places, these origins or pre-origins of language, are places we can map precisely because their limits have been named, they are therefore places we can visit rather than places "where (*wo, Ort, Wort*) it is impossible to go."[57] The challenge, for Derrida, is to think beyond the name, to think "what is still to come or what remains buried in an almost inaccessible memory".[58]

This 'impossible place', this difference which is no longer a difference *between* is approached by many words in Derrida's work, none of which could be said to name the difference *as such*. Here I use Derrida's reading of the word *Khōra* as a means to interrogate his own departure from Heidegger and Levinas, although this of course is only one way to read this departure. It is necessarily more than a little difficult to speak of *Khōra*; a placeless place which is in fact nothing. *Khōra* is other

---

[57] Jacques Derrida, *Sauf le nom*. (Paris: Galilée, 1993). Trans. by John P. Leavey Jr., 'Sauf le nom'. In *On the Name*. Stanford: Stanford University Press, 1995. pp. 35–85. [hereafter SN] p. 63 /trans. p. 59.

[58] Points p. 298 /trans. pp. 283–4: "In relation to whom, to what other, is the subject first thrown (*geworfen*) or exposed as hostage? Who is the 'neighbour' dwelling in the very proximity of transcendence, in Heidegger's transcendence, or in Levinas's? These two ways of thinking transcendence are as different as you wish. They are as different or as similar as being and the other, but seem to me to follow the same schema. What is still to come or what remains buried in an almost inaccessible memory is the thinking of responsibility that does not stop [*ne s'arrête*] at *this* determination of the neighbour, at the dominant schema of this determination."

beyond an understanding of other that would institute a relation. It is of a third genus, a *triton genos*; neither sensible nor intelligible, neither mythos nor logos, neither being nor nothing, nor even Being nor being: "but between all these couples and *another* which would not even be *their* other."[59] Its time, if I might speak of such a thing as 'the time of *Khōra*', is not that of being for *Khōra* is anachronistic. *Khōra* is without chronology without an order as such, it is the "inevitable" anachronism of the structure of being; it "anachronizes being."[60] Derrida claims it attempts to name 'imminence'; what is yet to come. Crucially, however, it does not name what we are *waiting for* to come since its imminence is alien to, other to, "every possible promise and threat."[61] The radical otherness of *Khōra*, the radical difference of *Khōra*, means that it escapes any horizon of expectation. *Khōra* thus names what is yet to come that cannot be expected and even in so doing, in naming an absolute imminence, in announcing the irruption of that which is other to its name and of the other more generally[62]; it still cannot be simply reduced to its name or to what it names. Without an essence as such, argues Derrida it cannot even be 'beyond its name' for this would be to place it in some definite place.

In what sense do these attempted descriptions echo the accounts of saying in Heidegger and Levinas? To begin with Heidegger; *Khōra* would seem very close to the Saying described above. It is a place which gives place to that whose laws it itself escapes.[63] It is beyond calculation, other to that which can be counted, just like Being (or Saying) which in giving beings their time and place "withdraws essentially from all calculation". But it would be 'risky', warns Derrida, to view *Khōra* in this way, as some sort of *es Gibt*.[64] Why? For one thing, it would be to re-inscribe *Khōra* in a logic of opposition which invariably leads to a logic of translatability (no matter how ambiguous or interminable); from Being to being, from Saying to the word of the poet, from one side to the other, one place to the other place. *Khōra* is exactly the other to these others – the third order, the excluded middle which remains beyond the name. Furthermore, the etymological links of *die Sage* to 'legend' or the oral tradition of story-telling, associates it with 'myth'. Yet Derrida is quite clear that *Khōra* is "beyond the retarded or johnny-come-lately opposition of *logos* and *mythos*".[65] *Khōra* remains untranslatable despite the play of translations operating within it – 'place', 'receptacle', 'nurse', 'imprint-bearer' – these 'translations' are but retrospective attempts to name what slips out of the grasp of thinking.[66] Unlike

---

[59] Jacques Derrida, *Khōra*. (Paris: Galilée, 1993). Trans. by Ian McLeod '*Khōra*', in Jacques Derrida, *On the Name* (Stanford: Stanford University Press, 1995) pp. 88–127 [hereafter *Khōra*] p. 46 /trans. p. 104.

[60] *Khōra* p. 25 /trans. pp. 93–4.

[61] *Khōra* p. 15 /trans. p. 89.

[62] *Ibid.*

[63] *Khōra* p. 18/ trans. p. 90.

[64] *Khōra* p. 30 /trans. p. 95.

[65] *Khōra* p. 18 /trans. p. 90.

[66] *Khōra* pp. 23–4 /trans. p. 93 Derrida notes that Heidegger too is led astray in attempting to name *Khōra* as the the place of the difference between Being and being in *Introduction to Metaphysics*.

Heidegger's Saying which is *appropriate to* (proper to) man, which gathers man to his ownmost belonging; *Khōra* is a "very singular impropriety" that "has nothing as its own".[67] In fact, it is precisely for this reason that Derrida converts what is traditionally rendered as '*the Khōra*' to '*Khōra*'; that Derrida translates common name (noun) to proper name. This paradoxical manoeuvre which at first glance would seem to make of *Khōra* a 'determined existent' a 'real referent' – the very thing that it 'is' not – in fact allows us to think *Khōra* as unique, singular. Moreover, by making '*the Khōra*' '*Khōra*' Derrida allows it to become not so much a 'proper' name but rather a *sur*-name. That is, an over-name, a more-than-name, a nickname, a metonym, "for all that is possible only as impossible".

With Levinas the parallels between the pre-original saying and *Khōra* seem to multiply. Saying in Levinas signifies a *disinterest* (against the *interest* of being) and likewise, Derrida claims that with *Khōra* one must "insist on its necessary *indifference* to receive all."[68] Levinas's saying designates a 'past which has never been present' and *Khōra*, too names a certain "pre-temporal *already* that gives place to every inscription."[69] Nonetheless, *Khōra*, can never have only been past, it must also be a future yet to come. In its imminence it must be conceived not only as *a past* that cannot be made present, but also a *future* that cannot be made present. As that which "anachronizes being" it plays the role of the "necessary disjointure, the de-totalizing condition of justice". This desert like messianism, without the promise or the threat of a messiah, "remains an ineffaceable mark".[70] Disjointed, anachronistic, imminent, ineffaceable; the mark of *Khōra* could not be effaced or transformed; like justice it could not be simply betrayed in a translation. *Khōra* does not find itself trapped in a said; it exceeds such a possibility. *Khōra* is more than Levinas's pre-original saying; for what cannot be named *as such* can also not be translated. "We would never claim to propose the exact word, the *mot juste*, nor to name it, *itself*".[71] In itself, *Khōra* remains somewhat unnameable, unsayable and hence un-translatable.

Translation offers a clue to reading the relation between Heidegger and Levinas by providing the *same* word for *die Sage* and *le dire*, namely 'saying'. This word translates the (pre-)origin of language and the meaning of that (pre-)origin in both thinkers, namely difference. Thinking this difference is to think the place of the human subject and this thinking is the very task of philosophy. For Derrida this is to name a place by calling forth its borders: Being and being, or, one and the Other.

---

[67] *Khōra* p. 37 /trans. p. 97.

[68] Jacques Derrida 'Comment ne pas parler, Dénégations'. In *Psyché: Inventions de l'autre* (Paris: Éditions Galilée, 1987). pp. 535–95. Trans. by Ken Frieden, 'How to Avoid Speaking: Denials'. In Budick, Sanford & Iser, Wolfgang (eds.) *Languages of the Unsayable, The Play of Negativity in Literature and Literary Theory*. (New York: Colombia University Press, 1989). pp. 3–70 p. 568 / trans. p. 37 (my emphasis).

[69] *Ibid*. p. 567/Trans. p. 36.

[70] *Khōra* p. 25/trans.p. 93.

[71] *Ibid*.

Khōra does not name the place *between* two limits, it does not even name as such; it is for this reason that it is untranslatable. For Derrida, there is no place (even a non-place) of the human subject, any more than there is a name that is 'proper' to a human subject. It is precisely in this insistence on the impossibility of propriety, on the impossibility of circumscription; that Derrida's departure from Heidegger and Levinas can be witnessed. A departure with consequences for thinking the political and justice.[72] A departure that marks for philosophy the challenge to think an impossible difference. In taking up this challenge philosophy might become that 'community of the question about the possibility of the question', if it can remain ever vigilant to the dangers of naming an answer.

References

Ciaramelli, Fabio. 1995. The riddle of the pre-original. In *Ethics as first philosophy: The significance of Emmanual Levinas for philosophy, literature and religion*, ed. Adrian T. Peperzak, 87–94. New York/London: Routledge.

Derrida, Jacques. 1992. Points de suspension, Entretiens. Paris: Éditions Galilée. Trans. Peggy Kamuf, and others, Points... interviews, 1974–1994. Stanford: Stanford University Press, 1995

Derrida, Jacques. 1967. L'écriture et la difference. Paris: Les Éditions du Seuil. Trans. Alan Bass, Writing and difference. London/New York: Routledge, 2001.

Derrida, Jacques. 1993. Sauf le nom. Paris: Galilée, 1993. Trans. John P. Leavey Jr., 'Sauf le nom'. In On the name. Stanford: Stanford University Press, 1995. pp. 35–85.

Derrida, Jacques. 1994. Khōra. Trans. Ian McLeod, in Jacques Derrida, On the name. Stanford: Stanford University Press. pp. 88–127.

Derrida, Jacques. 1989. 'Comment ne pas parler, Dénégations'. In Psyché: Inventions de l'autre. Paris: Éditions Galilée, 1987. pp. 535–595. Trans. Ken Frieden, 'How to avoid apeaking: Denials'. In Budick, Sanford & Iser, Wolfgang (eds.) Languages of the unsayable: The play of negativity in literature and literary theory. New York: Colombia University Press, 1989. pp. 3–70.

Heidegger, Martin. 1971. *Unterwegs Zur Sprache [GA12]*. Frankfurt am Main: Vittorio Klostermann, 1985. Trans. Peter D. Hertz, On the way to language. New York: Harper & Row

---

[72] Clearly an account of the political and justice far exceeds the scope of the current essay. However, it is intimately tied to the question of translation. The *polis* as place for Heidegger opens a primordial relation between man and Being and is the appropriate abode of them both. This place is governed by the 'jointure' of presence and absence, the order of Being – *dike*. (Heidegger, SA and *Parmenides* [GA 54] (Frankfurt am Main: Vittorio Klostermann, 1982). Trans. by André Schuwer & Richard Rojcewicz, *Parmenides*. (Bloomington: Indiana University Press, 1992). For Levinas, the arrival of the third party is the movement towards justice as the movement towards the ontological and thus calculable. For justice to be ethical it demands an unsaying to the primary signification of the infinite responsibility of the one to the other. (Levinas AQE, and *L'au-delà du verset* (Editions de Minuit, Paris: 1982); Ciaramelli, *op.cit.*). Yet for Derrida justice is always untranslatable and yet to come; called forth by *Khōra*. (Derrida, *Khōra*, in particular pp. 53–92 /trans. pp. 108–124). This paper then might offer a particular way into the question of justice between Heidegger, Levinas and Derrida.

Heidegger, Martin. 2006. 'Identität und Differenz'. In Identität und Differenz [GA 11] Frankfurt am Main: Vittorio Klostermann. pp. 27–80. Trans. Joan Stambaugh, Identity and difference. New York: Harper & Row, 1969

Heidegger, Martin. 1977. 'Der Spruch des Anaximander'. In Holzwege [GA 5]. Frankfurt am Main: Vittorio Klostermann. pp. 321–373. Trans. David Farrell Krell, and Frank A. Capuzzi, 'The Anaximander Fragment' in Martin Heidegger, Early Greek thinking. New York: Harper & Row, 1975. pp. 13–58.

Heidegger, Martin. 1982. Parmenides [GA 54]. Frankfurt am Main: Vittorio Klostermann, 1982. Trans. André Schuwer & Richard Rojcewicz, Parmenides. Bloomington: Indiana University Press, 1992.

Levinas, Emmanuel. 1994. 'La trace de l'autre'. In En découvrant l'existence avec Husserl et Heidegger,187–202. Paris: Vrin.

Levinas, Emmanuel. 2011. Totalité et infini. Paris: Le Livre de de Poche. Trans. Alphonso Lingis, Totality and infinity. Pennsylvania: Duquesne University Press, 1969.

Levinas, Emmanuel. 1998. Éthique comme philosophie première. Paris: Éditions Payot & Rivages. Trans. Seán Hand, and Michael Temple, 'Ethics as First Philosophy' In Seán Hand (ed) The Levinas reader. Oxford: Blackwell, 1989. pp. 75–87.

Levinas, Emmanuel. 2010. Autrement qu'être ou au-delà de l'essence. Paris: Le Livre de Poche. Trans. Alphonso Lingis, Otherwise than being or beyond essence. The Hague: Martinus Nijhoff, 1981.

Marx, Werner. 1971. Heidegger and the tradition. Trans. Theodore Kisiel, and Murray Greene Evanston: Northwestern University Press.

Of a Farcical *Deus ex Machina* in Heidegger and Derrida

Tziovanis Georgakis

> *Metaphysics has no choice [Der Metaphysik bleibt keine Wahl].*
> *(Martin Heidegger, 'Einleitung zu: "Was ist Metaphysik?",' in*
> *Wegmarken, ed. Friedrich-Wilhelm von Herrmann (Frankfurt*
> *am Main: Vittorio Klostermann, 2004), 379).*

> *Clov: Why this farce, day after day?*
> *Hamm: Routine. One never knows. [Pause.]*
> *(Samuel Beckett, Endgame (London: Faber and Faber, 2009), 21.)*

Abstract This essay argues that onto-theo-logy as articulated by Heidegger and Derrida is a farcical, machinating trick of a *deus ex machina*. For Heidegger, thinking in its entirety is onto-theo-logical and only articulates a rehabilitating event whereby ontological difference is both forgotten and remembered as the unthought. By discursively thinking for itself beyond itself, onto-theo-logy becomes hetero-tauto-nomical and executes a disjunctive justice that gives no serious ground for the double bind of heteronomy and tautonomy, which merely pretends to provide the relational order for identity and difference and, thus, remains an artificial hoax. For Derrida, in a similar fashion, hetero-tauto-nomy is inscribed in the onto-theo-logical re-appropriation of the gift of undeconstructible justice, the disjunctive condition for deconstruction. The rendering of the absolute singularity of a juridical other is the event of deconstruction, and, as an event, it becomes the order of denial that essentially denies any a priori juridical decision which could come as lawful precedence. But the event remains lawful and gets disseminated hetero-tauto-nomically as law, so deconstruction's 'neither-nor' aporia is still rendered lawfully, divinely, or mystically. Nonetheless, the mystique that delivers deconstruction is duplicitous and a farce beyond the disjunction between deconstruction and its necessary undeconstructibility. Therefore, both Heidegger and Derrida summon a *deus ex machina* which intervenes and delivers an elaborate hoax that deceives them.

Keywords Heidegger • Derrida • Farce • Machination • Ontological difference • Justice

---

T. Georgakis (✉)
Department of English Studies, University of Cyprus, Nicosia, Cyprus
e-mail: georgakis.tziovanis@ucy.ac.cy

© Springer International Publishing Switzerland 2016
L. Foran, R. Uljée (eds.), *Heidegger, Levinas, Derrida: The Question of Difference*, Contributions To Phenomenology 86,
DOI 10.1007/978-3-319-39232-5_6

1   Introduction: That Farce of a God of Machination

The question whether philosophy can understand itself by means of itself does not endure as a casual question. Rather, the question of the demarcation of philosophy by philosophy itself is assumed to be the grave question of philosophy per se, the eventual question of a discourse that wishes to delimit itself by simultaneously establishing and violating its limit. This question is hailed as the adamant difficulty of philosophy which endlessly returns to exhaust itself to its limit—extremity, beginning and end, or decisive point—since the demarcating point of philosophy is the incisive edge wherefrom philosophy is used and used up. But the problem that is the question of the enclosure of philosophy returns unabatedly and mercilessly with such a force that philosophy can only surrender to it. Hence, what is supposedly at stake for philosophy, in philosophical narrative, in thinking unravelled as reflective thinking as such; is the mechanics of the automatic generation, regeneration, and resignation of philosophy to its own most intimate difficulty.

But in effect there is nothing at stake here. Strictly speaking, there is no question to be asked by philosophy for philosophy's sake. The above narrative, which is the peremptory account of the deployment and overcoming of philosophy by philosophy, is a farce: a capricious pretence and a fancy mockery. But it is also a farce of a divine machination: a *deus ex machina*. Here, we employ a forgotten use of the noun 'machination' which, in addition to an instance of plotting, an intrigue or scheme, also implies something contrived or constructed or the use or construction of machinery, e.g., a mechanical appliance for war, a machine, a framework, or an apparatus.[1] The machine-like force that unabatedly questions philosophy is one of machination. It is mechanical but only in the sense of machination. It is a machination that machinates, so it is a ruthless farce in its order. It is not in any sense negative, so it renders nothing philosophical. In the same manner, it does not lead to an impossible eventuality—either a possible impossibility or an impossible possibility. As a matter of fact, the machinating farce is neither effective nor ineffective. It is not an event, so it appropriates a ploy of nothing and dispenses nothing. It neither arrives nor withdraws, so it is neither adventurous nor wonderful. It is nothing but not nothing in any sense. It is a farce beyond the tricks of farce, a farce that is neither farcical nor un-farcical. Machination remains unthought in the history of thinking because it tricks thinking into thinking the unthought, which is itself a ridiculous task. Said differently, the thought of a *deus ex machina* is a farcical machination and a ridiculous trick because it reduces thinking into a divine thinking that is neither divine nor mundane, neither thought nor unthought, neither possible nor impossible, neither necessary nor unnecessary. The farcical *deus ex machina* is a trick of thinking that traps thinking to its absurd perversion, and it does so in a way that is so deceptive that is left fully unrecognizable as well as disguised by thinking.

This essay speaks of a *deus ex machina*, of a divine machination that has been left masked and unquestioned in the discourses of phenomenology and deconstruc-

---

[1] *Oxford English Dictionary*, 2nd ed., vol. IX (Oxford: Oxford University Press, 1991), 156.

tion in particular, and in philosophy in general; insofar as both phenomenology and deconstruction claim that they heed the unquestioned in philosophy for philosophy's sake and stake.

2   Onto-Theo-Logy and the Trick of Hetero-Tauto-Nomy

In the essay entitled 'Introduction to "What is Metaphysics?",' Heidegger argues that the metaphysical question of Being, from its Greek inception, inquires into the first cause and ground of beings, in the sense of the highest and ultimate being, and, thus, becomes a question of the divine. He explicitly states that 'according to its essence, metaphysics is, at the same time, both ontology, in the narrower sense, and theology.'[2] In the history of philosophy, a type of such assimilation between ontology and theology occurs as early as Aristotle. In his work *Metaphysics*, he states that the 'science which studies Being qua Being [τὸ ὂν ᾗ ὄν]' is not the same as any of the other particular sciences because it investigates 'the first principles and the ultimate causes [τὰς ἀρχὰς καὶ τὰς ἀκροτάτας αἰτίας].' These principles and causes 'belong to something in virtue of its own nature,' so they are 'elements of Being not incidentally but qua Being.'[3] In the same work, Aristotle argues that theology is the most preferable science from all speculative sciences and even calls it 'primary philosophy [πρώτη φιλοσοφία].'[4] Likewise, G. W. F. Hegel considers theological thinking as the culmination of philosophical thinking. In his lectures on the philosophy of religion, given in 1827, he claims that the course of philosophy proves that the final result of all is god, 'this universal, which is in and for itself, embracing and containing absolutely everything, is that through which alone everything is and has subsistence.'[5] Hegel argues, hence, the following: 'The science of religion is one science within philosophy; indeed it is the *final* one.'[6]

Nonetheless, for Heidegger, there are no isolated instances in the history of thinking whereby the science of metaphysics as ontology is treated as theology; rather, thinking itself in its entirety, in its absolute and universal unfolding, in every breath of its portentous range; is onto-theo-logical. In the essay entitled 'The Onto-Theo-Logical Constitution of Metaphysics,' Heidegger at a point elaborates on the concepts of Being and god in Hegel and notes the following: 'But inasmuch as Hegel's thinking belongs to a period of history (this does not mean at all that it belongs to the past), we are attempting to think Being, as Hegel thought of it, in the

---

[2] Heidegger, 'Einleitung zu: "Was ist Metaphysik?",' 379.

[3] See Aristotle, *Metaphysics: Books 1–9*, trans. Hugh Tredennick (Cambridge, MA: Harvard University Press, 1933), 1003a20-32.

[4] See ibid., 1026a18-25.

[5] G. W. F. Hegel, *Lectures on the Philosophy of Religion: One-Volume Edition* (*The Lectures of 1827*), trans. R. F. Brown, Peter C. Hodgson, and J. M. Steward (Berkeley and Los Angeles, California: University of California Press, 1988), 115.

[6] Ibid., 113.

same manner, that is to think of it historically [geschichtlich zudenken].'[7] 'History [*Geschichte*]' here does not mean a chronological record of past events but the regenerative way in which Being is thought as authentic thought by means of the question of the meaning of Being. Heidegger decides to converse with Hegel because, as he states, 'for Hegel, the matter of thinking is: Being, as thinking thinking itself [*das Sein als das sich selbst denkende Denken*].'[8] Hence, the history of thinking is the history of Being which thinks thinking as such.

In fact, as Heidegger argues, the history of thinking is strictly ontological because as 'the language of tradition,' it speaks of the 'difference between Being and beings,' which, even though 'unthought [*Ungedachten*],' somehow directs us 'into what gives us thought [*in das zu-Denkende*].'[9] It is also theological because the Being of beings, as Heidegger writes, 'reveals itself as the ground that gives itself ground and accounts for itself,' as *'causa sui,' 'causa prima,'* and *'ultima ratio'* — all of which imply 'the metaphysical concept of God.' Again, even though theological thinking presents us with 'the original matter for thinking [*die ursprüngliche Sache des Denkens*],' its essence still remains to be thought since it, once again, speaks of the ontological difference that nonetheless remains unthought.[10] Finally, Being is logical since it 'becomes present [west] as Λόγος in the sense of ground [*im Sinne des Grundes*].'[11] When metaphysics inquires into the essence of beings in accordance with the ground that is common to all beings as such, then this logic is onto-logic. When metaphysics thinks of beings as a whole in accordance to the highest Being that accounts for every being, then this logic is theo-logic.[12] Hence, metaphysics corresponds to a logic that inquires into the ontological difference in terms of both the common ground and the highest Being of beings, so it is onto-theo-logic — a kind of logic that is nonetheless determined by that which differs in the thinking of the ontological difference, namely, the unthought as such.

Indeed, for Heidegger, the decisive event of the metaphysics as onto-theo-logy is articulated by the distinction between Being and beings which not only remains unthought and forgotten in the history of onto-theo-logy but also prescribes and determines it as such. The un-thoughtfulness of the ontological distinction is expressed as the singular and unique matter of metaphysical thinking: the event of the 'oblivion of Being [*Seinsvergessenheit*],' the forgetfulness of the difference between Being and beings. In an essay entitled 'The Anaximander Fragment,' Heidegger states that the oblivion of the ontological distinction is 'the richest [*das reichste*] and most prodigious [*weiteste*] event' in which 'the history of the Western world comes to be borne out'; 'it is,' as he declares, 'the event of metaphysics [*das*

---

[7] Martin Heidegger, 'Die Onto-Theo-Logische Verfassung der Metaphysik,' in *Identität und Differenz* (Stuttgart: Klett-Cotta, 2002), 35.

[8] Ibid., 34.

[9] Ibid., 40.

[10] See ibid., 48–51.

[11] Ibid., 61.

[12] See ibid., 63.

Ereignis der Metaphysik].'[13] Therefore, as Heidegger insists, 'the difference between Being and beings is the area within which metaphysics, Western thinking in its entire nature, can be what it is.'[14] In this sense, the onto-theo-logical constitution of metaphysics cannot be explained separately in terms of ontology, theology, or logic but only through the ontological difference and the event of its unprecedented oblivion. Heidegger explains:

> For it still remains unthought by what unity [*Einheit*] ontologic and theologic belong together, what the origin of this unity is, and what the difference of the differentiated which this unity unifies. All of this still remains unthought. The problem here is obviously not a union of two independent disciplines of metaphysics, but the unity of *what* [*was*] is in question, and in thought, in ontologic and theologic: beings as such in the universal and primal *at one with* [*Einemmit*] beings as such in the highest and ultimate. The unity of this One [*Die Einheit dieses Einen*] is of such a kind that the ultimate in its own way accounts for the primal, and the primal in its own way accounts for the ultimate. The difference between the two ways of accounting belongs to the still-unthought difference we mentioned.[15]

The unthought event that still remains unthought in onto-theo-logical metaphysical thinking is the unity of ontology and theology. That which binds them together as such is the unity of their exceptional constitution. Their unified constitution is of a difference since it lies within the realm of the oblivion of Being that has remained oblivious and still to be thought. It is difference constituted by differentiated difference: it is absolute difference undifferentiated by any kind of a signified difference, so it is neither differentiating nor differentiable. Consequently, for Heidegger, the question of the constitution of thinking remains a constant matter of thinking because it eternally awaits its own resolution, which will remain unthought since it is of a different origin and force, of a pure difference that is beyond the breath of thinking. Simply put, the matter of thinking, the thinking of Being, a self-thinking thought, absolutely thinks differently and assumes a difference beyond difference that itself remains unthought.

Exactly at the peculiar and unremarkable juncture whereupon thinking becomes a thoughtful whole, the critical jointure through which thinking thinks in itself and for itself and goes beyond itself towards that which can never think on its own, thinking becomes the subtle trick of a heteronomous tautonomy, or else: hetero-tauto-nomy. On the one hand, it seems to be tautonomic since the law of its unfolding is invariant and redundant.[16] It is invariant because it allows for every being whatsoever—every 'this' or 'that' being—to be accounted for in terms of its Being. It indeed grants the space for agreement because it makes beings absolutely agreeable in respect to their common ground. This invariant law has always and already been there for all beings, so it is pure and a priori invariance. As the invariant law of

---

[13] See Martin Heidegger, 'Der Spruch des Anaximander,' in *Holzwege*, ed. Friedrich-Wilhelm von Herrmann (Frankfurt am Main: Vittorio Klostermann, 2003), 365.

[14] See Heidegger, 'Die Onto-Theo-Logische Verfassung der Metaphysik,' 41.

[15] Ibid., 52.

[16] The word 'ταὐτόνομος' in Greek designates that which follows the same rule or law. See Henry George Liddell and Robert Scott, *A Greek-English Lexicon* (Oxford: Clarendon Press, 1996), 1761.

beings, it maintains eternity itself: the 'there is' as such, as it represented in time at all times. But such representation is indifferent because it cannot be represented timely in its invariance; in other words, it is invariantly pre-temporal. Hence, every thoughtful moment is a moment of the handing down of a difference that remains unrepresented *ad infinitum*. Every instance of thought, every designation and articulation of any being, without exception, is the same instance of an uncompromising reduction: the unconcealment of the oblivious oblivion of the Being of beings that nonetheless remains concealed. Thinking, thus, is unequivocally singular insofar as it is strictly employed by an invariant invariance. On the other hand, the invariant law that is thought as such is redundant in such a manner that it stubbornly remains a singularly excessive force that exceeds its absolute constancy. The point here is that this singular, absolute, and constant tautonomy unravels itself singularly and absolutely as heteronomy. Being as such, the order and law of presentation per se, is not represented by any representable instance, a being. No being whatsoever—neither 'this' nor 'that' being—accounts for Being. The law of presentation as such is foreign to every possible representation, so every representation renders impossible the presentation of its authoritative law. Every presentation, then, is a testament of a foreign rule that is absolutely and singularly unruly. Every presentation is an instance in which the presentative order fails to execute itself by means of itself, so it is a universal instance of the execution of presentative order. Each presentation is a moment of the surrender of the law of presentation to another foreign executive order, and this event happens every single time at any single moment of the tautonomous order of presentation.

Nonetheless, the hetero-tauto-nomy that pretends to be thinking as such is a farcical scheme. It is farcical because it cheats itself beyond the order of pretension and deception. The trick is played out in the following fashion: hetero-tauto-nomy, itself a ploy, tricks itself and does not execute by itself the tricky effect which appropriates itself. Hetero-tauto-nomy does not appropriate because it does nothing; however, since it is a trick, it is not nothing. It remains a trick, and, as a trick, it does not remain. In fact, the ploy of hetero-tauto-nomy pretends to be both tautonomous and heteronomous. The plot assumes that there is tautonomous hetero-tauto-nomy and heteronomous hetero-tauto-nomy which are exactly the same singularity: hetero-tauto-nomy. Simultaneously, the same posturing assumes that there is hetero-tauto-nomy which is neither tautonomous nor heteronomous. Hence, the assumption here is that there is an execution of the order 'both tautonomy and heteronomy, neither tautonomy nor heteronomy' which remains inexecutable in its execution. But the order of the inexecutable execution that executes hetero-tauto-nomy is a farce that does not give a serious ground for the double bind 'both/neither.' The farce deceives itself because it remains in any case un-assumed in its assumption of the law of the aforementioned double bind; after all, the law has been assumed as a cheating ploy but not executed as such. The pretention lies in the cheating event that assumes that the farce has been executed only by the farce. So, the farce assumes a farcical order which deceives order in a farcical way. As it turns out, this farcical play is assumed by both Heidegger and Derrida, and it does so in a way that tricks them both.

3 Heidegger: Machination and the Disjunction of the Last God

The trick of the hetero-tauto-nomy is entertained by Heidegger in the following sentence: 'Instead, "repetition [*wiederholung*]" here means to *let* the *same* [*das selbe*], the uniqueness of Beyng become a plight *again* and *thereby out of a more original truth*. "Again" means here precisely 'altogether otherwise [*ganzanders*].'[17] For Heidegger, the order of the same is represented again and again ad infinitum, but it does so uniquely and in excess. The 'same' names the uniqueness of Being itself whose uniqueness is always unique, thus, altogether foreign and excessive. Tautonomy, the order of the same, gets repeated heteronomously; the order of Being is eternally administered both indistinctly and anew, but it is dispensed as neither something indistinct nor something new. In 'The Anaximander Fragment,' Heidegger discusses the question of the oblivion of the ontological difference in terms of the dispensation of a tricky term: the 'ἔσχατον' [*eschaton*]. He writes:

> What once occurred in the dawn of our destiny would then come, as what once occurred, at the last (ἔσχατον) [*eschaton*], that is, at the departure of the long-hidden destiny of Being. The Being of beings is gathered (λέγεσθαι, λόγος) [*legesthai, logos*] in the ultimacy of its destiny. The essence of Being hitherto disappears, its truth still veiled. The history of Being is gathered in this departure. The gathering in this departure, as the gathering (λόγος) [*logos*] at the outermost point (ἔσχατον) [*eschaton*] of its essence hitherto, is the eschatology of Being. As something fateful, Being itself is inherently eschatological [*Das Seinselbst ist als geschickliches in sich eschatologisch*].[18]

The ancient Greek term 'ἔσχατον' is tricky because it nominates both the highest and the lowest in terms of degree. In addition, the term was used in geometrical analysis, and it designates the last step or 'the ultimate condition of action.' As an adverb, the word 'ἐσχάτως' [*eschatós*] means exceedingly.[19] The first occurrence in the history of Being is also its last, and it signifies the departure of the long-hidden destiny of Being that still remains hidden. The order of the trick is the following: the first and final dispensations of the order of Being are dispensed with permanently; what finally remains is pure excess itself, the ultimate order of dispensation that is so thoroughly excessive that ultimately exempts order itself.

Elsewhere, in *Contribution to Philosophy (Of the Event)*, Heidegger names the order of dispensation as 'the last god [*der letzte Gott*].' He states the following:

> The last god is not the end; the last god is the other beginning of the immeasurable possibilities of our history. For the sake of this beginning, the previous history must not simply cease but must instead be brought to its end. The transfiguration of its essential basic positions has to be carried by us into the transition and the preparation.

---

[17] Martin Heidegger, *Beiträge zur Philosophie (Vom Ereignis)* (Frankfurt am Main: Vittorio Klostermann, 1989), 73.

[18] Heidegger, 'Der Spruch des Anaximander,' 327.

[19] Liddell and Scott, *A Greek-English Lexicon*: 699–700.

> The preparation of the appearance of the last god is the extreme venture [*äußerste Wagnis*] of the truth of Beyng. Only in virtue of this truth is the human being successful in retrieving beings.[20]

Indeed, this last god that names the extreme risk of the unconcealment of Being is another name for hetero-tauto-nomy itself. Hetero-tauto-nomy prepares its own dispensation insofar as it awaits the coming of its order. But the awaiting itself is tricky because this order could not be ordered by any order. A preparation for Being's risky venture implies absolute surrender to the order of ultimate execution. However, and most importantly, the endpoint for the last god's preparation is called 'machination [Machenschaft].' Heidegger states:

> The last god is the beginning of the longest history on its shortest path. Long preparation is needed for the great moments of its passing. And for preparedness for god, peoples and states are too small, i.e., already too much torn from all growth and nonetheless delivered only to machination.
> Only the great and unrevealed individuals [*Einzelnen*] will provide the stillness for the passing of the god and among themselves for the reticent accord [*Einklang*] of those who are prepared.[21]

Machination here does not designate a characteristic of undeserving populations and governments. Indeed, Heidegger insists that 'it does not name a kind of human conduct but a mode of the essential occurrence of Being insofar as it 'does promote the *non*-essence [*Un*wesen] of Being.'[22] He also writes the following astonishing sentence: 'Machination itself withdraws, and thus Beyng itself withdraws, since machination is the essential occurrence [*Wesung*] of Beyng.'[23] In the context of the question of the meaning of Being, machination names the mode of the essential occurrence of Being. This modality, as Heidegger states, is '*non*-essence itself, since it is essential to the essence (of Being).'[24]

In fact, machination is another scheme for the tricky and farcical 'ἔσχατον.' [*eschaton*] Heidegger asserts that 'machination is the early [*das frühe*] but for a long while to come [*langehin*] hidden non-essence of the Beingness of beings.'[25] Machination is devious excess that not only constitutes but also overwhelms the endpoints, beginning and end, of the order of presence. The great and unseen prophets who will prepare the coming of the last god eventually remain silent and in reserve since they are suspended in their speech: the excess of onto-theo-logy. The silent accord of those soothsayers who linger in anticipation is the 'ἔσχατον,' which accords only in discordance. Indeed, Heidegger adds the following:

> What does machination mean? That which is let loose into its own shackles. Which shackles? The pattern of general calculable explainability, by which everything draws nearer to

---

[20] Heidegger, *Beiträge zur Philosophie (Vom Ereignis)*: 411.

[21] Ibid., 414.

[22] Ibid., 126.

[23] Ibid., 128.

[24] Ibid., 126.

[25] Ibid., 128.

everything else equally and becomes completely alien to itself—yes, totally other than just alien. The relation of non-relationality.[26]

Heidegger describes machination as a self-operating or automatic apparatus that contrives itself and schemes a ridiculous state of affairs whereby it is left free while it is still lay bound to its own fetters. Machination is a modality of a chain that essentially chains itself. It is a cunning trap because it is, as Heidegger informs us, 'the pattern of general calculable explainability,' a scientific modality that constantly assumes causality and eternally claims verifiability. It operates in terms of constancy and presence and, thus, reduces all beings to an indistinguishable and indifferent state of abandonment in which Being and beings bear no difference. It is a trap because Being and beings are chained together by a relation that does not relate presently in a presentable manner. Therefore, a possible untangling of the ontological difference cannot be revealed, and a possible escape from the trap cannot be provided. A possible intervention that could weigh the ontological difference and cut the bond between Being and beings is out of the question.

In 'The Anaximander Fragment,' Heidegger turns to the concepts of justice and injustice to further elaborate the notion of the relation of non-relationality. He states that 'ἀδικία [adikia 'injustice'], disjunction, is disorder.[27] Here, disjunction names the modality of the ontological distinction. Heidegger claims the following:

> Coming to presence in the jointure [Fuge] of the while, what is present abandons the jointure and is, in terms of whatever lingers awhile [*Je-Weilige*], in disjunction [*Un-Fuge*]. Everything that lingers awhile stands in disjunction. To the presence of what is present [*Anwesen des Anwesenden*], to the ἐόν of ἐόντα, ἀδικία belongs.[28]

In this case, ontological difference as injustice is expressed by means of adjudication, by what Heidegger calls a 'twofold absence [*zwiefaches Ab-wesen*].' The unjust and absent, the 'ἔσχατον,' or the last god—the relation of Being and beings as a relation of difference—'emerges by approaching and passes away by departing.' Once again, devious adjudication is captured by a double bind, an emergence and a passing away that are both absent. But this double bind is again a relation of conjunction and, thus, a recorded instance and distance between two presentable and presenting ends because, as Heidegger insists, what is present 'lingers [*weilt*],' and its duration (or its 'while [*Weile*]') 'occurs essentially in jointure [*Fuge*].'[29] Heidegger's double bind is trapped by its own pretension, a posturing which assumes a double condition that nonetheless remains single in its appropriating effect, which is to order doubly. Again, there is an indivisible remnant that cheats Heidegger, and that is pure, undivided, and uncompromising division itself which can never be put into a relation of conjunction. Heidegger's phenomenology is ruined by the farce of thinking because the last god can only assume or feign, fabricate as so to deceive, its own hetero-tauto-nomy.

---

[26] Ibid., 132.

[27] Heidegger, 'Der Spruch des Anaximander,' 357.

[28] Ibid., 355.

[29] See ibid.

Hence, justice cannot be done for Heidegger's diagnosis of metaphysics as onto-theo-logy. Actually, the question whether onto-theo-logy could possibly speak of the arrival of a righteous, last god who will redeem it from its forgetfulness and abandonment is ridiculous in its unfolding. The question of the meaning of Being is a machination of farcical order because it leaves metaphysics without a divine arbitrator whose eventual appearance is simultaneously promised and disavowed. At the same time, what is constantly snarled within the plot acted out by this farcical trap is nothing other than the trap itself. In a sense, the farcical trap of machination traps itself. This ludicrous sort of *deus ex machina* that is machination executes the farce of representation as farce, as an artifice that ridicules beyond distortion the ridiculous order we call 'representation.' The *deus ex machina* derides representation beyond confusion and disguise, beyond and before the artificial intervention of derision itself. The farce that we call machination is beyond and before the making of a farce, and that makes it farcical because the notions of 'beyond' and 'before' become themselves farcical. In other words, the *deus ex machina* is still enclosed in its trap door, but its enclosure is performed in an unlikely and extravagantly way in terms of a mischievous hoax that mischievously remains a hoax.

4   Derrida: Mystique and Ridicule Between Deconstructibility and Undeconstructibility

Two proclamations by Derrida that could expose the core of the project of deconstruction deserve attention. The first comes from a lecture on negative theology entitled 'How to Avoid Speaking: Denials.' Derrida states:

> What 'différance,' 'trace,' and so on, 'mean-to-say'—which consequently *does not mean to say anything*—would be 'something' 'before' the concept, the name, the word, that would be nothing, that would no longer pertain to being, to presence or to the presence of the present, or even to absence, and even less to some hyperessentiality. Yet the ontotheological reappropriation always remains possible—and doubtless *inevitable* insofar as one is speaking, precisely, in the element of ontotheological logic and grammar.[30]

Derrida here presents us with the double risk of onto-theo-logy's venture. On the one hand, onto-theo-logy, the schema of the presentative order, cannot be schematic in any way. It cannot be schematized because it is the schema of all schemas, a 'schema' before the order of presentable schemas. So, it is 'something' that means to say 'nothing'; it is that 'nothing' that cannot be schemed. In this sense, onto-theo-logy is 'nothing,' a scheme that is absolutely heteronomous. On the other hand, as proper order, as a discourse that inevitably schematizes the impossibility of its schema, albeit in a non-schematizing way, onto-theo-logy has no other option than to be ordered as 'nothing.' It has no other alternative other than to be always and

---

[30] Jacques Derrida, 'How to Avoid Speaking: Denials,' in *Psyche: Inventions of the Other, Volume II*, ed. Peggy Kamuf and Elizabeth Rottenberg (Stanford, CA: Stanford University Press, 2008), 148.

already the impossible 'nothing,' a schema that is absolutely tautonomous in its configuration.

Derrida's second proclamation that is of importance here comes from *Specters of Marx* in which he discusses Heidegger's notion of disjunction. He writes:

> In this interpretation of the Un-Fug (whether or not it is on the basis of Being as presence and the property of the proper), would be played out the relation of deconstruction to the possibility of justice, the relation of deconstruction (insofar as it proceeds from the irreducible possibility of the Un-Fug and the anachronic disjointure, insofar as it draws from there the very resource and injunction of its reaffirmed affirmation) to what must (without debt and without duty) be rendered to the singularity of the other, to his or her absolute *prece*dence or to his or her absolute *pre*viousness, to the heterogeneity of a *pre-*, which, to be sure, means what comes before me, before any present, thus before any past present, but also what, for that very reason, comes from the future or as future: as the very coming of the event. The necessary disjointure, the de-totalizing condition of justice, is indeed here that of the present—and by the same token the very condition of the present and of the presence of the present. This is where deconstruction would always begin to take shape as the thinking of the gift and of undeconstructible justice, the undeconstructible condition of any deconstruction, to be sure, but a condition that is itself in deconstruction and remains, and must remain (that is the injunction) in the disjointure of the Un-Fug.[31]

For Derrida, deconstruction is shaped by rendering the absolute singularity of a juridical other. It is initiated in terms of a singular relation with the other, in terms of the law of the other. This initial appropriation remains a relation, but it is a relation of the denial of relation and a law that denies lawfulness. It is a singular denial that speaks of the law of the other. But the other as the absolute jurisdiction of denial is that which becomes of onto-theo-logy. Onto-theo-logy is rendered as the law of the other, so it becomes the order of denial that denies absolutely. Deconstruction is deployed exactly at this denying juncture that is irreducibly disjunctive. It is hence drawn and interpreted from the precedent of the other that denies an a priori judicial decision which could come as precedence. Deconstruction is pronounced from the same heteronomous order of onto-theo-logy, so it is indistinguishable from onto-theo-logy. It is onto-theo-logy as other, another onto-theo-logy, onto-theo-logy interpreted again as the law of the other.

But deconstruction is tricky in its rendering since the law of the other cannot be re-rendered again lawfully. In a paradoxical way, the law remains lawful and favours a lawful rendition. Deconstruction, therefore, is also rendered from this unjust favour. It reads and interprets from the scheme of this injustice. So, Derrida interprets Heidegger in the following way:

> Has not Heidegger, as he always does, skewed the asymmetry in favor of what he in effect interprets as the possibility of favor itself, of the accorded favor, namely, of the accord that gathers or collects while harmonizing (*Versammlung, Fug*), be it in the sameness of differents or of disagreements [*differends*], and before the synthesis of a sys-tem?[32]

---

[31] Jacques Derrida, *Spectres of Marx*, trans. Peggy Kamuf (London: Routledge, 1994), 24–8.
[32] Ibid., 27.

Derrida's verdict here is that Heidegger's asymmetrical justice reconverts into absolute symmetry, an accorded judgment. Heidegger is tricked by ontological difference itself because it reads it again as a sign of partiality and prejudice, an indistinct possibility that singularly justifies the singular order of the forgetfulness of Being. For Derrida, Heidegger's interpretation of ontological difference is singularity favouring the singular, so it distorts heteronomy itself, the law from which the order of the same is decreed. Heidegger is tricked by the order of the double bind, which is disjunctive in its interpretation. Derrida asserts the following: 'The *neither-nor* can no longer be reconverted into *both-and.*'[33]

However, the trick remains, and it renders deconstruction interpretable. In 'Force of Law: The "Mystical Foundation of Authority"', Derrida names deconstruction's rendition as 'the mystical.' He explains: 'Discourse here meets its limit—in itself, in its very performative power. It is what I propose to call here the *mystical.* There is here a silence walled up in the violent structure of the founding act; walled up, walled in because this silent is not exterior to language.'[34] Analogous to Heidegger's 'ἔσχατον,' [*eschaton*] the mystical is the first and final dispensation of discourse itself: the silent speech of the other that remains the constitutive core of language itself. It is also walled up, that is to say, trapped in the silence that performs. Indeed, Derrida's deconstruction is committed to a peculiar divine thinking that remains unthought in its unfolding. Derrida states that 'deconstruction is already pledged, engaged [*gagée, engagée*] by this demand for infinite justice, which can take the aspect of this "mystique" I spoke of earlier.'[35] The task of deconstruction is to strip thinking down to its bare founding limitation and reveal that such a foundation is an aporia, a secret impasse through which nothing essentially becomes, a differential force that does not act and does not found, a performing event that suspends thinking and suspends itself. So, deconstruction is a kind of a *deus ex machina* because it intervenes for the sake of thinking, through means provided by thinking itself, and brings thinking to its own resolution. This intervening event is divine since it is eternally expected to emerge from within a mystical place unknown to any order of signification; however, it is also empty of divinity since it is infinitely unenforceable, unforeseeable, and undecidable. Still, the *deus ex machina* that plots the intervening and disrupting event of deconstruction is a tricky and farcical since it attests a bizarre and deceptive god. Derrida notes: 'God: the witness as "nameable-unnamable," present-absent witness of every oath or of every possible pledge.'[36] Derrida's god is indeed ridiculous: both present and absent but, at the same time, impossible, without presence or absence, hence, neither present nor absent. Deconstruction compromises thinking by thinking the unthought as the aporetic divinity of the impossible.

---

[33] Derrida, 'How to Avoid Speaking: Denials,' 172.

[34] Jacques Derrida, 'Force of Law: The "Mustical Foundation of Authority",' in *Acts of Religion*, ed. Gil Anidjar (New York: Routledge, 2010), 242.

[35] Ibid., 248.

[36] Derrida, 'Faith and Knowledge: The Two Sources of "Religion" at the Limits of Reason Alone,' 65.

In fact, the farce that sketches deconstruction is played out in terms of difference, specifically, that of justice and law and, in turn, that of deconstructibility and undeconstructibility. Firstly, Derrida defines as follows the 'difficult and unstable' difference between justice and law:

> between justice (infinite, incalculable, rebellious to rule and foreign to symmetry, heterogeneous and heterotropic) on the one hand, and, on the other, the exercise of justice as law, legitimacy or legality, a stabilizable, statutory and calculable apparatus [dispositif], a system of regulated and coded prescriptions.[37]

The law as a body of edicts and verdicts cannot found itself by means found in itself for the following simple reason: the force that founds law cannot be a part of law because, if it were a part of law, it would not have the higher authority to found and enforce law. In this sense, law, as a sovereign body of superior authority, is impotent because it cannot justify itself by decree. What justifies law is incalculable justice, yet justice is the exercise of law as an enforcement that is in itself impotent. Following the above syllogism, a set of different facts presents itself for the sake of deconstruction. The fact that law as law is impotent is the fact of deconstruction; it makes deconstruction possible. The fact that justice, as the exercise of impotent law, is foreign to law makes justice unlawful. The fact that justice is unlawful makes justice immune from legal enforcement, impotent or not. Therefore, the fact that justice is immune from either impotent or potent legal action makes justice undeconstructible. The fact that justice is undeconstructible is the fact of deconstruction; it is the fact that makes deconstruction impossible. Indeed, Derrida puts forward the following three propositions:

1. The deconstructibility of law (for example) makes deconstruction possible.
2. The undeconstrucibility of justice also makes deconstruction possible, indeed is inseparable from it.
3. *Consequence*: Deconstruction takes place in the interval that separates the undeconstrucibility of justice from the deconstructibility of law. Deconstruction is possible as an experience of the impossible, there where, even if it does not exist, if it is not *present*, not yet or never, *there is* justice.[38]

The above propositions leave deconstruction encaged in the trap door of a *deus ex machina* because they iterate the ridiculous difference between deconstructibility and undeconstructibility. There is deconstruction—that is to say, deconstruction takes place—if and only if the following occur: (a) law remains deconstructible, (b) justice remains undeconstructible, and (c) law remains necessarily conjunctional to justice by means of an impossible disjunction. This impossible conjunction stands as the event proper of deconstruction since it allows for the 'both-and' conjunction to be automatically reconverted into the 'neither-nor' disjunction. In other words, the event of the impossible that is deconstruction itself is a mechanic reconversion, a duplicitous conversion of a former conversion, a conversion in which 'this or that'

---

[37] Derrida, 'Force of Law: The "Mystical Foundation of Authority",' 250.
[38] Ibid., 243.

conversion—the conversion of deconstructibility into undeconstructibility, possibility into impossibility, necessity into contingency, and vice versa—is reconverted into another conversion that is 'neither this nor that nor any other conversion.' The impossible event of deconstruction is a duplicitous reconversion because it deliberately demands a prior conversion that has always and already been reconverted into its own disjunctive impossibility. The impossible, the automatic reconversion into nothing, unravels only if it pretends that an a priori conjunction has already been posited as a disjunctive nothing. Deconstruction is two-faced because it assumes that an impossible nothing, the disjunctive impossibility of every possible conjunction, has always and already been reconverted into an 'other' impossible disjunction. In this sense, the event of deconstruction is an assumption since it allegedly accepts that the impossible proceeds impossibly. However, it is a cunning assumption because, in any event, the allegation remains without proof, so the assertion that deconstruction takes place as an impossible act outlasts deconstruction. Deconstruction needs an assertion to take place, but an assertion immediately implies conjunction. Hence, the assertion that 'the prior assertion is impossible' reappears again anew, but, again, it does so assertively. At any time, at all times, deconstruction is in absolute need of a first assertion which is to be denied, and this is, in turn, the one and only assertion that deconstruction cannot deny. But such an assertion is duplicitous because neither its employment nor its demonstration is a matter of affirmation or denial. The proposition 'the impossible proceeds impossibly' cannot in any case be proposed because no proceeding can ever proceed. There is no impossible condition that overcomes the impossible because the impossible itself can neither be associated nor be disassociated by impossible conditions. What remains in thinking is not the impossible departure of the impossible but the mocking drop of a farcical *deus ex machina* who jokingly and unbelievably boasts that the impossible first condition exists impossibly. But this exceptional god, the only possible god one could boastfully assert, can never possibly be believed. Its word remains inarticulated in the most deviating way, so it is a mere artifice, a trickery of artifices, a labyrinth of insidious stratagems in which philosophical thinking is played out inescapably. The ridiculous puzzle that is the consequence of deconstruction is that Derrida could not possibly articulate the play of the farce that overwhelms his thought.

5 Conclusion: The Machinating Return

Heidegger's phenomenology and Derrida's deconstruction wish to alleviate thinking by thinking the unthought as either possible or impossible. But the thought of the unthought only invites a *deus ex machina* that intervenes foolishly and renders it foolish. The matters of phenomenology and deconstruction do not matter since they are *contrivances* of an artificial hoax that is delivered as an artificial hoax in its machinating return. The dilemma that traps them, the inconvertible law of 'both/ neither,' is duplicitously performed, doubly-dealt in terms of a deception that is 'beyond' and 'without' deception, a fraudulence that deceives the already unfavourable and disjunctive 'beyond' and 'without.' It is a tricky dilemma since it does not order a judgment between two options that seem equally unfavourable. It is a dilemma constituted by fraud and tricked by fraud, so it is fanciful, virtually divine.

References

Aristotle. 1933. *Metaphysics: Books 1–9*. Trans. Hugh Tredennick. Cambridge, MA: Harvard University Press.

Beckett, Samuel. 2009. *Endgame*. London: Faber and Faber.

Derrida, Jacques. 1994. *Spectres of Marx*. Trans. Peggy Kamuf. London: Routledge.

Derrida, Jacques. 2008. How to avoid speaking: Denials. In *Psyche: inventions of the other, volume II*, ed. Peggy Kamuf and Elizabeth Rottenberg, 143–195. Stanford: Stanford University Press.

Derrida, Jacques. 2010a. Faith and knowledge: The two sources of "Religion" at the limits of reason alone. In *Acts of religion*, ed. Gil Anidjar, 42–101. New York: Routledge.

Derrida, Jacques. 2010b. Force of law: The "Mustical Foundation of Authority". In *Acts of religion*, ed. Gil Anidjar, 230–298. New York: Routledge.

Hegel, G.W.F. 1988. *Lectures on the Philosophy of Religion: One-Volume Edition (The Lectures of 1827)*. Trans. R.F. Brown, Peter C. Hodgson, and J.M. Steward. Berkeley/Los Angeles: University of California Press.

Heidegger, Martin. 1989. *Beiträge zur Philosophie (Vom Ereignis)*. Frankfurt am Main: Vittorio Klostermann.

Heidegger, Martin. 2002. Die Onto-Theo-Logische Verfassung der Metaphysik. In *Identität und Differenz*, 31–67. Stuttgart: Klett-Cotta.

Heidegger, Martin. 2003. Der Spruch des Anaximander. In *Holzwege*, ed. Friedrich-Wilhelm von Herrmann, 321–373. Frankfurt am Main: Vittorio Klostermann.

Heidegger, Martin. 2004. Einleitung zu: Was ist Metaphysik? In *Wegmarken*, ed. Friedrich-Wilhelm von Herrmann, 365–383. Frankfurt am Main: Vittorio Klostermann.

Liddell, Henry George, and Robert Scott. 1996. *A Greek-English Lexicon*. Oxford: Clarendon.

Oxford English Dictionary, vol. IX, 2nd ed. Oxford: Oxford University Press, 1991.

The Paradoxical Listening to the Other: Heidegger, Levinas, Derrida – And Gadamer

Carlos B. Gutiérrez

Abstract In the light of outstanding philosophical theories, listening to the other turns out to be the paradoxical task of addressing an unreachable absolute, which nonetheless embodies all interlocutors and all vital and affective belongingness of human beings at one time. Thus, the philosophy of the second part of the twentieth century is marked by the strong contrast that goes from absolute otherness, from an other that is completely other; to the belonging otherness to which we are bound in our being. This contrast determines the various nuances of listening to the other which I intend to address in this paper.

Keywords Heidegger • Levinas • Derrida • Gadamer • Alterity • Dialogue • Language

In the light of outstanding philosophical theories, listening to the other turns out to be the paradoxical task of addressing an unreachable absolute, which nonetheless embodies all interlocutors and all vital and affective belongingness of human beings at one time. Thus, the philosophy of the second part of the twentieth century is marked by the strong contrast that goes from absolute otherness, from an other that is completely other; to the belonging otherness to which we are bound in our being. This contrast determines the various nuances of listening to the other which I intend to address in this paper.

1 Ontological Difference Only

Let us begin by saying that it is very difficult to talk about listening to the other in Heidegger's philosophy, since it is precisely the other who in the initial existential analytic is notable for its absence. The idea of the other is so tenuous there that it demands as its counterpart the overwhelming omnipresence of the anonymity of the public realm. In addition, the dissonant introduction of "being-with" as a structure of

---

C.B. Gutiérrez (✉)
Universidad de los Andes, Bogotá, Colombia
e-mail: cgutierr@uniandes.edu.co

© Springer International Publishing Switzerland 2016
L. Foran, R. Uljée (eds.), *Heidegger, Levinas, Derrida: The Question of Difference*, Contributions To Phenomenology 86,
DOI 10.1007/978-3-319-39232-5_7

being of human beings contradicted the *existential* that was sketched in paragraphs 4 and 9 of *Being and Time* in terms of concern for one's own being. I share Derrida's appreciation that the reference in paragraph 34 of *Being and Time* to hearing as *Dasein*'s authentic opportunity for its most proper possibility of being, in terms of "hearing the 'voice of the friend which every *Dasein* carries together with it'," is no more than an exemplary reference "an exemplarity which carries in itself all the features of being-with as hearing-one-another" (Derrida et al. 1998, 357). Not even the call of consciousness in *Being and Time* has anything to do with the others, since in Heidegger's voice of consciousness it is *Dasein* who calls itself to its most proper self; the invoker and the interpellated coincide in such a way that the internal dialogue of Christian morality is eventually reduced to an edifying ontological monologue.

In Heidegger's later works, moreover, *voice* is identified with the historical-destining interpellation of Being. There, not even the reference to a common destining may palliate the loss of the voice of the other, since the community subjected to destining is, as Levinas well pointed out, a "neutral intersubjectivity," inasmuch as being as *logos* is no one's verbum (Levinas 1957). Thus, while there is more ontological difference than real alterity in *Being and Time*, in Heidegger's later philosophy, being is the instance that interpellates us and towards which the essence of speech is displaced. Heidegger undoubtedly posed the question of being of human beings with the radical intention of overcoming the modern philosophy of subjectivity as self-founding selfhood. Nonetheless, in "subordinating the relation to the other to the relation to being in general" and inserting human beings into the appropriating event of the historical destining of the very truth of being, Heidegger's philosophy, according to Levinas, displays the "imperialism of the self", proper to western thought. Reducing what is to being is an exertion of logocentric violence that abolishes the incommensurability of everything other—just as Hegel did in overcoming all difference in absolute knowledge.

2 Absoluteness and Relinquishment of One's Own Being

For Levinas, on the contrary, at the beginning of philosophy is the primal event of encountering the absolute otherness of the other human being, an encounter which, instead of founding closeness, rather evidences the remoteness of 'the incommensurable,' of that which is irreducible from itself to selfhood, for it lies beyond any identity I may assign to or impose upon it. The initial happening is thus a belittlement of my power and the disappointment of all power of unifying assimilation. The wonder of infinitude that I experience in the face-to-face when I become fully aware of my finitude turns me into being-for-the-other, into a prodigal decentering, into an asymmetric commitment to deliver unlimited aid to the other in its helplessness (Gutiérrez 2001). The Lithuanian thinker attributes to the "totally other" (a traditional Jewish expression of divine transcendence) an absolute, original and distant present, whose arrival occurs in the manner of infinite exteriority, that when it is welcomed interrupts certainties and habits, dislocates self-consciousness and opens an irreparable tear within it.

The ethical question of violence emerges for Levinas wherever the infinitude of the other's presence is rejected, denied, or fought, not only as a result of a threat to the other's existence but as long as it is understood from perspectives alien to that of the absoluteness of the other's difference. It may well happen, for example, that certain forms of solidarity conceal violent discriminatory attitudes, such as demanding membership in a certain group or adherence to a particular set of values as a condition for their provision. Violence lurks as soon as the relation to the other stops being lived as the initial event of encountering an absolute otherness in favor of any totalitarian order that, in the name of homogeneity, abolishes differences and imposes the economy of the identical, of the same.

And it is precisely around this violence that Levinas, as is known, critiques the dominant tendency of Western thought. Violence is not something external or accidental; it is in fact something that pulsates in European philosophy and which, throughout its history and in the continuity of ontological motives, eliminates the incommensurability of the other, making use of a homogenizing knowledge or the determinant power of objectivity, as well as of scientific knowledge. In this sense, Hegel's philosophy is the one that makes thoroughly patent the violence that throbs in the European tradition in its determination to overcome all differences in the totality of absolute knowledge. Let us remember that what the *Phenomenology of Spirit* basically describes is the process of emancipation of consciousness from the forgetting of itself into the knowing of itself in everything it knows, i.e., the transit from consciousness to *logos* that is mediated with itself in everything. The structure of this knowledge is analyzed later through the *logic of reflection* in which Hegel tries to demonstrate that the other of reflection is necessarily the expression of reflection, and that reflection is absolute negativity, the unity of which articulates the unity of *logos*. Herein lies the logocentrism that, in Levinas' opinion, animates the transformation of everything other into the same, in turning every human attitude into a category because of what he calls "the profound allergy of philosophy" to reality (Levinas 1992). This is also valid for the Hegelian philosophy of history since history, which was the realm of violence and conflict for the philosopher, was conceived as the unfolding of absolute spirit. Let us finally mention that, in the philosophical tradition of violence against alterity, Levinas includes Husserl — who addressed the topic of the other only from the perspective of intentionality of the self, capable of recognizing the other as if it were another me — and Heidegger — whose ontology he finds openly authoritarian.

In trying to think of the other outside the concept which encloses the realm of meaning within a totality, Levinas collides with the limits of language. His contemporaries took an important step by thinking *différance* but they basically did not go further than knowing it as that which selfhood excludes; thus it was selfhood that continued to determine *différance*. It is not a matter, either, of insisting in thinking objectively the essence of the other, for one would continue to search for that which encloses it within a totality that lessens its otherness. Much less is it a matter of finding its self foundation. The only way to preserve radical otherness is to let one's self be affected in passivity by its anarchic interpellation, not subjugated by any principle, which has always been. But, how is it possible, under such conditions, to give a place to the other within language? In *Otherwise than Being* we read that I can only respond to the interpellation of the other with the *saying* that presents itself "turning [consciousness] inside out, like a cloak, which by itself would have remained *for-itself* even in its intentional aims [...] The subject in saying approaches a [fellow-man] in expressing itself, in being expelled, in the literal sense of the term, outside of any locus, no longer *dwelling*, not stomping any ground [...] The subject of saying does not give signs, it becomes a sign, turns into an allegiance" (Levinas 1994, 48–49). Relinquishment is total.

Levinas makes use of the vocative case in order to stress that it is the other who calls for and to whom one alludes in the enunciation of words, without it being either a subject or an object; what is at stake is the call of the other and the self exposed to it "like a skin to that which hurts it." Only thus, listening to the interpellation of the other before all representation that I may elaborate for myself, does language stop being appropriation and disappearance of the other. Unnoticeably, infinity makes its entrance into language outside of all dialogue. Listening predominates. As is well suggested by Argentinean philosopher Miguel Gutiérrez:

> "It is in the exposure to the other that our hearing sharpens and it is possible to hear the knuckles of that otherness knocking on my door. And if I manage to hear them and I open the door, it is not for the other to enter my dwelling and become my tenant or my guest, but in order to keep that door open and closed at the same time, so that the other is not the only one who enters, but rather I the one who exits, not only from the comfort of my home but from the comfort of my being. It is in the *exit from being* that interpellation of the other, concern for the other, the epiphany of its face, become possible" (Gutiérrez 2008, 110).

Listening to the other is only possible as my relinquishing of being. The face of the other is imposed on me from its infinite height and I welcome the unilateral obligation that its helplessness imposes on me—at the margin of language, at the margin of dialogue. The arrogance of one's self gives place to the other that I enthrone, in a welcoming in which I fade away to the point of being no one. Levinas' philosophy, in his retracing of European logocentrism, thus consummates the turn "from being to the other".

3   A Relationship of Interruption

Derrida's thought is largely akin to that of Levinas. Even though he agrees with the idea of an infinite otherness, he dissents from the characterization of otherness as absolute (Derrida et al. 1989). In order for otherness to be embraced as such, it has to manifest itself, it must announce itself and be perceived, which presupposes that I be able to recognize the other in its otherness. Derrida does not reject the idea of an infinite otherness that withdraws itself from the power of understanding, the idea of a difference that exceeds the limits of the identity which it troubles from the very beginning; neither does he deny that ethics be precisely the recognition of such excess in which difference is disseminated. Nevertheless, he thinks that it is precisely the effectiveness of such dissemination which presupposes that otherness may be experienced as such. Thus, Derrida accepts the irreducibility of otherness but refuses to grant it the nature of absolute difference and immediacy. Therefore, he makes an effort to promote a difficult and contradictory reflection in the light of which a relation with the other without reducing it to selfhood or extinguishing its difference becomes possible.

Altérités, a work composed by Derrida and three of his French colleagues, sketches such relation as

> "a respect-to someone that in virtue of its otherness and its transcendence makes the respect-to impossible. Such is the paradox. It is a relation without relation, to say it in the words of Blanchot. In order to enter into a relation with the other, interruption must be possible. The relation has to be a relation of interruption. And here the interruption does not interrupt the relation to the other but opens it instead. It all depends on the way in which one determines the mediation that concerns us here. If one makes of it mediation in the Hegelian sense of appeasement, reconciliation, totality, etc., one only reaches the extinction of the other through such mediation. It is possible, nonetheless, to think of another experience of mediation, in the manner of a dislocated relation that understands the other as other in a certain incomprehension. This is not ignorance, or darkening or giving up all desire of comprehensibility. It is necessary, however, for the other to continue to be other at some point, and when it is the other, it is thus another. At that moment the respect-to the other as such is a respect-to of interruption. Such is also the condition of desire" (Derrida et al. 1986, 81–82).[1]

A good example of this relation which is possible through interruption is that of his friendship with Gadamer, a friendship which Derrida characterized as an *interrupted dialogue*. Said dialogue was only possible by clearing out for it a space of suspension from all mediation, in which the affirmation of meaning is interrupted and in which interrupting finitude liberates the movement of an endless interior dialogue. A similar non-habitual space was that of the *text*, a name Derrida gave to the other, to that which exceeds all experience, a space akin to what Gadamer called the *eminent text*, "text to a special degree" (Gadamer 1992a, 339).[2] Eminent, because, unlike any other text referred to a single unity of meaning, it displays a total negativity that prevents it from entering into any given project of meaning and suspends all interpretive mediation.

This paradoxical mediation, which is relation to what makes impossible a relation—impossibility of which there can be an ethical experience—, led Derrida to interpret the phenomenon of violence differently from Levinas. The latter counterposes the pure and absolutely non-violent ethical relation to the absolutely violent realm of negations of alterity, which comprehends knowledge, thematizing discourse and history as a totality. Derrida rejects such counter-positioning because for him there is no choosing between pure violence and absolute non-violence, given that human existence flows between the two—human existence being the condition of possibility of the worst actual violence but also of all resistance to violence and, above all, to all interruption of it. History takes place in this realm, a scenario in which our existences enter into reciprocal relation at the margin of all absolute con-

---

[1] My translation.
[2] My translation.

ditions, in a sort of never-resolved conflict between the dominant violence and recognition of difference and alterity. Discourse takes place here as well, an ever-impure form in which violence and opposition to it intermingle, and where mediation—and the relation that makes ethics possible, prohibiting the postulation of a transcendental and absolute otherness—are articulated.

Opposite political implications also follow from these two ways of thinking of otherness. For Levinas, politics begins where ethics ends, which is the welcoming of absolute otherness; thereby making politics the space of domination and violence that must be controlled from the standpoint of ethics. For Derrida, on the contrary, absolute otherness imposes total quietism and conservatism that, by excluding all possibility of change and mediation, finally decide the extinction in rigidity of otherness itself (Derrida et al. 1986). Thus the need to free ourselves from the straightjacket of absolute identities and to open ourselves up to transformation and negotiation in order to assume the risk of articulating differences and overcoming identities.

We are not, therefore, doomed to choose between the absolutely violent discourse and the absolutely silent welcoming of the other. We are always talking between these two extremes, addressing one another, sharing phrases and a language without phrases, deprived of all predication for having been deprived of the circulation of the verb *to be* as a concept of concepts of the same, a language which thus says nothing. "Which would be entirely coherent if the face was only glance, but it is also speech; and in speech it is the phrase which makes the cry of need become the expression of desire" (Derrida 2001, 185). And it is precisely in the phrase, i.e., in articulation, mediation and relation where Derrida encounters the possibility of an ethics that prohibits the affirmation of absolute and transcending otherness: in human existence there is also listening, paying attention, commitment to and caring for, giving and receiving. Is it possible then that the interruption of all relation ends up revealing itself as a superfluous artifice?

4   The Other Which Is the Other of Ourselves

Finally, I want to present a different reading of otherness which results from Gadamer's hermeneutic philosophy. For hermeneutics, as is well known, comprehension flows in the counter-tensionality of familiarity and strangeness. "*The true locus of hermeneutics is this in-between*" (Gadamer 2006b, 295). Regarding the comprehensibility of the other, hermeneutics does not start from suspicion but rather from openness, while it nonetheless knows its own limits: there is a "potential of alterity" in the dialogical experience that cannot be exhausted by any comprehensive participation (Gadamer 1992a). The willingness to understand is limited in its pretension by the indissoluble alterity of the other. The knowledge that "[t]he very humanity of our existence depends, finally, upon whether we have learned to see the limits which our own nature has set for us, over against the nature of others" (Gadamer 1992b, 152) comes into play here.

Gadamer's notion of the other has paradoxical Hegelian roots: the other is the other of our selves. That is why it is possible, according to Hegel, to know oneself in the other. Such clarity also inspires the idea of *formation* assessed by German humanism. *Formation* as the basic human task of increasingly ascending towards a greater generality of one's own point of view, of elevating ourselves towards a knowledge which, by virtue of including more different points of view — of others and of several possible others — constantly overflows both our own particularity and that of the other. Such ascent is thus a broadening of our own horizon, due to the encountering of 'the other' and others, which irritates our prejudices and allows us to recognize ourselves in the different and strange that become familiar. In the face of this incessant broadening and retro-referring activity, the inadequacy of both the mere contemplation of one's self in the other, incapable of grasping its otherness, as well as the inadequacy of the total mediation of the other with one's self, become evident. The fundamental movement of the spirit as belonging in which one partici- pates is that of knowing our own in what is alien and from what is alien returning each time to one's self.

The dialectics that take place when one situates comprehension between famil- iarity and strangeness is also displayed in the concept of the other. The other as simple and totally incomprehensible other is, from the perspective of hermeneutics, an abstraction; the other as other and at the same time as other of one's self is, rather, subject to the ever-open effort to comprehend. Apropos "The Diversity of Europe", Gadamer suggests a process of learning in order to avoid subjecting this compre- hension of the other to domination purposes, as is usually done in the name of the scientific method. "So it may not be unjustified to conclude from our discussion a final political consequence. We may perhaps survive as humanity if we would be able to learn that we may not simply exploit our means of power and effective pos- sibilities, but must learn to stop and respect the other as an other, [...] and if we would be able to learn to experience the other and the others, as the other of our self, in order to participate with one another" (Gadamer 1992b, 236–237).

4.1 The Mirror That Is the Friend

In order to justify this call we might go back to the interpretation of the idea of friendship in Aristotle given by Gadamer at the beginning of his academic career as an inaugural lecture. The Stagirean knew that the plenitude of human beings lacks something essential if one gets by completely on one's own depriving oneself of the gain represented by friendship. He therefore also invokes the argument — anti- Cartesian, we might say — that the essence of a friend is the fact that it is easier to know an other than to know oneself; we know well how easy it is to fool ourselves about ourselves and how endless the task of knowing ourselves is.

Knowing oneself in the mirror that is the friend points to what is common to one and the other regarding the good. It is not the particularity of one's own being that each one sees in such a mirror, but what is approvingly or disapprovingly valid for oneself and for the other, and what one sees in the mirror is that which one cannot otherwise see accurately in oneself and one's own weaknesses. Furthermore, the encounter in the mirror of the friend is not experienced as a demand, but rather as a fulfillment; what we encounter in the mirror is nothing of the sort of a Kantian duty but rather a flesh-and-bone vis-à-vis. And since it is not one's own image reflected but that of a friend, all the forces of growing familiarity and commitment to the-best-oneself-that-the-other-is-for-ourselves then come into play—which is always much more than the interiorization of good intentions or scrupulous impulses. All these forces grow to the point of becoming the powerful stream of communities and affinities that start taking shape and in each of which one begins to feel and know one's self. What is thus partaken in is a real intertwining in the weave of human beings, always living with one another (Gadamer 1990).

4.2 The Dialogue That We Are

Distancing himself from Heidegger and his noticeable lack of interest in the other, Gadamer started out on his own path, well aware of the need to move on from an existential analytics to an existential dialectics from which hermeneutics arises. In one of his last interviews, Gadamer declared that he wanted to show Heidegger "that the genuine meaning of our finitude or our 'thrownness' consists in the fact that we become aware, not only of our being historically conditioned, but especially of our being conditioned by the other. Precisely in our ethical relation to the other, it becomes clear to us how difficult it is to do justice to the demands of the other or even simply to become aware of them. The only way not to succumb to our finitude is to open ourselves to the other, to listen to the "thou who stands before us" (Gadamer 2006a, 29). What does the dialogical nature of language consist of?

We are a dialogue, as Hölderlin well noticed. "But this being-in-dialogue means being beyond oneself, thinking of the other and turning back to oneself as to an other." (Gadamer 1992a, 356). This is why we are all, at all times, concerned with the gigantic task of keeping our biases and the plethora of our desires, impulses, interests, and old opinions under control, to the point where the other does not become invisible or stops being the other. It is not easy, of course, to understand that we could acknowledge that the other may be right, that oneself and one's own interests may not be right… We must therefore "learn to respect the other and what is other. Or, in other words, we must learn not to be right. We must learn to lose the game –those who do not learn this at an early age will not be able to fulfill the great tasks in later life" (Gadamer 1990, 37).[3]

That is why, in the face of the old and the new ideologies of consensus, hermeneutics represents the culture of dissent; it is about recognizing the radical and incommensurable singularity of the other and recovering a sense of plurality that defies any easy total reconciliation. Knowing that it is always possible to not do

---

[3] My translation.

justice to the other's alterity, we should resist the double temptation of superficially assimilating the other to the same, and to reject alterity as being insignificant or harmful. Lyotard goes back to Hannah Arendt's claim that "it seems that a man who is no more than a man has lost precisely the qualities that make it possible for others to treat him as an equal," to remind us that man is only more than a man if he is also the others. As Schleiermacher realized, what makes humans alike is that each one carries in himself the figure of the others (Lyotard 1994).[4] Their sameness proceeds from their dissimilarity.

4.3   We Are Ever-Increasingly What We Are Because We Are Ever-Increasingly the Others

We cannot, of course, avoid the profound paradox that was posed to Levinas when he foresaw that the totalizing metaphysics that eliminates all alterity can only be confronted through an absolutization of the other, who imposes on us—from the heights of its ineffability—the infinite obligation of welcoming and assisting it. We admit that philosophy has been the alchemy that transforms alterity into selfhood through the power of the philosopher's stone of the transcendental self, and that, after so many abuses, philosophy must take place today in resistance of the other to the same—a resistance of a fundamentally ethical nature, in the form of an asymmetrical openness to the other. However, if the original face-to-face relation to the other always occurs in language, it is not clear why this relation would be beyond all comprehension, unless comprehension is assimilated to objective knowledge. As interlocutor of all comprehension and endless source of surprised amazement that moves us to experience, we will always encounter the other on both the side of familiarity and on the side of strangeness. Willingly or unwillingly, we know about the other, who always manages to surprise us, for at the moment of truth there is really not much that we might know about him; recognizing this rupture of our epistemological arrogance may also entail the beginning of trust and the alleviation of old tensions. However, there is so much that I share with the other that is our own in common (legacies and traditions, languages, trades, hopes and even shared secrets), and so much that binds me to him, that it is legitimate to talk about participating in being and comprehension with him, which results, in turn, in mitigating or lessening both his and my own subjectivity.

One must, undoubtedly, stop the excessive assimilation of the others—and what is other or different—to the same, which is always our own, within the overflowing universal homogenization of the world in which we live. We will always have to be alert to the risk of simplistic stereotypes of all kinds, but we cannot do without the force which results from belonging together and to each other, with all the others. Neither can we do without the gratifying and wonderful experience of knowing that

---

[4] My translation.

oneself is one with another him or her—for otherness has gender!—however limited or short-lived that experience may be. The little we know about the other smuggles a great deal of light into our lives. On the side of *strangeness* are the voices and glances of the others who incessantly interpellate us with questions and demands, often startling ones, which keep us alive in the interpretative flow of the sense of living. Those voices and glances are fresh air in the prison of ownness and sameness to which we condemn ourselves in everyday life; fresh air that from time to time liberates us from the high pre-determination of what we are and what we comprehend. But also on the side of *familiarity* there is the other in the whole vast social realm in which human existence comes to pass, without forgetting that it is through love and care that we make possible the best in others and in ourselves. Sometimes we think we are gaining familiarity with the other; soon, however, the reality of otherness imposes itself once again. It is thanks to the others, nonetheless, that we are constantly changing, that is, becoming others. Learning in this way, we are ever-increasingly what we are because we are ever-increasingly the others; the notion of ownness only makes sense in a contrastive relation with others and with becoming other. And this is a never-ending process. The others reveal to us what is our own and they also reveal to us that if we take only the course that leads towards us, we never reach ourselves: the path to one's own identity goes through the others. It is the path of welcomed alterity, that is, of listening.

References

Derrida, Jacques, Stanislas Breton, Francis Guibal, and Pierre-Jean Labarrière. 1986. *Alterités*. Paris: Osiris.

Derrida, Jacques, Stanislas Breton, Francis Guibal, and Pierre-Jean Labarrière. 1989. *La escritura y la diferencia*. Trans. Patricio Peñalver. Barcelona: Anthropos. English edition: Derrida, J. 2001. *Writing and Difference* (trans. Bass, Alan). London: Routledge.

Derrida, Jacques, Stanislas Breton, Francis Guibal, and Pierre-Jean Labarrière. 1998. *Políticas de la amistad seguido del oído de Heidegger*. Madrid: Trotta.

Derrida, Jacques. 2001. *Writing and Difference*. (trans. Bass, Alan). London/New York: Routledge.

Gadamer, H.G. 1990. *La herencia de Europa*. Barcelona: Península.

Gadamer, H.G. 1992a. *Verdad y Método II*. Salamanca: Sígueme.

Gadamer, H.G. 1992b. In *Hans-Georg Gadamer on education, poetry, and history*, ed. Dieter Misgeld and Graeme Nicholson. Albany: State University of New York Press.

Gadamer, H.G. 2006a. *A century of philosophy. Hans-Georg Gadamer in conversation with Riccardo Dottori*. New York: Continuum.

Gadamer, H.G. 2006b. *Truth and method*. London: Continuum.

Gutiérrez, Carlos B. 2001. Del solipsismo al descentramiento prodigante. El desbordamiento dialógico de la subjetividad en el humanismo hebreo del siglo XX. *Palimpsestus* 1: 24–37.

Gutiérrez, Miguel. 2008. ¿Qué un otro *otro*? *Ideas y valores* 136(57): 105–115.

Levinas, Emmanuel. 1957. *Totalidad e Infinito*. Salamanca: Sígueme.

Levinas, Emmanuel. 1992. *Die Spur des Anderen*. Freiburg i. Br: Alber.

Levinas, Emmanuel. 1994. *Otherwise than being, or beyond essence*. Dordrecht: Kluwer Academic Publishers.

Lyotard, Jean-François. 1994. *Los derechos del otro*. Lecture at the Universidad Nacional de Colombia, March 1994, translated into Spanish by Diana Muñoz.

Echoes…Before the Other

Sinéad Hogan

Abstract In his essay "Jacques Derrida: Wholly Otherwise",1 Lévinas asks "[does] Derrida's work constitute a line of demarcation running through the development of Western thought in a manner analogous to Kantianism, which separated dogmatic from critical philosophy?" A line of demarcation running through Western thought could also be written as Western thought. In this essay I will ask what might such a form of demarcation mean for reading Derrida in relation to Heidegger and Lévinas? If this line of demarcation also separates a dogmatic from a critical philosophy, might the dogmatism be one that holds fast to an authoritative yet naïve belief in the ideal of a separation between aesthetics and critical thinking?

Keywords Derrida • Levinas • Heidegger • Aesthetics • Thinking • Erasure • Critical • Art

In his essay "Jacques Derrida: Wholly Otherwise",[1] Lévinas asks "[does] Derrida's work constitute a line of demarcation running through the development of Western thought in a manner analogous to Kantianism, which separated dogmatic from critical philosophy?" A line of demarcation running through Western thought could also be written as ~~Western thought~~. In this essay I will ask what might such a form of demarcation mean for reading Derrida in relation to Heidegger and Lévinas? If this line of demarcation also separates a dogmatic from a critical philosophy, might the dogmatism be one that holds fast to an authoritative yet naïve belief in the ideal of a separation between aesthetics and critical thinking?

---

[1] Emmanuel Lévinas, 'Jacques Derrida: Wholly Otherwise,' in *Proper Names*, trans. Michael B. Smith (California: Stanford University Press, 1996), 55–62.

S. Hogan (✉)
Department of Art and Design, Institute of Art, Design and Technology,
Dun Laoghaire, Ireland
e-mail: sinead.hogan@iadt.ie

© Springer International Publishing Switzerland 2016
L. Foran, R. Uljée (eds.), *Heidegger, Levinas, Derrida: The Question of Difference*, Contributions To Phenomenology 86,
DOI 10.1007/978-3-319-39232-5_8

101

1   Critical Aesthetics?

Lévinas describes Derrida's work by noting its quality of intense precision and indicates that its mode of questioning appears as a "new style of thought…exceptionally precise yet very strange texts". Identifying 'style' here, where 'precision [*précis*]' meets the 'strange [*étranges*]'[2] is significant for at least three reasons. (1) Precision would most often be associated as indicating a form of stylistic clarity in western thinking, structured on what we might call the *aesthetics of rationality*, (2) When *precision* meets the strange, *an aesthetics of unheimlichkeit* is evoked, (3) *précis* also evokes the form and style of *an aesthetics of condensed critical analysis*. By evoking precision, *unheimlichkeit* and criticality, Lévinas in effect describes Derrida's "calling into question" as an act of placing us in a different space where "nothing is left inhabitable for thought [rien n'est plus habitable pour la pensée]".[3] Therefore, thought after Derrida, according to Lévinas, becomes peculiarly dislocated, its style removed from a character of (at)homeliness with corresponding securities of the familiar comforts of assured and clear territorial and analytical demarcations. 'Critical clarity' itself comes 'into question', and becomes identified *as a question of 'style'* when Lévinas asks whether Derrida's thinking points us towards "the end of a naïvety, an unsuspected dogmatism that slumbered in the depths of what we took to be the critical spirit?"[4] Such naïvety is perhaps the naïvety that presumes a 'clear style' as something natural to critical thinking, a possibility or command 'to say what we mean'. However a naïvety is merely something that has become 'naturalised' in, or native to a culture and therefore may be founded on a set of pre-judged identifications.

Lévinas continues in his essay to specifically identify in Derrida's work, "all philosophical significance aside, a purely literary effect, a new *frisson*, Derrida's poetry".[5] This description emphasizes that, in Lévinas' reception of Derrida's thinking, an aesthetic, affective sense is heard that indicates a combination of excitement with trembling, such as '*frisson*' evokes. However, Lévinas' comment also indicates this as something potentially separable for him from what he calls 'philosophical significance'.

In Lévinas' great writings on 'the other', the separation between philosophical significance, *Being* and the aesthetic may at first appear to be a presumed, necessary and radical difference, one intimately related to the complex discourses of his theological-Judaic tradition on interdiction, aniconicity, naming and representation. In the 1947 text, *Existence and Existents*[6] and in the 1951 text 'Is Ontology

---

[2] The title of Lévinas' essay in French was 'Jacques Derrida/Tout Autrement', see Emmanuel Lévinas, *Noms Propres*, (Fata Morgana, 1976), 65–72.

[3] Lévinas, 'Jacques Derrida: Wholly Otherwise,' 56.

[4] Ibid.

[5] Ibid.

[6] Emmanuel Lévinas, *Existence and Existents*, trans. Alphonso Lingis (The Hague: Martinus Nijhoff, 1978), 19.

Fundamental?' ontology is to be escaped, art is an "event of obscuring",[7] of passivity, magic and exoticism and radically different from ethics (which is first philosophy). It is also radically different from concept (philosophy) or 'testimony' (theological). For Lévinas '*Saying (le dire)*' is an irreducible ethical mode of exposure (always 'to the other') in contrast to the determining closure in the 'known' of a represented '*said (le dit)*'. In the way Lévinas uses the notion of 'exposure and openness' in relation to *le dire*, we would need to ask whether and how this relates to Heidegger's deconstruction of ontotheology, and specifically to the latter's project of rejecting 'aesthetics' as a 'metaphysical' term.[8] Lévinas proffers 'prophetism' as "a moment [of answering for the Other]of the human condition itself".[9] Heidegger in place of the 'aesthetic' proffers 'poetic saying', *Dichtung* and thinking *Denken*. How does Lévinas' sense of 'exposure to the other' relate or differ from how Heidegger evokes the sense [*Sinn*] of being-in-the-world as an interplay between '*disclosingness* [*Erschlossenheit*]' and, what is related yet differentiated, the responsibility of *resoluteness* [*Entschlossenheit*] in *care* [*Sorge*], (most specifically outlined in *Being and Time* of 1927)?[10]

If ethics is first philosophy in Lévinas' work, then does *thinking as ethics* exclude or include aesthetics? It may seem clearly demarcated in Lévinas' writings that aesthetics is not ethics, yet Lévinas' writing itself is profoundly artful, crafted and stylistically distinct and therefore, in this sense, profoundly aesthetic. If, in 1973, Lévinas reads Derrida's 'new style of thought' as taking place through the 'frission' of its poetry, then this opens up the implication that the *frisson* for Lévinas may come from the co-dependence of aesthetics and criticality to be found in Derrida's writings.

Lévinas defines his own approach as one differentiated from the phenomenological and ontological through another separation, the 'exception of the Other'. It is perhaps the use of this specific term 'Other' that is at first the most obvious differentiation between the style of Lévinas' writings and Heidegger's. For Lévinas, the 'Other' is never synchronous with the phenomenological or ontological. His thinking and writing on the 'Other' therefore requires that he posit a notion of a quasi-phenomenological 'face-to-face' encounter. This, through his writings, therefore produces a paradoxical *sense*; that is must indicate a sense of the non-phenomenological and non-ontological. The Other is not given to our understanding in the way that 'things' are, therefore our phenomenological experience of alterity must take a different form than that of things in the world. Saying, *le dire*, for Lévinas is this intimacy, through *exposure* and *exteriority*, it is not 'related to' but a 'to the Other'. And yet it is written and spoken of.

---

[7] Emmanuel Lévinas, 'Reality and its Shadow' in *The Levinas Reader*, ed. Seán Hand (Oxford: Basil Blackwell, 1989), pp. 129–143.

[8] For example in the 1942 lecture course *Holderlin's Hymn: 'Der Ister'*.

[9] Emmanuel Lévinas, *Ethics and Infinity*, trans. Richard A. Cohen (Duquesne University Press, 1985), 113.

[10] Martin Heidegger, *Being and Time*, Trans. John Macquarrie and Edward Robinson. (San Francisco: Harper & Row publishers, 1962).

In *Being and Time*, Heidegger also specifically differentiated the *Mit-Dasein*[11] of Being-towards-others from both the ready-to-hand and the present-to-hand of ontological being towards things. *Mit-Dasein* is a primordial existential phenomenon constituting *Dasein* that operates before any phenomenon of the positivity of 'empathy'. The latter is a form motivated through the encounter with its opposite, i.e. when negative modes of unsociability dominate and cause a resistance to the other.[12] *Dasein* does not resist the other, nor is there a projection or attempt to understand the other as a 'duplicate self'. Rather, "Being towards Others [is] an autonomous, irreducible relationship of Being: this relationship, as Being-with, is one which, with *Dasein's* Being, already is."[13] *Dasein* is always already co-constituted as *Mit-Dasein* and as so, Being-with is intimately and existentially differentiated from both 'empathy' and the alienation of "the neuter, the "They" [*das Man*]."[14] The critique and deconstruction of the privileging of presence is founded on such principles. If we consider it through the context of Derrida's description of *différance*, as "the entirely other relationship that apparently interrupts every economy",[15] this irreducible relation of *Mit-Dasein* may be considered a place of constituting *différance*.

2 How Might This Appear?

According to Lévinas, Derrida's thinking broaches a new style for thought, one where the history of philosophy is shown to be a developing sense of the sheer difficulty of thinking. Lévinas, with his image of a "no-man's land", evokes a sense of marginal space that has opened up. An uncanniness, an *unheimlichkeit* is inevitably evoked by the 'nothing inhabitable' there. Lévinas points out that what may be to come, after the critique of presence, is a sign of the privileging of what is 'otherwise' in language. That is, a writing otherwise to the kind of signification that would accord and synchronise directly with the reciprocal economy of presence. But Lévinas' questions in relation to Derrida's thought also pose the problem of how such a demarcation in thinking may resonate with the supreme non-accordance, which is the 'exception of the Other'? In its differentiation from the ontologically conditioned of a 'Said', *the sign*, in the disruption that occurs through Derrida's thought of *différance*, can be aligned with what Lévinas calls 'Saying [*le dire*]'.

---

[11] Heidegger, *SZ* 113–130.

[12] Heidegger, *SZ* 125.

[13] Heidegger, *SZ* 125.

[14] Ibid. 126.

[15] "How are we to think *simultaneously*, on the one hand, *différance* as the economic detour which, in the element of the same, always aims at coming back to the pleasure or the presence that have been deferred by (conscious or unconscious) calculation, and, on the other hand, *différance* as the relation to an impossible presence, as expenditure without reserve [...]?". Jacques Derrida, 'Différance' in *Margins of Philosophy*, trans. Alan Bass (Chicago: University of Chicago Press, 1982), 19.

Lévinas proposes that in Derrida's writing "the sign, like the Saying, is the extra-ordinary event (running counter to presence) of exposure to others, of subjection to others; i.e. the event of subjectivity."[16] In a significant and clear-sighted observation, this 'subjectivity otherwise' is also differentiated from a mere *absence* of presence.

What is obviously indicated yet unspoken in 'Jacques Derrida: Wholly Otherwise' is the difference and space Lévinas wants to put between his thought and what was represented for him by 'Heidegger's climate.' Yet, in the sentence from "Jacques Derrida: Wholly Otherwise" where Lévinas says, "the history of philosophy is probably nothing but a growing awareness of the difficulty of thinking,"[17] it is hard not to hear echoes of Heidegger's "most thought-provoking in our thought-provoking time is that we are still not thinking".[18]

Therefore, if we were to follow Lévinas' claim that there is a reason, before the kind of knowledge that gives us classical intellectualism, and that would be 'ethics as first philosophy' and we were to hear the *frission* effect of 'Derrida's poetry' and further, we were to enquire into Heidegger's question 'what is called thinking?'[19]… then we may need to trace the chiasmic and *unheimlichkeit* relation between ethics and aesthetics.

3   A Different Climate

In *Totality and Infinity*, in 1961, Lévinas defined his approach as an engaged analysis of the unique and different "intentionality" of transcendence, experienced in "the gleam of exteriority…in the face of the Other [le visage d'autrui]".[20] Insisting, purposefully, in contrast to how he reads Heidegger, on retaining a sense of the 'humanism of the Other'. Yet with this insistence on 'humanism', the question arises of how might the 'other' potentially operate as a term of exclusion and differentiation? This is one of the later questions for Derrida in relation to both Heidegger and Lévinas, when his deconstruction turns towards 'humanism, *Dasein* and the question of 'the animal'.[21] Yet it could also be asked, is not the 'wholly other' to the 'human' excluded in any 'humanism of the other'? Derrida's approach to this Lévinasian conundrum is encapsulated in the phrase *tout autre est tout autre*.[22] The double '*tout autre*' pivots on the contradictions that differently inform *both* phenomenality and transcen-

---

[16] Lévinas, 'Jacques Derrida: Wholly Otherwise,' 61.

[17] Lévinas, 'Jacques Derrida: Wholly Otherwise,' 55.

[18] Heidegger 2004.

[19] Martin Heidegger, *What is called thinking?*, Trans. J. Glenn Gray (Perennial: Harper Collins, 2004).

[20] Lévinas, *Totality and Infinity*, 24.

[21] Jacques Derrida, *The Animal That Therefore I Am*, Ed. Marie-Louise Mallet, Trans. David Wills (Fordham University Press, 2008).

[22] Jacques Derrida, *The Gift of Death and Literature in Secret*, Trans. David Wills (Chicago: Chicago University Press, 2008).

dence. What this may mean is that ontology and phenomenality may not necessarily be thought as *opposites* to transcendence and alterity. To think them as such would entwine them in a 'togetherness,' through a reciprocal logic of negation and co-defining assimilation. Instead they could be thought of as *contra-dictory*, utilising a sense of non-reciprocality that exposes a *saying* 'against' a *said*. In this way the critique of presence and *logocentricism* institutes a new 'logic of inherent contradiction'. *Contra-diction* becomes an operative mode rather than a logical description. The 'against' of the *contra* would not be an 'oppositional-being-at-war' but the point where a lever of *différance* provides a place for a 'non-reciprocal exposure of *saying*' to work *with*.

In *Totality and Infinity*, Lévinas' key task was to outline "*the difference between objectivity and transcendence*".[23] For Lévinas, in 1974, in *Otherwise than Being*,[24] the 'dis-interested desire of transcendence' is opposed to 'war'. War is the reduction of the "other of being" ("*l'<<autre>>de l'etre*") through the totalisation that comes about in being-interested, the positivity of *conatus*, the impulse to exist of the 'my place in the sun' an *ethos* of self-preservation, knowing and confirmation, where "essence is interest". Lévinas defines the theatrics of oppositionality as the place where,

> Being's interest takes dramatic form in egoisms struggling with one another, each against all, in the multiplicity of allergic egoism which are at war with one another and are thus together. War is the deed or the drama of the essence's interest. No entity can await its hour. They all clash, despite the difference of the regions to which the terms in conflict may belong. Essence is thus the extreme synchronism of war.[25]

A form of hospitality may have to open up here to certain inhospitalities occasioned, for Lévinas, by Derrida's event and *style* of criticality. Identifying the operations of *différance* acts to dissolve the dogmatic impression and effect of any synchronism and shows it to be apparently *contra-dictory* in character. In *différance* the realisation of 'essence as extreme synchronism' becomes highlighted as a logical impossible. An apparent synchronism in its privileging of presence is shown as a 'clash, between different regions to which the *différance*, in conflict, may belong'. The form of hospitality required to open up to this quasi-logic is perhaps the hospitality to the event of an aesthetic-criticality. I propose that this demarcation is opened up by Derrida, in response to Lévinas' work, through the phrase '*tout autre est tout autre*'. A crucial detour and spacing between *tout autre* and *tout autre* is exposed by this saying. We could then also consider this as representing the space 'in question' between hearing Heidegger and Lévinas' thought together, where the absence of a specific constant term for the non-phenomenological other in Heidegger's writings is chiasmically marked by the dominance of the term 'other' in Lévinas' writings.

---

[23] Lévinas, *Totality and Infinity*, 49.

[24] Emmanuel Lévinas, *Otherwise than Being*, trans. Alphonso Lingis (Pennsylvania: Duquesne University Press, 2008).

[25] Lévinas, *Otherwise than Being*, 4.

4   Why *tout autre est tout autre*?

In relation to his reading of Lévinas, (but also of Kierkegaard and Heidegger),[26] and most specifically on the topic of 'responsibility', Derrida proposed this chiasmic formula, '*tout autre est tout autre*', to be at the heart of his deconstruction of ethics. By doing so Derrida provided a phrase that evidences a dissymmetry and non-synchronicity within what is also read as a tautology (in French). In English 'every other is wholly other' can only paraphrase one aspect of the saying's equivocity and it loses the tautological form and effect. The phrase is a formula that calls on us to think the conditions of a multitude of impossible synchronies.[27] A further impossible synchrony takes performative effect when we hear or speak '*tout autre est tout autre*'. Aurally we cannot distinguish it from '*tout autre et tout autre*'. The *est* and *et*, the *is* and *and*, when heard in French, accord with each other. This is one of the extended aesthetic effects and *frissions* of Derrida's thought on *tout autre*. It is an aesthetic companion to the intervention of the *a* in *différance*, which is also only evident when written and is non-differentiated when heard. These are not effects for the sake of 'aesthetics' per se, in the sense of auxiliary flourishes, but ones constitutively necessary for thinking through an aesthetic-criticality.

It should be noted here that in the phrase *tout autre est tout autre* Derrida does not use the Lévinasian capitalized *Autrui*. Why? In 'Violence and Metaphysics', Derrida identifies the difference between *autre* and *Autrui* as residing in the (Latinate) derivation of the *alter-huic*. The '*huic*', he considers, brings in a dangerous ontological 'this' to the realm of alterity, potentially positively instating a hypostasis. This would be a *reduction to presence* in relation to what should remain foreign to sense. Derrida asks "what does *autre* mean before its Greek determination as *heteron*, and its Judeo-Christian determination as *autrui*?"[28] He considers that what is concealed in and by the Greek *heteron* (what is differentiated only through a differentiation from 'being'), operates at the same time as an irreducible signifier. There is an act of concealment *in the word* that signifies a pre-comprehension in a general sense, a 'conciousness' of *alterity*. Yet alterity must remain irreducible to conceptualisation. It is this irreducibility that is fundamental and for Lévinas is what makes 'first philosophy' an ethics. The concealments that Derrida points out are also however, (in a move that echoes Heidegger), a revealing of the "irreducible

---

[26] See, Jacques Derrida *The Gift of Death and Literature in Secret*, trans. David Wills (Chicago and London: Chicago University Press 2nd Ed. 2008).

[27] That is between 1. the irreplaceable, unsubstitutable and untranslatable singularity of the unique of every <u>other</u> (*tout autre*) 2. the exemplarariness of iterability, that is the shared constitution of *tout autre*, the exemplarary and singular *Da of every Da*-sein that 'we' are, that is of <u>every</u> other (*tout autre*) 3. the incommensurability of each and every *Da-sein* with every *autre* (*tout autre*) and also 4. of the incommensurability of any and all other (*tout autre*) with what may be wholly other (*tout autre*).

[28] Jacques Derrida, 'Violence and Metaphysics' in *Writing and Difference*, trans. Alan Bass (Chicago: University of Chicago Press, 1978), 105.

centre of meaning (the other *as* Other [l'autre *comme* autrui])".[29] It is this notion of what we could call here an *'aesthetics* of irreducibility' that Derrida considers both contested by Lévinas, when the latter himself privileges the phrasing of 'Other,' but also may evoke the very *metaphysical desire* that is the founding context of Lévinas' thought.

It could be proposed that the non-synchronistic *at the same time* of an apparent tautology opens up an *unheimliche* contra-diction as the *différance* of the *'tout autre est tout autre'*. It provides an 'instantaneous dissociation' from any presentation and synchronism in the *said* of the 'Other/tout autre'. The *aesthetics of Being* in any 'is/*est*', escapes the ontology of its *said* in the *différance* evoked by its Saying, *le dire*. The *est* between each *tout autre* thinks and says the *tout autre* otherwise than as tautological... *tout autre est* (*is*) [*at the same time*] *tout autre*... The *différance in its spatialising and temporalising* of the ontological copula *is* displays a phenome-nological contra-diction. This contra-diction is both aesthetic and existential. Any 'at the same time' that may operate at the heart of every divisibility-of-presence is infused with an *aesthetics of différance*. This disrupts any attempt, any intentional or unintentional effect, to reduce the *other* to an ontic or ontological entity.

This is an *aporetic* contra-diction at the heart of any thinking or saying of 'the other'. It is an aporia because the condition of the experience of alterity is that there is no 'the experience' of what is other; "it is this absurdity, denounced in the self-evidence of the "at the same time," that constitutes the *aporia* as the *aporia*".[30] It is simply and purely impossible to appropriate or represent the other, *tout autre*. This is not evidence of 'the difficulty' of representation or even a demand to search for better forms of representation, it is simply a founding condition of any *saying*. There can be no 'said' [*le dit*] as other, all evocation of 'the other' must *succeed in failing*. In a way, there is no contra-diction here but rather a crediting of the signifi-cance of *impossibility*. But can there then still be a Saying [*le dire*] of the other? Does '*l'autre*' name? If a term can 'be a Saying [*le dire*] of the other' does this exclude other terms, other names from the Saying [*le dire*] of *alterity*? How do we find ourselves in the situation that we can think *of* alterity without reducing this through a representation?

I propose that the brilliance of Derrida's intervention of *différance* is that it allows the thought of the unity of difference and identity to pivot on the aesthetic intervention of the *a*. Thus the *a* acts not as an erasure, but as a disruptive point that arrests and opens up infinite dimensions and disseminatory effects, *in its saying and its said*. 'Infinite' here can be heard in its full range of evocations, including what resists any synthesising closure in presence and in so doing opens out the grounds for difference, substitution, and iterability. These are merely the grounds and critical-aesthetics of language and saying. Both the most gentle and the most 'vio-lent' attempts to appropriate that which is inappropriable, including what may be

---

[29] Jacques Derrida, *Writing and Difference*, trans. Alan Bass (Chicago: University of Chicago Press, 1978), 105. Derrida, *L'écriture et la différence* (Paris: Éditions du Seuil, 1967), 155.

[30] Jacques Derrida, '*Ousia* and *Grammé*: Note on a Note from *Being and Time*', in *Margins of Philosophy*, trans. Alan Bass, (The Harvester Press: University of Chicago, 1982), 56.

said by the term 'other,' will necessarily experience an *aesthetics of impossibility*. For in the experience of any attempt to represent is the quasi-phenomenological realisation of the 'nothing to be grasped,' where there is no ontological register and what remains is untouched as *alterity*: the erotic point of impossibility.

5 Precision Is Without Clarity or Obscurantism

In *Acts of Literature*, Derrida proposed that resistance to the impossible synchrony of an apparent contradiction is a form of "modern obscurantism".[31] We can add this to Lévinas' observation of a 'slumbering dogmatism,' as a way of identifying Derrida's thought of *différance* as that 'line of demarcation running through the development of Western thought … separating dogmatic from critical philosophy'. I propose that *différance* provides a conceptual and phenomenological breakpoint in the specularity of language, in what Lévinas calls the 'said' [*le dit*]. It institutes what Derrida called *literature*, Heidegger called 'poetic thinking' and Lévinas called 'saying'.

One of the questions that then comes to mind is whether it is possible to speak of the term 'other,' as *sous rature*, in the way that Heidegger in 1956, in *Zur Seinsfrage*,[32] put ~~Sein~~ under erasure (with an X), and as developed extensively by Derrida? There is a breakpoint to any ontological synthesising when the taking place of the term ~~Being~~ is an 'under erasure'. Current typesetting conventions now operate with a graphic strikethrough, however Heidegger's graphic X evokes the notion of the 'fourfold' of his later thinking. In such a way, ~~Being~~ under erasure would (at the same time) be otherwise to what it 'is' as a 'saying'. This eminently obvious intervention operated to essentially both highlight and disturb the presenting power of all representation and emphasise language's relation to the impossibility of the reduction of a sign to an *according with presence*. The realisation of which would be nihilism as 'totality'. Would the practice of *sous rature* enhance or undermine how the 'Saying' [*le dire*] and 'said' [*le dit*] of 'other' also operates? Or is the X of erasure (as a literal graphic or implied modality) a visual way of the very same differentiation between the 'Saying' [*le dire*] and 'said' [*le dit*]? Is this 'other' a word or placeholder for the always already *under erasure*?

Significant here is that the principle of identity is symbolically represented as A is A, providing an initial tautological empty foundation and principle for any classic logical proposition which must be subject to non-contradiction. But what we could now call the *aesth-ethics of saying* sunders this first principle. There is a hospitality to contradiction in every saying (of *alterity*) because of the necessary inadequacy of the *said*. A saying therefore does not say the said, *tout autre ~~est~~ tout autre*. Both the principle of identity and the phrase *tout autre est tout autre* pivot on the is/*est* and in

---

[31] Jacques Derrida, *Acts of Literature*. ed. Derek Attridge, (New York: Routledge, 1992), 43.

[32] Martin Heidegger, *The Question of Being*, trans. William Kluback and Jean T. Wilde (New York: Twayne Publishers Inc., 1958).

this way are extensions of the Heideggerian ~~ist~~ and ~~Sein~~. Most evidently *autre* does not here escape its being as signifier and therefore as signifier cannot escape from the *aesthetics of iterability*. The phenomenological *said* of *tout autre* must betray *tout autre* in both its resistance and submission to the phenomenological.

5.1   Is There a Need to Escape from This Term 'Other'?

In his early text *De l'évasion* (1935) translated as *On Escape* (Lévinas 2003),[33] Lévinas didn't use the term 'other'. There he writes "the need for escape is found to be absolutely identical at every juncture [*point d'arrêt*] to which its adventure leads it as need; it is as though the path it travelled could not lessen its dissatisfaction."[34] A *point d'arrêt* is translated as "juncture" and significantly is kept in the English translation [in square brackets] indicating at the same time therefore an untranslatable. Also possible were terms such as *breakpoint* or *holding point*. While its constellation of references has many more possibilities, it is generally a graphic marked point that puts a stay on an action. For example, a *point d'arrêt* is the name of a three-pronged tip-end used in the classic form of fencing. In that context, it acts as a 'stopping point' that the *épée* fencer has at the end of the sword, to stop it piercing his opponent. It is also a term for an act in sewing that prevents a thread from unravelling and a graphic in musical notation which is placed over a note to indicate a rest or extended pause, 🎵 a shift, a breakpoint or durational stay in the tempo.[35] It can also indicate a breaking disturbance point for a flow in an aerodynamic context. In this context here, we could consider it as a marked disturbance point that puts a durational stay on the activity of representation, in relation to any presumption of accessing the other as a phenomenological presence. Could then the term 'other' be a juncture that Lévinas' adventure led to as a need, yet the path it travelled does not lessen a dissatisfaction in what is *said*? Is there also therefore a need then to ethically escape the dominance of a *said* such as operates in "the other"?

I propose that Lévinas' brief early mention of the *point d'arrêt* could be considered already as this escape and to be a pre-echo of the graphic mark of the *sous rature's X*. I propose that this internal pause in the development of a movement describes the absolute necessity of failure, breakdown and risk in any representation, writing or thinking of *ethics* or the *other*. Hence in what Derrida calls 'literature' we must hear at all times the double act of *errature* (going astray) and *rature* (erasure) of language. The style, so-called hyperbolism and particular mode of quasi-phenomenology that operates in the writings of Heidegger-Lévinas-Derrida, provides in this sense an alternative to any 'modern obscurantism' that *would*

---

[33] Emmanuel Lévinas, *On Escape, De L'évasion*, trans. Bettina Bergo, (California: Stanford University Press, 2003).

[34] Ibid. 53.

[35] It is a species of 'fermata' an articulation mark in musical notation that allows a note to be held longer at the discretion of the musician.

seek stabilization and clarification (as reduction to a representing power) of what *must* and can only remain bound by the constitutively undecidable status of a singularity∞iterability bind. This would therefore (to be faithful to Lévinas' thinking), by necessity, include any appropriation, stabilizing or moralising of the term 'Other' as a privileged terminology, designed to invoke a *sacrosanct style* of writing. The dogmatic presumption here would be of a predetermined ethics of representation, presumed ethical because 'free from aesthetics'.

5.2   The Aesthetic Conditions of the Law of the 'Other'

I would like to paraphrase Derrida from 'Before the Law' and ask then 'what if the law that constitutes '*Dasein*' and what if the law of the '*Other*', without being itself transfixed by literature, or *Dichtung* or Saying, 'shared the conditions of its possibility with the literary object?'[36]

A mode of 'poetic thinking' is elaborated by Heidegger in relation to the question nominated by the essay '*Why poets?*', in which he ultimately proposes a critique of capitalism and nihilism's reduction of everything to a present-to-hand resource. There he calls 'poets', those that "*in a desolate [dürftiger] time*", "risk more […by willing more] in that they will in another mode than the deliberative self-assertion of the objectification of the world…[and] experience defenselessness in unwholeness."[37] Lévinas, in the 1966 essay 'The Servant and her Master', writing in relation to his friend Blanchot, describes poetry as "the disruption of immanence" and he posits that "poetic language gives sign … To introduce [this] meaning into Being is to go from the Same to the Other (Autre), from Self to Other (Autrui), it is to give sign, to undo the structures of language. Without this, the world would know only the meanings which inspire official records or the minutes of the board meetings of Limited Companies." Here Lévinas seeks to escape from the categories of 'art' and commerce that would be seen to be a reduction of this 'disruption to immanence,' if poetry is not distinguished from "a purely aesthetic event"; "There is no question of considering this disruption as a purely aesthetic event. But the word poetry does not after all name a species whose genus is referred to by the word art. Inseparable from speech (*le verbe*), it overflows with prophetic meanings."[38] In question then may be the style of an *aesthetics of thinking*.

We can take Heidegger's definition of dis-interested, defenseless willing or desire, with all its echoes of *or for* Lévinas' 'dis-interested desire of transcendence', as the definition of the 'poematic-thinker' rather than as a reference to any model of formal art practice (including poetry *as such*). I would proffer that in this way, Heidegger, Lévinas and Derrida are exemplary poematic thinkers, but more impor-

---

[36] Derrida, *Acts of Literature*, 191.

[37] Martin Heidegger, *Off the Beaten Track*, trans. Julian Young and Kenneth Haynes, (Cambridge: Cambridge University Press, 2002), 239–240.

[38] Emmanuel Lévinas, 'The servant and her master' in *The Levinas Reader*, ed. Seán Hand (Oxford: Basil Blackwell, 1989), 159.

tantly the conversation between their thinking is a poematic one of invention and intervention necessary for a thinking of alterity… without possible object. These would provide the *aesthetic conditions* of the law of the '*Other*'.

Invention, as Derrida elaborates the term, is a calling upon or coming upon the "singular structure of an event [ie…of a] speech act…[that will] on the one hand be [an event] insofar as it is singular, and, on the other hand, inasmuch as its very singularity will produce the coming or the coming about of something new."[39] In 'Violence and Metaphysics', Derrida stressed in his discussion of Lévinas' writings how "despite all appearances there is no concept of the Other, [and therefore] we would have to reflect upon this word "Other" [*Autrui*] in an artisan-like way."[40] Such a way would have to respect the irreducibility to thematisation and conceptualization while submitting to the finitudes and inhospitalities of 'being-in-language'.

Lévinas' recognises such a literary inhospitality in his description of Derrida's writing as a "no-man's land." Derrida recognized the aesthetic in the thinking of ethics when he called *Totality and Infinity* "a work of art not a treatise."[41] Heidegger relatedly proposed another no-man's land between aesthetics and ethics, with the notion of *Bewahrung*, preservation, as intimately related to the work of art as what founds "being-with-one-another [*Miteinandersein*]…from out of the relation to unconcealment,"[42] …ie. founding being 'with the otherness of the other', rather than on any concept that claims the mastery of *understanding* the other. We can hear in these echoes, the aesthetic-work of thinkers who are most definitely not proposing art, aesthetics or any *connoisseurship* as an ethical answer, nor proposing any mode of aesthetic access to the other, but are perhaps calling up a virtual conversation around the 'aesthetic-ethic object', as an impossible object negated and doubled and divided by the *sous rature of the X*.

5.3   (In)Hospitalities of Language as Condition of Possibility for Thinking the Other

Is there then a hospitality to be broached between Heidegger's language of *Dasein* and Lévinas' language of *l'autre*? Between these thoughts that reject aesthetics *as such*, and another way of thinking aesthetics?

As Derrida reads it, literature began under the same conditions of possibility that a thought of alterity initiates. That is a strong claim. He expands it by proposing that literature participates in this shared constitution as it "began with a certain relation to its own institutionality, i.e., its fragility, its absence of specificity, its absence of

---

[39] Jacques Derrida, *Psyche: Inventions of the Other, Volume 1*, ed. Peggy Kamuf and Elisabeth Rottenberg (California: Stanford University Press, 2007), 5.

[40] Derrida, *Writing and Difference*, 104.

[41] Derrida, ibid. 312, footnote no. 7.

[42] Heidegger, *Off the Beaten Track*, 41.

object."[43] We can ask then: is an institution with an absence of object impossible, or is the openness of this impossibility and non-objectification an exemplary foundation? We might ask, bringing Heidegger into the conversation, what kind of relation does all this have to the institutionality and phenomenology of *Dasein*, since both a thought of *Dasein* and a thought of *l'autre* are both founded on a deconstruction and invention of a sense of subjectivity requiring an 'absence of object'. That is, *Dasein* and *l'autre* can be considered structurally *unheimlichkeit* as "possibility of the impossibility" of experience. Death constitutively opens *Dasein* to the "non-relational [*unbezügliche*]."[44] *L'autre* is the non-relational. In Heidegger's thinking, the interruption and non-according *as Dasein's* constituting non-experience "gives Dasein nothing to be 'actualised'..."[45] In Lévinas' thinking, the interruption and non-according *of the other* is non-experience and with *l'autre* nothing is given to be 'actualised'. Thus both thoughts point to a phenomenology that is otherwise to any determined ontology and is a holding rupture, suspension or *point d'arrêt* producing a disturbance in the phenomenological.

It is important to keep in mind here the great double resonances of the word *expérience* in French, where both experience and experiment can be heard. In doing so we could then speak of the 'experiment of the experience' or the 'experience of the experiment' of literature as constitutive risk taking with this disturbing absence of object. And we can hear there echoes with the *transcendence* of Lévinas' impossible *dis-inter-estedness as desire*, as the "deformalization of the idea of infinity, this wholly empty notion. The infinity in the finite....a desire perfectly disinterested."[46]

5.4   What Kind of Experience *Can This Poematic, Aesthetic or Desiring Disinterested Thinking Be?*

Heidegger proposed that his writing in, *On the Way to Language*, is "intended to bring us face-to-face with a possibility of undergoing an experience [*Erfahrung*] with language."[47] In German *Erfahrung* can also be a term for experiment. Heidegger nuances what "'*Erfahrung*" signifies, and in this passage we can hear the *Erfahrung* in the sense of *expérience* not as intentional experimenting but as almost an experiment done *on* us... *Erfahrung* of language is "this something that befalls us, strikes us, comes over us, overwhelms and transforms us...[It] is not of our own making... we endure it, suffer it, receive it as it strikes us and submit to it. It is this something itself that comes about, comes to pass, happens."[48] This phenomenological descrip-

---

[43] Derrida, *Acts of Literature*, 42.

[44] Heidegger, *Being and Time*, 294, (*SZ*, 250).

[45] Ibid. 307, (*SZ*, 262).

[46] Lévinas, *Totality and Infinity*, 50.

[47] Martin Heidegger, *On the Way to Language*, trans. Peter D. Hertz (SanFrancisco: Harper & Row, 1971), 57.

[48] Ibid.

tion of the event of being-subject-to-'the call of language' fundamentally disrupts our notion of agency and authorship and institutes the hyperbolic and aporetic impossibility *and* necessity of a response-ability. Therefore in the experience of language we 'enter into the experiment of its capacity to overwhelm and transform and we submit to this', we are hostage to this *expérience/experiment*. No more so than when we are dumbfounded, stunned or astonished and held '*in* contra-diction'.

In this way, I propose that in Heidegger, as well as more explicitly in Lévinas and Derrida, there is a thought or unthought of language and authorship as within the aporia of impossible hospitality, its *Unheimlichkeit*. Perhaps then the phrase 'language is the house/temple/precinct of being' could be rephrased after Lévinas' and Derrida's work, yet keeping its Heideggerian echoes, as 'Language is hos(ti) pitality'. In doing so, we must first remember that one of the first laws of hospitality is that the host should not ask 'who' or 'what' the guest is [or means?] Instead in hospitality, as in reading, we must extend the affirmative welcome of 'learning to exist in the nameless' of a 'yes, come...' there must be a 'knowing not to know', and an openness "before any identification", projection, pre-judged-ness or *ressentiment*.[49]

Derrida pointed out in his engagement with the aporias of unconditional/conditional hospitality that this is also a space of antinomy, i.e. of two mutually exclusive, non-symmetrical <u>and</u> inseparable laws. The law (universal singular and exemplary) of unconditional hospitality is to welcome without condition, the laws that hospitality is conditional upon (plural, specific and iterable) are necessary to effectively recognize the offer of hospitality or its institution; "They both imply and exclude each other, simultaneously. They incorporate one another at the moment of excluding one another... (... instant of impossible synchrony, ...)".[50]

Derrida proposes that for absolute hospitality to be "offered beyond debt and economy" it would have to go beyond the Kantian notion of the categorical imperative *as duty*. It would require therefore responsibility *as not responding* to the compulsion to act out of duty, to risk being inhospitable, so as to avoid being trapped by a reductive '*language of ritual and duty*' leaving us free for the affirmative binds of '*language and ritual*.'[51] And therefore hospitality becomes hostipitality; both hostage and host to a hostility of being duty bound before the other. Hostipitality as *open to the other as irreducibly and non accessible other, tout autre*. Could we write this essential *unheimlichkeit* as ~~hospitality~~?

To avoid reducing the '*language of ritual and duty*' to all the knowingness of negative or positive representation, with the violence and petty cruelties inherent in mechanistic determinations, in the words of Heidegger, "a transformation of language is needed...This transformation does not result from the procurement of

---

[49] Jacques Derrida, *Of Hospitality*, trans. Anne Dufourmantelle (California: Stanford University Press, 2000), 77.

[50] Ibid. 81.

[51] Jacques Derrida, *On The Name*, trans. Thomas Dutoit (California: Stanford University Press, 1995), 7.

newly formed words and phrases."[52] Hence an experience *of* language becomes an experiment *in* language. Language must seek out a hospitality to the aesthetic contradictions of 'impossible synchrony'. No perfect word or phrase or saying, is out there to be found, all words, as Lévinas has pointed out, in their 'said' betray the saying. Instead what must be risked in this hostipitality for saying, is precisely the singularity of 'unconditional saying'. This could be considered as the epiphany of an inter-*face* that shows itself in the poematic, a no-man's land where aesthetics and ethics meet.

As per the logic of under erasure and *point d'arrêt*, we are ethically structured and haunted by the poematic in all language as our impossible *being otherwise before the other*:

> we are structured by the phantasmic ...in particular ... we have a phantasmic relation to the other, and that the phantasmicity of this relation cannot be reduced, this pre-originary inter-vention of the other in me.
>
> It is here that exemplarity, universality and singularity cross each other's paths.[53]

Such a phantasmic, echoic constitution requires a foundation based on a law of contra-*diction*, to do justice to alterity's necessary resistance to the phenomenological. Such a space would be evident as a disturbance where the point of demarcation between aesthetics and critical thinking had previously appeared to clearly exist and be delimited. This would place Heidegger, Lévinas and Derrida's work as a chiasmic line of demarcation running through the development of Western thought in a manner analogous to Kantianism, separating dogmatic from critical philosophy. As Derrida pointed out, in his 1965 lectures on Heidegger and the Question of Being & History in relation to Heidegger's 'Zur Seinsfrage', "[t]his crossing out, this negative writing, this trace erasing the trace of the present in language is the unity of metaphoricity and non-metaphoricity as unity of language". Hence $X = ...$[54]

References

Derrida, Jacques. 1967. *L'écriture et la différence*. Paris: Éditions du Seuil.

Derrida, Jacques. 1978. *Writing and Difference*. Trans. A. Bass. Chicago: University of Chicago Press.

Derrida, Jacques. 1982. *Margins of Philosophy*. Trans. A. Bass. The Harvester Press: University of Chicago.

Derrida, Jacques. 1992. In *Acts of literature*, ed. Derek Attridge. New York: Routledge.

Derrida, Jacques. 1995. *On The Name*. Trans. Ed. T. Dutoit. Stanford: Stanford University Press.

Derrida, Jacques. 2000. *Of Hospitality*. Trans. A. Dufourmantelle. Stanford University Press.

---

[52] Martin Heidegger, *On the Way to Language*, trans. Peter D. Hertz (SanFrancisco: Harper & Row, 1971), 135.

[53] Jacques Derrida and Maurizio Ferraris, *A Taste for the Secret*, trans. Giacomo Donis (Cambridge: Polity Press, 2002), 89.

[54] Jacques Derrida, Heidegger: *The Question of Being & History*, Trans. Geoffrey Bennington (Chicago University Press, 2016), p. 224.

Derrida, Jacques. 2007. In *Psyche: inventions of the other*, vol. 1, ed. Peggy Kamuf and Elisabeth Rottenberg. Stanford: Stanford University Press.

Derrida, Jacques. 2008. *The Gift of Death and Literature in Secret*. Trans. D. Wills. Chicago: Chicago University Press.

Derrida, Jacques. 2008. *The Animal That Therefore I Am*. Ed. Marie-Louise Mallet, Trans. D. Wills. Bronx: Fordham University Press.

Derrida, Jacques. 2016. *Heidegger: The Question of Being & History*, Trans. Geoffrey Bennington. Chicago: Chicago University Press.

Derrida, Jacques, and Maurizio Ferraris. 2002. *A Taste for the Secret*. Trans. G. Donis. Cambridge: Polity Press.

Heidegger, Martin. 1958. *The Question of Being*. Trans. W. Kluback and J.T. Wilde. New York: Twayne Publishers.

Heidegger, Martin. 1962. In *Being and time*, ed. John Macquarrie and Edward Robinson. San Francisco: Harper & Row publishers.

Heidegger, Martin. 1971. *On the Way to Language*. Trans. P.D. Hertz. San Francisco: Harper & Row.

Heidegger, Martin. 2002. *Off the Beaten Track*. Trans. J. Young and K. Haynes. Cambridge University Press.

Heidegger, Martin. 2004. *What Is Called Thinking?* Trans. J. Glenn Gray. Perennial: Harper Collins.

Lévinas, Emmanuel. 1969. In *Totality and infinity*, ed. Alphonso Lingis. Pittsburgh: Duquesne University Press.

Lévinas, Emmanuel. 1976. *Noms Propres*. Fata Morgana.

Lévinas, Emmanuel. 1989. In *The Levinas reader*, ed. Seán Hand. Oxford: Basil Blackwell.

Lévinas, Emmanuel. 1996. *Proper Names*. Trans. M.B. Smith. California: Stanford University Press.

Lévinas, Emmanuel. 2003. *On Escape De L'évasion*. Trans. B. Bergo. California: Stanford University Press.

Lévinas, Emmanuel. 2008. *Otherwise than Being*. Trans. A. Lingis. Pennsylvania: Duquesne University Press.

The Impossible Force of "Mightlessness": Translating Derrida's *impouvoir* and Heidegger's *Machtlose*

Oisín Keohane

Abstract This paper examines how Derrida, in *The Beast and the Sovereign, Volume II*, examines the notion of *Walten* in Heidegger. I argue that while Derrida has provided us in his seminar with invaluable insights into Heidegger's early work – dating from the late 1920s to the early 1930s – he has missed something essential in Heidegger's thought towards the end of the 1930s, namely, Heidegger's turn towards *das Machtlose*, the 'unpower' which is beyond power and lack of power, as described in his 1938 *Mindfulness*. This turn, I claim, cannot be separated from Heidegger's turn towards Nietzsche in his seminars post-1935. It also demonstrates that Derrida remains blind to his own proximity to post-1935 Heidegger when he himself tries to separate the forceful unpower (*im-pouvoir*) of unconditionality from the majestic power (*pouvoir*) of sovereignty. It thus discusses the connections, as well as the differences, between Derrida's *impouvoir* and Heidegger's *Machtlose*.

Keywords *Walten* • *Pouvoir* • Power • *Machtlose* • Heidegger • Derrida

Can one speak of a phenomenology of force – is such a thing possible? Jacques Derrida, in one of his earliest essays, "Force and Signification," gives what may seem to be a disappointing answer – he states that "one would seek in vain a concept in phenomenology which would permit the conceptualisation of intensity or force."[1] Thus according to early Derrida, the Derrida of 1963, phenomenology does not have the power to conceptualise force, especially force in all its intensity. However, exactly 40 years later, in 2003, Derrida seems to change his mind, or at least complicate his position, in the second set of his *The Beast and the Sovereign* seminars upon examining Martin Heidegger's use and description of *Walten*, which plays a

---

[1] Jacques Derrida, "Force and Signification," in *Writing and Difference*, trans. Alan Bass (Chicago: University of Chicago, 1978), 32.

O. Keohane (✉)
Department of Philosophy, University of Dundee, Dundee, UK

University of Johannesburg, Johannesburg, South Africa
e-mail: o.keohane@undee.ac.uk

© Springer International Publishing Switzerland 2016
L. Foran, R. Uljée (eds.), *Heidegger, Levinas, Derrida: The Question of Difference*, Contributions To Phenomenology 86,
DOI 10.1007/978-3-319-39232-5_9

117

significant role, Derrida highlights, in the emergence and vocabulary of not only sovereignty, but also of Heidegger's account of the ontological difference.

Having introduced the word *Walten* in German, I want to state from the beginning that I will not attempt to translate this word, because as Derrida himself notes, it is difficult, if not impossible, to translate the intensity of this word, whose manifold and potential connotations are always growing and swelling. Indeed, *Walten*, one might say, is always engendering further forces which give birth to a myriad of possibilities – Derrida will speak of "virtual connotations, potential, precisely, potentially potent"[2] – befitting the fact that swelling is linked to force, since the Greek *kuéo* (to be pregnant) and *kúros* (force, sovereignty) are related terms, as Derrida notes in one of his footnotes in 'Faith and Knowledge' that cites Émile Benveniste on this matter.[3]

Walten is consequently one of the principal or chief words of what we might call the politico-ontological thought of Heidegger. I say politico-ontological thought so as to distinguish it from what is traditionally called, and studied (sometimes too narrowly) under the title of, political philosophy. Three texts occupy Derrida in his analysis of *Walten* – Heidegger's 1929 seminar *The Fundamental Concepts of Metaphysics*, his 1935 seminar *Introduction to Metaphysics*, and his 1957 publication *Identity and Difference*. I will argue that while Derrida has provided us in his seminar with invaluable insights into Heidegger's early seminar work (dating from the late 1920s to the mid-1930s), he has missed something essential in Heidegger's thought towards the end of the 1930s. This something is Heidegger's turn towards *das Machtlose*, "unpower," or what I will call "mightlessness" – since I am interested in the possibilities and potentialities of "might" as a *verb* as well as the power of the *noun* "might" – that which is beyond not only power and might, but impotence or a lack of power, as described in Heidegger's work *Mindfulness* (*Besinnung*), composed in 1938–1939. A text I should note that was only published in German in 1997, and translated into English in 2006 (thus perhaps Derrida's unfamiliarity with it, since it has not, at the time of writing, been translated into French). As we will see though, whilst Derrida would have needed to consult the original German if he wished to read *Besinnung* – since it was not available in an English or a French translation when he was writing his seminars in 2002–2003 – there are other texts that Derrida could have (re)read and that would have intimated the problem surrounding the notion of power or force in Heidegger's work post-WWII, namely, those that speak of 'the quiet (or still) force of the possible', such as the 1947 "Letter on Humanism". This gap in Derrida's account of Heidegger will be demonstrated to be significant not only because it complicates Derrida's understanding of *Walten*, but because Heidegger's account of *das Machtlose* will be shown to have some important and uncanny points of affinity with Derrida's own account of *impouvoir* – a neologism he borrows from Artaud and Blanchot – to

---

[2] Jacques Derrida, *The Beast and the Sovereign*, volume II, trans. Geoffrey Bennington (Chicago: University of Chicago Press, 2011), 281.

[3] Jacques Derrida, "Faith and Knowledge," in *Acts of Religion*, ed. Gil Anidjar, trans. Samuel Weber (London: Routledge, 2002), 84.

signal the forceful mightlessness of unconditionality which Derrida contrasts with the majestic power of sovereignty.

It will also be maintained that Heidegger's turn towards "unpower" cannot be separated from his engagement with Nietzsche in his seminars post-1935. It is thus significant that the proper name "Nietzsche" and Heidegger's reading of the Nietzschean notion of "the will to power" appear nowhere in the second volume of *The Beast and the Sovereign*, even if the adjective "Nietzschean" briefly appears twice in these seminars. This is despite the fact that Derrida, from the 1960s, always linked difference to force through none other than Nietzsche, so as to avoid turning force into a substance. He thus writes in the 1988 "Afterword" to *Limited Inc* – I stress the date to recall that this is only one year after Derrida's *Of Spirit* was published, and two after his lecture on Foucault entitled "Beyond the Power Principle" (*Au-delà du principe du pouvoir*)[4] – that:

> I never resort to these words [namely, force and power] without a sense of uneasiness, even if I believe myself obligated to use them in order to designate something irreducible. What worries me in them is that which resembles an obscure substance, that could, in a discourse, give rise to a zone of obscurantism and of dogmatism. Even if, as Foucault seems to suggest, one no longer speaks of Power with a capital P, but of scattered multiplicity of micropowers, the question remains of knowing what the unity of signification is that still permits us to call these decentralised and heterogeneous microphenomena "power".[5]

Moreover, even if one should still think the unity of this signification in a way other than substance according to Derrida, one should also hold "that there is never any thing called power or force, but only differences of power and of force [...] in short [...] one must start, as Nietzsche doubtless did, from difference in order to accede to force and not vice versa."[6] The same gesture can already be seen to be at work in his earlier piece "Scribble (power-writing)," published in 1977. In that piece Derrida argues against interpreting power as something external to or separate from writing. On the contrary, he maintains, "writing and power [*pouvoir*] never work separately, however complex the laws, the system, or the links of their collusion may be [...] Writing does not come to power. It is there beforehand, it partakes of and is made of it."[7] Yet, Derrida insists, whilst we must acknowledge what he calls "writing-power," the danger is still that we will forget about the need to speak about it differentially and speak instead of "the singular abstraction, power [*le* pouvoir]" and so run "the risk of reproducing that political operation which, to heap blame on something like *power* [*le* pouvoir] in general, assimilates all kinds of power for whatever purposes they may serve."[8] He hence declares that "There is not *one* power, *the* power of the mark. This singular would still lead to some mystification: fostering the belief that

---

[4] Jacques Derrida, "Au-delà du principe de pouvoir," *Rue Descartes*, 2014/3, no. 82, 4–13.

[5] Jacques Derrida, *Limited Inc*, trans. Samuel Weber (Evanston: Northwestern University Press, 1988), 149. Translation modified.

[6] Derrida, *Limited Inc*, 149.

[7] Jacques Derrida, "Scribble (power-writing)," *Yale French Studies*, no. 58 (1979), trans. Cary Plotkin, 117.

[8] Derrida, "Scribble (power-writing), 117–118.

one can do otherwise than to oppose powers to powers and writings to other writings, or again that the unity of *power* (and of *knowledge*) is always itself, the same, wherever it is and whatever force it represents."[9] Throughout Derrida's career, he has thus always spoken of differential force through (or at least within earshot) of Nietzsche, of a force that would contest the completion, the closure, and the cohesiveness of force (the noun, the substantive), of a closed power identical to itself, until, without explanation, Nietzsche fails to appear in the second set of *The Beast and the Sovereign* seminars.

Let me start by retracing Derrida's attempts to ensnare his elusive quarry or prey – the word *Walten*. He first of all notes its neglect in most readings of Heidegger, and that the French translation of Heidegger's *Walten* "banalizes, neutralizes and muffles" this German word by excluding a notion of violence. Let me note that since the English translations often render *Walten* as "to prevail" or "to hold sway," we might think Derrida would hold the same opinion about English translations – that they too neutralise, somewhat violently, the potential violent connotations of *Walten*. He explains firstly that as a verb *walten* (it can be both a verb and a noun) means "to reign, to govern" and that the verb is linked with "authority, power [*pouvoir*], reigning and sovereign potency [*puissance*] in *Walten* or *Gewalt*. This is a reigning and sovereign potency that is often emphasized in the political order, even though the meaning of *Walten* or *Gewalt* is not limited to that, and finds in that order only one of its figures."[10] There is thus a marked political dimension to the word *Walten*, but Derrida, while insisting that it should *not* be totally removed from this field, notes that the political dimension does *not* exhaust its meaning. The trick will then be how to knot and untie these two "nots" – how not reduce it to the political and how not to forget the political. Derrida attempts this by outlining how Heidegger's 1929 seminar *The Fundamental Concepts of Metaphysics* equates, and, indeed, translates the Greek word *physis* as *Walten*, and how this:

> *Walten* is [understood as] dominant, governing power [*puissance*], as self-formed sovereignty, as autonomous, autarkic force, commanding and forming itself, of the totality of beings, beings in their entirety, everything that is. *Physis* is the *Walten* of everything, which depends, as *Walten*, only on itself, which forms itself sovereignly, as power [*pouvoir*], receiving its form and image, its figure of domination, from itself.[11]

Hence if *physis* is best understood as *Walten*, it has three essential characteristics: one, it is about everything that is, two, it is self-forming, and three, it is a power. But this *Walten*, according to Derrida's reading of Heidegger, is not commanded by man, rather, "humans themselves are dominated, crushed, under the law of this sovereign violence. Man is not master, he is traversed by it, 'gripped [*transi*],' says the French translation of *durchwaltet*, man is dominated, seized, penetrated through and through by the sovereign violence of *Walten* that he does not master, over which he has neither power nor hold."[12] Moreover, since *Walten* "covers the totality of

---

[9] Derrida, "Scribble (power-writing), 144.

[10] Derrida, *The Beast and the Sovereign*, volume II, 32.

[11] Derrida, *The Beast and the Sovereign*, volume II, 39.

[12] Derrida, *The Beast and the Sovereign*, volume II, 41.

what is, its meaning [*signification*] also covers animals [note the English translation skips the adjective 'living' (*vivant*), *le vivant animal*], man and the gods [...]. In other words, this all-powerful [*toute-puissance*] sovereignty of *Walten* is neither solely political nor solely theological. It therefore exceeds and precedes the theologico-political."[13]

I want to highlight this point – *Walten* cannot be subsumed under the usual category of the theologico-political, precisely because it is linked with *physis*, which is taken by Heidegger to be ontologically *prior* to distinctions like the divine and the profane, or man and the non-human animal. Accordingly, Derrida says that "This is not the sovereignty of God, it is not the sovereignty of a king or a head of state, but of sovereignty more sovereign than all sovereignty."[14] This is what makes *Walten* a principal or chief word of Heidegger's politico-metaphysical logic, *Walten* concerns sovereignty *more* sovereign than all sovereignty, than sovereignty as traditionally understood and categorised in political philosophy, be it the political philosophy of Bodin, Hobbes or Rousseau. Note the paradox – to be more sovereign than the sovereign, that which is traditionally defined as having no superior, nothing higher than itself. Hence though Derrida speaks of the force of *Walten* and *Walten* as a force, he also adds that "I put the word 'force' in quotation marks because it does not satisfy me, anymore than the word 'violence', in any case, it [*Walten*] is something that is not a thing."[15] Remember the two "nots" that threaten to constantly trip us up and create a scandal: one should not reduce *Walten* to the political and one should not forget its political dimension. One will, to use a famous Nietzschean image, have to walk a tightrope between these two "nots".

Now, as Derrida dramatises it, there are three stages of *Walten* in Heidegger. Act I opens with its almost complete absence in *Being and Time*. In Act II, we have its swelling use in the 1929–1930 seminar, and five years later again in *Introduction to Metaphysics*, where it is tied and allied to *physis*. Finally, in Act III, we have its reappearance in Heidegger's 1957 publication *Identity and Difference*, when Heidegger speaks of the ontological difference. But this staging of *Walten*, misses, or so I claim, Heidegger's post-1935 material which explicitly discusses power through the theme of *Gelassenheit*, a release, a letting go, a letting be – and I emphasise the notion of possibility, of might, of letting something *potentially* be so that something might happen – which Heidegger will associate with a gentle force *without* weakness in a way akin to Derrida's own analysis of *impouvoir*. Let us examine two citations from Heidegger's 1938 work *Mindfulness*, bearing in mind that in this work Heidegger tries to separate the forceful *Machtlose* of Being from what he calls the *Machenschaft* of the modern age, everything to do with machination, makeability, and manipulative domination:

Be-ing – unpower [*das Machtlose*] – beyond power and lack of power [*Unmacht*] – better, what is outside power and lack of power, and fundamentally unrelated to such [...] Unpower

---

[13] Derrida, *The Beast and the Sovereign*, volume II, 41.

[14] Derrida, *The Beast and the Sovereign*, volume II, 123f.

[15] Derrida, *The Beast and the Sovereign*, volume II, 94f.

[*Macht-lose*] is not the same as what is without-power [*Ohn-mächtige*], which while it is deprived of power and lacks power nevertheless and simply remains related to power.[16]

Being here is not posited as something that is powerful or powerless; it is beyond or before both, beyond or before, one might say, the power principle as such. Being is not dictated to *by* power, but nor does it dictate *to* power. Being is a releasement (*Gelassenheit*) from the workings and trappings of power – it is a force of mightlessness. Let me briefly note that my translation of *Machtlose* as "mightlessness" suffers from the fact it can sound like it is naming a loss, since it utilises the suffix -ness. This is why Krzysztof Ziarek prefers to translate it as "power-free". His translation has the great advantage of no longer sounding like a loss, but it does lose what interests me, namely, the relationship between *Machtlose* and the impossible – since one way of reading the im-possible, or translating it, is literally might-lessness. As Krzysztof Ziarek writes – and we should note that it is he and Fred R. Dallmayr who have, almost uniquely, stressed this theme of unpower in Heidegger – "The suffix -*less* (-*los*) in *Machtlos* (literally, power-less) does not have, as Heidegger explains, the connotations of lack or absence: it is not powerlessness in the sense of the lack of power, impotence, or disempowerment. Rather the German suffix -*los* indicates a release and a freeing. Thus it may be best to render *das Machtlose* into English as the power-free, as Heidegger himself suggests, when at one point he supplements *machtlos* with *machtfrei*."[17] Not that, we should be quick to note, Heidegger completely eliminates every notion of violence, since Heidegger does not let go, release, at least in 1938, the notion of *Herrschaft*, that is, mastery. Indeed, he links *Herrschaft* to nothing less than the Latin for majesty – *maiestas*, a rare word in Heidegger – in the following quote:

We name Be-ing unpower, this cannot mean that Being is deprived of power [that it dispenses with power]. Rather the name unpower should indicate that given its essence [*Wesen*], Being [*Seyn*] continues to be detached [or released: *losgelöst*] from power. However, this unpower is master [*Herrschaft*]. And mastery in the inceptual sense does not need power. Mastery prevails out of dignity [*waltet aus der Würde*]; [....] on occasions we use the word "power" in the transfigurative sense of *maiestas*, which means the same as mastery.[18]

So on the one hand, we have power and impotence, and on the other, we have mightlessness and a mastery that does not need power, and which in fact "reigns" or "prevails" – Heidegger uses, notably, a conjugation of *walten* – from dignity, that is, the famous attribute associated with majesty. In other words, Heidegger is here seeking to disassociate power, *Macht*, from the majesty of *Walten*. He is looking for a majestic *Walten*, one which does not need power. A majestic mastery that would

---

[16] Martin Heidegger, *Mindfulness*, trans. Parvis Emad and Thomas Maly (Continuum/ Bloomsbury Academic: London, 2006), 166.

[17] Krzysztof Ziarek, "Trading in Being: Event, Capital, Art," http://heideggercircle.org/Gatherings2012-01Ziarek.pdf, page 4, accessed 01 Feb. 2013. See also his "*Das Gewalt-lose Walten*: Heidegger on Violence, Power, and Gentleness," Proceedings of the Forty-Fifth Annual Meeting of the Heidegger Circle, Marquette University, Milwaukee, http://antihumaniste.files.wordpress.com/2011/07/2011proceedings.pdf

[18] Heidegger, *Mindfulness*, 170.

be a higher power precisely because it would not be dependent on power. This process of disassociation between *Macht* and *Walten* is furthered over the next year or two, for example, in the work (or series of works) entitled *The History of Beyng* (*Die Geschichte des Seyns*), composed in 1938–1940 and published in German in 1998 and translated into English in 2015. In this text, Heidegger speaks of the:

> Event and the gentleness of the highest mastery, which does not need power and "struggle," but originary con-frontation [*Ereignis und die Milde der höchsten Herr-schaft, die nicht der Macht und nicht des "Kampfes" bedarf, sonder ursprüngliche Auseinander-setzung*]. The violence-free reign [*Das Gewalt-lose Walten*].[19]

As Ziarek notes, Heidegger in this passage turns *Gewalt*, a noun, into a modifier of *Walten*. Heidegger thus disrupts, through syntax, what we may expect – *Gewalt* becomes an adjectival, and, moreover, is presented in negative form, while *walten*, a verb, becomes a verbal substantive (*Walten*). *Gewalt* is, accordingly, displaced as a gathering point. Additionally, and perhaps even more intriguingly, during the course of *The History of Being* Heidegger eventually relinquishes the term *Herrschaft* ("mastery" or "authority") as something still too deeply involved with power and violence. In other words, by 1940, Heidegger arrives at a notion of an eventual gentleness (*Milde*), or what I will call a gentle mightlessness, which is neither potent nor impotent. Now let me be clear, I do not think that Heidegger has necessarily eradicated every problematic notion of might or violence in his work post-1940 – and I do think that Krzysztof Ziarek lets Heidegger here off the hook too easily, ignoring, say, the violence that Heidegger does to violence itself, his homogenisation of it, in his work post-1940 – but this turn towards *das Machtlose* does introduce a development which Derrida ignores at his peril. In sum, even if we have good reasons to think that a *gesture* of violence continues on in Heidegger's work after 1940, we should nevertheless recognise that Heidegger has removed – or rather, transformed – the vocabulary of violence in his work post-1940.

Likewise, this turn, as I stated earlier, cannot be divorced from Heidegger's reading of Nietzsche. I cannot, for the sake of brevity, discuss here the voluminous seminar material on Nietzsche that Heidegger worked on after 1935, but I will briefly mention his abortive seminar on Nietzsche in 1941–1942, but composed in 1940, entitled "Nietzsche's Metaphysics". There Heidegger states that the essence of power, as revealed by Nietzsche's will to power, is that power is the constant need for more power, to attain more *not* simply because it wants more, but so as to ensure it continues to exist – "Power is only power as long as it remains an increase in power and commands itself the "more" in power. The mere pausing within the increase of power, the standing still [*stehenbleiben*] at a level of power, already

---

[19] Martin Heidegger, *Die Geschichte des Seyns, Gesamtausgabe* vol. 69 (Frankfurt am Main: Vittorio Klostermann, 1998) 8. I have used Ziarek's translation of this passage, as contained in his aforementioned paper "*Das Gewalt-lose Walten*: Heidegger on Violence, Power, and Gentleness". The same passage in the 2015 History of Beyng reads: 'Propriation and the gentleness of supreme sovereignty, which does not require power or "struggle", but originary critical setting apart. Powerless holding sway". Martin Heidegger, History of Beyng, trans. Jeffrey Powell and William McNeill (Indiana University Press: Bloomington, 2015), 8.

initiates powerlessness [*Ohnmacht*]. The overpowering [*Übermächtigung*] of itself belongs to the essence of power."[20] To return to the imagery of the tightrope walker, power cannot stand still, it must constantly push on or it falls to its death. We might think that Derrida had little chance of knowing Heidegger's loss of faith in the power of *Macht* and even *Herrschaft* in his work from the late 1930s, since the work I am talking about was only published in German in the late 1990s. However, I think there is evidence for this loss of faith in the power of *Macht* in one of Heidegger's most well-known texts, namely, his 1947 "Letter on Humanism," as when he speaks of "the quiet [or still] force of the possible [*die stille Kraft des Möglichen*]," a phrase which originates from *Being and Time*, but which Heidegger returns to and reinterprets in the "Letter" so as to undo the usual distinction between possibility (and the Greek to Latin translation of *dynamis* as *possibilitas* or *potentia*) and actuality (and the Greek to Latin translation of *energia* as *actus* or *actualitas*).[21] There is no space to take up the immense question of how Heidegger and Derrida reconfigure our notions of modality and the (im)possible, especially when dealing with the topic of death and the "power" to die, but I do want to highlight two things in the passage "the quiet force of the possible," namely, that Heidegger has switched to talking of force (*Kraft*), rather than power (*Macht*), and that once again he uses a non-equivalent synonym for mightlessness and gentleness: something quiet, something still, but not without force, still force. "What is stillness? (*Was ist Stille?*)" Heidegger asks in his 1950 lecture "Language":

> Stillness stills by the carrying out, the bearing and enduring, of world and things in their presence. The carrying of the world [*Das Austragen von Welt*] and things in the manner of stilling is the appropriative taking place of the difference [*das Ereignis des Unter-Schiedes*].[22]

In sum, by the 1940s, force, unlike the will to power, still *carries* possibilities for Heidegger. I mention the significant import of carrying since Derrida highlights the notion of carrying throughout the second volume of *The Beast and the Sovereign*, especially when discussing words related to the German verb *tragen*, to carry or bear something, as one carries or bears a child, or in this case, the carrying of the world. It is the force carried aloft by *stillness* that Derrida has failed to observe, even when he singles out the *Austrag*, with its connotations of "bearing" as well as "(re) conciliation," as that "in" which *Walten* reigns. The same *Austrag* used in the lecture "Language" to translate the Greek word *diaphora*, which literally means "to carry away," but which is primarily used to convey difference, disagreement, or conflict.

---

[20] Martin Heidegger, "Nietzsche's Metaphysics," *The Heidegger Reader*, ed. Günter Figal, trans. Jerome Veith, (Bloomington, Indianapolis: Indiana University Press, 2009). The corresponding passage in the Stambaugh, Krell and Capuzzi translation of Heidegger's *Nietzsche* can be found on page 195 – *Nietzsche, Volume III: The Will to Power as Knowledge and as Metaphysics*, ed. D. F. Krell (San Francisco, Harper & Row, 1987).

[21] Martin Heidegger, "Letter on Humanism," trans. F. A Capuzzi and J. Glenn Gray, in *Martin Heidegger: Basic Writings*, revised and expanded edition, ed. D. F. Krell (London: Routledge, 1993), 220.

[22] Martin Heidegger, "Language," in *Poetry, Language, Thought*, trans. Albert Hofstadter (New York: Harper and Row, 1971), 207.

It is stillness, the force of stillness, and not power, that ensures the world is born aloft. The link between *Austrag* and "the quiet [or still] force of the possible" is evident when Heidegger says in *Identity and Difference*, "The only thing which matters for our task is an insight into a possibility [*Möglichkeit*] of thinking of the difference as the dif-ference [*Differenz als Austrag*]."[23]

It should also be recalled that Heidegger actually conjoins force to bearing as early as his lectures on Aristotle in 1931 – a series of lectures we will return to when speaking of the suffering that Derrida links to *impouvoir* – since Heidegger will speak in 1931 of suffering or enduring as a kind of bearing or bearance (Heidegger uses the neologism *Ertragsamkeit*, coming from *ertragen*, "to bear"). However, it should also be observed that while Heidegger speaks of unforce (*Unkraft*) and im-potentia in his 1931 lectures, they do not, despite first appearances, perform what his texts later in the decade do when he comes to talk of *das Machtlose*, since in these earlier lectures Heidegger maintains that "unforce is nevertheless *bound* to the realm of force that remains withdrawn from it."[24] In other words, not only are we dealing with a difference between *Kraft* and *Macht* during Heidegger's lectures in the 1930s, but the logic of the *un-* in contrast to the logic of the *-lose*.

Nevertheless, this notion of non-impotent force, of mightlessness that still has force, still has some affinity with Derrida's dynamic use of the word *impouvoir*, a neologism Derrida picks up from Artaud and Blanchot and which is notable for being homophonic with 'a power' or 'one power', *un pouvoir*. The word *impouvoir* can be found several times in his writings, first in "La Parole soufflé," and then sub-sequently in texts such as "Scribble (power-writing)," *Spurs*, *The Animal that Therefore I am*, "The University Without Condition" and *The Beast and the Sovereign*. What is more, Derrida associates *impouvoir not, as we might expect, with das Machtlose, a German term to my knowledge Derrida never mentioned, but rather, problematically, with Entmachtung (Of Spirit)* and *die Ohnmacht* ("Heidegger's Ear"). In chapter 7 of *Of Spirit*, Derrida examines the notion of *Entmachtung* as found in the 1935 *Introduction to Metaphysics* and links it with the Heideggerian emphasis on world and spirit. Derrida cites the following passage from Heidegger: "What does 'world' mean, when speaking of the darkening of the world? World is always spiritual world [*geistige Welt*]. The animal has no world (*Welt*), nor any environment (*Umwelt*). The darkening of the world contains within itself a disempowering [*Entmachtung*] of the spirit."[25] Derrida comments in his reading that he will translate *Entmachtung* as "'destitution' from now, because spirit thereby loses a power [*pouvoir*] which is not 'natural'."[26] In other words, it is not a matter of material, physical, biological or natural power. He adds that:

---

[23] Martin Heidegger, *Identity and Difference*, *trans.* Joan Stambaugh, bilingual edition (New York: Harper & Row, 2002, 68. Translation modified.

[24] Martin Heidegger, *On the Essence and Actuality of Force*, *trans.* Walter Brogan and Peter Warnek (Bloomington: Indiana University Press, 1995), 94. My emphasis.

[25] Martin Heidegger, *Introduction to Metaphysics*, trans. Gregory Fried and Richard Polt (New Haven: Yale University Press, 2000), 47.

[26] Jacques Derrida, *Of Spirit*, translated by Rachel Bowlby and Geoffrey Bennington (Chicago: University of Chicago, 1989), 59.

If *Entmachtung* dooms spirit to impotence [as Bennington translates *impouvoir* – I want to suggest that a better translation might be "mightlessness"] or powerlessness [*impuissance*], if it deprives it of its strength [*force*] and the nerve of its authority [...] what does this mean as far as force is concerned? That spirit *is* a force and *is* not a force, that it has and has not power [*pouvoir*]. If it were force in itself, if it were force itself, it would not lose force, there would be no *Entmachtung*. But if it were not this force or power [*pouvoir*], the *Entmachtung* would not affect it essentially, it would not be *of spirit*. So one can say neither the one nor the other, one must say both, which doubles up each of the concepts: world, force, spirit.[27]

Derrida, while thus carefully complicating our understanding of force in Heidegger in 1935 (since he both ties and severs it from spirit) nevertheless associates *impouvoir* with *Entmachtung* rather than *Machtlose*. This is unfortunate *because Entmachtung* signifies a loss of power, a deprivation of power, hence one uses the word in German to speak of the dethronement of the monarch, the sovereign king, as opposed to *Machtlose*, which Heidegger stresses is not a loss, not a matter of deprivation, of impotence. One cannot behead, overthrow, oust or uncrown *Walten* like one can a king. The same problem arises in "Heidegger's Ear," which explicitly mentions *Walten*, when Derrida speaks of *die Ohnmacht* in *Being and Time*. Derrida associates this time *impouvoir* with *Ohnmacht*, "the impotence [*im-pouvoir*] (*die Ohnmacht*) of the turning way or of the being-turned away (*Überlassenheit*) [that one can make when one faces a choice]."[28] The unfortunate tethering of *impouvoir* to *Ohnmacht* is, however, corrected in the second volume of the *Beast and Sovereign*, when Derrida writes that Heidegger grants in his *Introduction to Metaphysics* "the predicate of sovereignty or superiority (*Überlegenheit*) is granted not to potency [*puissance*] but to a certain impotence [*impuissance*] (*Ohnmacht*)."[29] Nonetheless, Derrida does not seem aware of his earlier association of *Ohnmacht* with *impouvoir*, nor the fact that Heidegger distinguished, from the late 1930s, *die Ohnmacht* from *das Machtlose*, precisely because Heidegger claims that *die Ohnmacht* only mirrors the reverse of power, while *das Machtlose* escapes the dynamics of power insofar as it attempts to withdraw itself from power in a non-disempowering fashion, which is to say, by means of *loslassen*.

Furthermore, in Derrida's 1999 Athens-based address "Unconditionality or Sovereignty," Derrida separates the forceful mightlessness (*im-pouvoir*) of unconditionality, which he associates with the imp- of the impossible, from the majestic power (*pouvoir*) of sovereignty, just as Heidegger tries to separate the forceful *Machtlose* of Being from the *Machenschaft* of the modern age (machination, makeability, manipulative domination). Derrida states:

For thought thereby, the one that finds its place of freedom there, also finds itself, to be sure, *without power*. It is an unconditionality without sovereignty, which is to say at bottom a freedom without power. But without power does not mean 'without force'. And there, discreetly, furtively, another frontier is *perhaps passed through, at once inscribing itself and resisting the passage*, the barely visible frontier between the unconditionality of thought

[27] Derrida, *Of Spirit*, 61–62. Italicisation in the original.

[28] Jacques Derrida, "*Heidegger's Ear*: Philopolemology (*Geschlecht* IV)," trans. John P. *Leavey* Jr., in *Reading Heidegger: Commemorations*, ed. John Sallis (Bloomington, Indiana University Press, 1993), 177.

[29] Derrida, *The Beast and the Sovereign*, volume II, 248.

[...] and the sovereignty of power, of all powers, theologico-political power down to its national or democratic guises, economic-military power, the power of the media, and so forth. The affirmation I am speaking of remains a principle of resistance or of dissidence: *without power [pouvoir] but without weakness [faiblesse]. Without power but not without force, be it a certain force of weakness.*[30]

So like the Heidegger of the late 1930s, Derrida links force and non-impotent mightlessness together, and contrasts them to sovereignty, the theologico-political and power. The same distinction between non-impotent mightlessness and sovereign power can also be witnessed in *Rogues* (originally delivered in 2002) and the earlier piece "The University Without Condition" (delivered in the same year as "Unconditionality or Sovereignty") when Derrida speaks of a *"weak force".*[31] As he puts in *Rogues*: "This vulnerable force, this force without power, opens up *unconditionally* to what or who *comes* and comes to affect it. The coming of this event exceeds the condition of mastery".[32] In "The University Without Condition," one finds an earlier reiteration of this distinction when Derrida asks: "How to dissociate sovereignty and unconditionality, the power [*pouvoir*] of an indivisible sovereignty, the powerlessness [or mightlessness: *im-pouvoir*] of unconditionality."[33]

Moreover, in that last piece, he also links this weak force of the event – to what or who *comes* – to the force of the perhaps: "The event belongs to a *perhaps [peut-être]* that is in keeping not with the possible but with the impossible".[34] I highlight this because Derrida is signalling in this passage, though his invocation of the event, the "dangerous 'perhaps'" which Nietzsche spoke of in *Beyond Good and Evil* and which Derrida had earlier analysed in *Politics of Friendship*, especially in its second chapter, "Loving in Friendship: Perhaps – the Noun and the Adverb". It is also not without a certain import that Heidegger himself recalls this "perhaps," this *vielleicht*, in his work from the 1950s, and more importantly for my purposes, at crucial stage in *Identity and Difference*, when speaking of the *Austrag* and the diaphora of difference – recall the importance of bearing and carrying – that *Walten* occurs "in". Heidegger writes: "Perhaps coming [*Vielleicht kommt*] from this discussion [*Erörterung*], which assigns the difference [*Differenz*] of Being and beings to

---

[30] Jacques Derrida, "Unconditionality or Sovereignty," *Oxford Literary Review*, Volume 31 (2009), translated by Peggy Kamuf, 129–130.

[31] Speaking of years and dates, it should be mentioned that there is one text I will not be able to discuss in this piece, again for reasons of space, and that is Derrida's *H.C for Life, That is to Say...*, which was originally given as a lecture in 1998. In this piece, Derrida, via his reading of Cixous, places much more stress on *puisse* (and its associates, *puissance* and *puissant*), and even the English words "might" and "may," than *pouvoir* or *impouvoir*, even if *impouvoir*, which is translated as "unpower" by Derrida's translators, is mentioned at one point in the text when discussing the "mighty power of the 'might' (*la puissance de 'puisse'*)". Jacques Derrida, *H.C for Life, That is to Say...*, trans. Laurent Milesi and Stefan Herbrechter, (Stanford: Stanford University Press, 2006), 132.

[32] Jacques Derrida, *Rogues*, trans. Pascale-Anne Brault and Michael Naas (Stanford, CA: Stanford University Press, 2005), xiv. My emphasis.

[33] Jacques Derrida, "University Without Condition," in *Without Alibi*, edited, translated, and with an introduction by Peggy Kamuf, (Stanford: Stanford University Press, 2002), 232.

[34] Derrida, "University Without Condition," 235.

Austrag, a *bearing* that holds together by holding apart [....] one brings to light something all-pervading which pervades Being's destiny [*Geschick*] from its beginning to its completion."[35] This should signal to us that Derrida's reading of Heidegger's *Identity and Difference* in the second volume of *The Beast and the Sovereign* remains unsatisfactory, and that he remains blind to his own proximity to Heidegger, as well as the role Nietzsche bears – and it is precisely a question of bearing, what weight or import we assign to Nietzsche – in any discussion of *Walten*.

But it should also not be forgotten that Derrida's discussion of *Walten* takes places under the heading of *The Beast and the Sovereign*, and while we have frequently mentioned the masculine noun in the title (the sovereign, *le souverain*), we have hardly discussed the feminine noun (the beast, *la bête*). Indeed, it has no doubt not escaped you that I recalled, somewhat too fleetingly, like an animal on the run, the figure of "the animal" that Derrida pursues in these discussions of *Walten*, as when we find Heidegger talking of force though the animal "poor in world" and so deprived of spirit, or when I discussed *le vivant animal* that *Walten* reigns over. The penultimate instance of *impouvoir* that I want to consider comes from this fabulous bestiary of Derrida's (and indeed, one should not forget that *impouvoir* already had, from "La Parole soufflé" onwards, a relationship to the animation of *anima* and the breath of life).[36] A bestiary which speaks of mightlessness as a species of suffering, namely, the confessional bestiary, the bestiary without condition, the one entitled – and one should note that it is a profound mediation on entitlement – *The Animal that Therefore I am*. In this text, Derrida invokes Bentham's great question about suffering, namely, can animals suffer, and Derrida notes that:

> The question is disturbed by a certain *passivity*. It bears witness, manifesting already, as question, the response that testifies to a sufferance [*passibilité*], a passion, a not-being-able [*un non-pouvoir*]. The word *can* [pouvoir] changes sense and sign here once one asks, "Can they suffer?" [...] "Can they [non-human animals] suffer?" amounts to asking "Can they *not be able*?" And what of this inability [*impouvoir*]? What of the vulnerability felt on the basis of this inability? What is this nonpower [*non-pouvoir*] at the heart of power? What is its quality or modality? How should one take it into account? What right should be accorded it? To what extent does it concern us? Being able to suffer [*pouvoir souffrir*] is no longer a power; it is a possibility without power, a possibility of the impossible.[37]

In this passage, passivity (from Latin *passivus* "capable of feeling or suffering") is understood not as a power, a being able to, or a capacity, but as something tied to mightlessness, and this, in turn, is linked to the bearing of pain. What "we" share with non-human animals is not the capacity to suffer, but a shared vulnerability to suffering, a shared burden which manifests itself as a possibility of mightlessness. I mentioned earlier that Heidegger spoke in 1931 of suffering as a kind of bearing or

---

[35] Heidegger, *Identity and Difference*, 67. Translation modified.

[36] One way of connecting Derrida's emphasis on respiration to Heidegger's emphasis on stillness would thus be to talk of "whist," an old English word that speaks of quietness, the wind, respiration and silence, which is to say, stillness.

[37] Jacques Derrida, *The Animal that Therefore I am*, trans. David Wills (New York: Fordham University Press, 2008), 27–28. Emphasis in the original.

bearance (*Ertragsamkeit*). Heidegger does this so as to highlight Aristotle's two notions of passive power, namely, the notion of *dynamis tou pathein*, the power to be affected, the power to suffer and undergo change, which can be contrasted to *hexis apatheia*, the power to resist said change. We might thus say that Derrida in connecting *impouvoir* to suffering reconfigures the relationship between (non) power and bearing, and so the relation of what was previously called *dynamis tou pathein* (suffering) to *hexis apatheia* (resistance). Indeed, the very Aristotelian notions of *dynamis* and *hexis* are invoked by Derrida when discussing Bentham's question, with Derrida reminding his readers that the passivity he is talking about is not yet another species of *dynamis* or *hexis*.[38] The explicit potentialities in the off-ing for this reconfiguration between (non)power and bearing are not spelt out in *The Animal that Therefore I am*, but I do think they show up a little later in Derrida's 2001 "Provocation" to *Without Alibi*, when he asks: "what is passitivity? The passitivity of resistance resists thought because it is what *does* the most, *makes* the most happen, more than the most, the impossible itself, at the heart of the possible. In fact, one may say of the impossible that it marks the limit of a possible or a power, more precisely, of an 'I can' or a 'we can'."[39] Recalling his earlier words about unconditionality, namely, that it is "a principle of resistance," we might say unconditionality as the possibility of mightlessness is what, for Derrida, does the most, more than what is otherwise possible with the possible. Mightlessness, as the impossible, is a possibility with force but without power.

I will conclude by considering one final instance of *impouvoir* in Derrida's writings. This time, it is from "Scribble (power-writing)," or what can also be translated, since Derrida follows *pouvoir* with an infinitive – "*Scribble (pouvoir/écrire)*" – as "Scribble: being able/ to write." Derrida writes that "what is astonishing is not writing as power but what comes [*ce qui vient*], as if from within a structure, to limit it [that is, writing] by a powerlessness [*impouvoir*] or an effacement".[40] This sentence is in itself pretty astonishing in light of Derrida's later preoccupations and writings. For it suggests that what is astonishing is not writing *as such*, writing from the perspective of the "as such," the *als-Struktur* which for Heidegger distinguishes man from "the animal," nor writing *as* power, writing understood from the perspective of the analogical and oft-regimented "as," but what comes, what arrives – which Derrida would later associate with the name "event" – under the modality of an "as if" (an "as if" that echoes, but which is not identical to, or reducible to, the Kantian *als ob* that Derrida would talk about decades later in pieces such as "The University Without Condition" and *Rogues*). Mightlessness or *impouvoir*, in relation to writing, would arrive, *if* it arrives, only under the conditions of the "as if".

---

[38] Jacques Derrida, *The Animal that Therefore I am*, 27.

[39] Jacques Derrida, "Provocation," in *Without Alibi*, edited, translated, and with an introduction by Peggy Kamuf (Stanford: Stanford University Press, 2002), xxxiii. Italicisation in the original.

[40] Derrida, "Scribble (power-writing)," 117.

What is more, the fact that Derrida associates *impouvoir* not with Being, but with writing, or "writing-power," is in itself instructive. As David Farrell Krell notes, one can distinguish Heidegger's history of Being (which concerns, and is constituted by, the ontological difference) from Derrida's history of writing (which concerns, and is constituted by, traces).[41] We should, accordingly, trace not only what notion of mightlessness Derrida and Heidegger both shared, but also the different uses to which they put mightlessness. For instance, while Heidegger associates mightless-ness first and foremost with Being, Derrida associates it with a whole range of topics, including unconditionality, writing and animals. One lesson we can gain from this juxtaposition of contexts in Derrida is that animals are not incapable of writing from his viewpoint, especially when one thinks of the trace. As he puts it in "Violence Against Animals":

> [T]he elaboration of a new concept of the *trace* had to be extended to *the entire field of the living*, or rather to the life/death relation, beyond the anthropological limits of "spoken" language (or "written" language, in the ordinary sense), beyond the phonocentrism or the logocentrism that always trusts in a simple and oppositional limit between Man and the Animal. At the time I stressed that the "concepts of writing, trace, gramma or grapheme" exceeded the opposition "human/nonhuman."[42]

That writing exceeds the anthropological limit is perhaps best shown by the interplay of *les animots* and *les animaux* in his numerous works, and his refusal, to which we are still indebted, to write off animals, to write off the *Schuld*. Which is another way of saying we need to start asking ourselves about the link between *ertragen* ("to carry") and *Ertrag* ("profit, produce, yield, return") when it comes to animals. What will we stomach – and it precisely a question of the stomach, of what we will swallow, of what we will bear – when it comes to animals, including the animal known as man? As Derrida asks: "What is power if all it can do is un-power [*im-pouvoir*], if all it can do is what it cannot do [*s'il ne peut que ce qu'il ne peut pas*] – namely, the impossible?"[43]

References

Derrida, Jacques. 1967. *L'Ecriture et la différence*. Paris: Seuil.
Derrida, Jacques. 1977. *Scribble (pouvoir/écrire)*. Preface to *l'Essai sur les hiéroglyphes des Egyptiens* by William Warburton. Paris: Aubier.
Derrida, Jacques. 1978. Force and signification and La Parole soufflé. In *Writing and Difference* (trans: Bass, Alan). Chicago: University of Chicago.

---

[41] See the closing pages of David Farrell Krell's latest book, *Derrida and Our Animal Others: Derrida's Final Seminar, the Beast and the Sovereign* (Bloomington, Indiana: Indiana University Press, 2013).

[42] Jacques Derrida, "Violence Against Animals," in *For What Tomorrow … A Dialogue*, trans. Jeff Fort (Stanford: Stanford University Press, 2004), 63. My emphasis.

[43] Derrida, *The Beast and the Sovereign*, volume II, 235.

Derrida, Jacques. 1979. Scribble (power-writing) (trans: Plotkin, Cary). *Yale French Studies* 58: 117–147.

Derrida, Jacques. 1981. *Spurs: Nietzsche's Styles/Eperons: Les Styles de Nietzsche* (trans: Harlow, Barbara). Chicago: University of Chicago Press.

Derrida, Jacques. 1987. *De l'esprit*. Paris: Galilée.

Derrida, Jacques. 1988. *Limited Inc* (trans: Weber, Samuel). Evanston: Northwestern University Press.

Derrida, Jacques. 1989. *Of Spirit* (trans: Bowlby, Rachel). Chicago: University of Chicago.

Derrida, Jacques. 1993. Heidegger's Ear: Philopolemology (Geschlecht IV) (trans: by Leavey Jr., John P). In *Reading Heidegger: Commemorations*, ed. John Sallis. Bloomington: Indiana University Press.

Derrida, Jacques. 2002a. Faith and Knowledge (trans: Weber, Samuel). In *Acts of Religion*, ed. Gil Anidjar. London: Routledge.

Derrida, Jacques. 2002b. University Without Condition (trans: Kamuf, Peggy). In *Without Alibi*, edited and with an introduction by Peggy Kamuf. Stanford: Stanford University Press.

Derrida, Jacques. 2003. *Voyous: Deux essais sur la raison*. Paris: Galilée.

Derrida, Jacques. 2004. Violence Against Animals (trans: Fort, Jeff). In *For what Tomorrow ... A Dialogue*. Stanford: Stanford University Press.

Derrida, Jacques. 2005a. *Rogues* (trans: Brault, Pascale-Anne and Michael Naas). Stanford: Stanford University Press.

Derrida, Jacques. 2005b. *Politics of Friendship* (trans: Collins, George). London: Verso.

Derrida, Jacques. 2006a. *L'animal que donc je suis*. Paris: Galilée.

Derrida, Jacques. 2006b. *H.C for Life, That is to Say...*, (trans: Laurent Milesi and Stefan Herbrechter) Stanford: Stanford University Press.

Derrida, Jacques. 2008. *The Animal that Therefore I Am* (trans: Wills, David). New York: Fordham University Press.

Derrida, Jacques. 2009. Unconditionality or Sovereignty (trans: Kamuf, Peggy). *Oxford Literary Review* 31: 115–131.

Derrida, Jacques. 2011. *The Beast and the Sovereign*, vol. II (trans: Bennington, Geoffrey). Chicago: University of Chicago Press.

Derrida, Jacques. 2014. *Au-delà du principe de pouvoir. Rue Descartes* 2014/3(82): 4–13.

Heidegger, Martin. 1971. Language. In *Poetry, Language, Thought* (trans: Albert Hofstadter), 187–210. New York: Harper and Row.

Heidegger, Martin. 1985 [originally published in 1959]. *Unterwegs zur Sprache, Gesamtausgabe*, vol. 12. Frankfurt am Main: Vittorio Klostermann.

Heidegger, Martin. 1991. Nietzsche's Metaphysics. In *Nietzsche, Vol. 3, The Will to Power as Knowledge and Metaphysics* (trans: Krell, David F.). New York: Harper & Row.

Heidegger, Martin. 1993. Letter on Humanism (trans: Capuzzi, F. A and J. Glenn Gray). In *Martin Heidegger: Basic Writings*, revised and expanded edition, ed. D. F. Krell, 217–265. London: Routledge.

Heidegger, Martin. 1995a. *On the Essence and Actuality of Force* (trans: Brogan, Walter and Peter Warnek). Bloomington: Indiana University Press.

Heidegger, Martin. 1995b. *The Fundamental Concepts of Metaphysics* (trans: McNeill, William and Nicholas Walker). Bloomington: Indiana University Press.

Heidegger, Martin. 1997. *Besinnung, Gesamtausgabe*, vol. 66. Frankfurt am Main: Vittorio Klostermann.

Heidegger, Martin. 1998. *Die Geschichte des Seyns, Gesamtausgabe*, vol. 69. Frankfurt am Main: Vittorio Klostermann.

Heidegger, Martin. 2000. *Introduction to Metaphysics* (trans: Fried, Gregory and Richard Polt). New Haven: Yale University Press.

Heidegger, Martin. 2002. *Identity and Difference* (trans: Stambaugh, Joan). Bilingual edition. New York: Harper & Row.

Heidegger, Martin. 2006. *Mindfulness* (trans: Emad, Parvis and Thomas Maly). London: Continuum/Bloomsbury Academic.

Heidegger, Martin. 2009. Nietzsche's Metaphysics. In *The Heidegger Reader*, ed. Günter Figal (trans. Jerome Veith). Bloomington: Indiana University Press.

Martin, Heidegger. 2015. *History of Beyng.* (trans: Jeffrey Powell and William McNeill). Bloomington: Indiana University Press.

Krell, David Farrell. 2013. *Derrida and our animal others: Derrida's final seminar, the beast and the sovereign.* Bloomington: Indiana University Press.

Ziarek, Krzysztof. 2002. Art, power, and politics: Heidegger on *Machenschaft* and *Poiesis*. *Contre-Temps* 3: 175–186.

Ziarek, Krzysztof. 2011. *Das Gewalt-lose Walten*: Heidegger on violence, power, and gentleness. In Proceedings of the forty-fifth annual meeting of the Heidegger Circle, Marquette University, Milwaukee, 155–163. http://antihumaniste.files.wordpress.com/2011/07/2011proceedings.pdf. Accessed 1 Feb 2013.

Ziarek, Krzysztof. 2012. Trading in being: Event, capital, art. *Gatherings: The Heidegger Circle Annual* 2: 1–23. http://heideggercircle.org/Gatherings2012-01Ziarek.pdf, page 4, accessed 1 Feb. 2013.

Responsibility for a Secret: Heidegger and Levinas

François Raffoul

Abstract In thinking the question of responsibility between Levinas and Heidegger, it is both a movement of expropriation towards the other and a relation to a secret that come to the fore. Levinas' entire itinerary of thought has been structured by the effort to escape the closure of philosophies of totality, to exceed the horizon as such, to move beyond ontology, a movement towards exteriority or towards the other that has taken with it and redefined the very concept of responsibility. No longer a responsibility for oneself, or for one's actions, but a responsibility for the other and for the sake of the other. However, can the other only be said to lie beyond being, if being, as Heidegger would show, is itself the beyond, the transcendent pure and simple? Being might include a relation to the other, which explains why Heidegger thematizes being-with as a constitutive feature of existence. To that extent, one may seek to inquire into the ontological senses of responsibility. Heidegger's thought of being entails a profound philosophy of responsibility. But it is no longer developed in terms of subjectivity, even in its reversal. Rather, Heidegger shows that one is ultimately responsible for an inappropriable, a secret or mystery. This secret of being represents a sense of otherness that is not reduced, as in Levinas, to the "other human being," that is, within a subjectivist, anthropocentric horizon. I will explore in the following pages the terms of this debate.

Keywords Responsibility • Otherness • Secret • The face

In thinking the question of responsibility between Levinas and Heidegger, it is both a movement of expropriation towards the other and a relation to a secret that come to the fore. Levinas' entire itinerary of thought has been structured by the effort to escape the closure of philosophies of totality, to exceed the horizon as such, to move beyond ontology, a movement towards exteriority or towards the other that has taken with it and redefined the very concept of responsibility. Levinas' corpus presents an extraordinary revolution in the thought of responsibility, a peculiar "reversal," to use

F. Raffoul (✉)
Faculty of Philosophy, Louisiana University, Baton Rouge, LA, USA
e-mail: fraffoul@yahoo.com

© Springer International Publishing Switzerland 2016   133
L. Foran, R. Uljée (eds.), *Heidegger, Levinas, Derrida: The Question of Difference*, Contributions To Phenomenology 86,
DOI 10.1007/978-3-319-39232-5_10

his terms, of the concept of responsibility: far from assigning responsibility to the actions of an agent, on the basis of the freedom of the subject, following an entire tradition, Levinas reconceptualizes responsibility as a being "for-the-other". No longer a responsibility for oneself, or for one's actions, but a responsibility for the other and for the sake of the other. In fact, for Levinas, the other "is above all the one I am responsible for".[1] Levinas approaches responsibility as that which could not have begun from me, going so far as to write that responsibility "is not mine" (Levinas 1996).[2] A responsibility "of the other," anticipating what Derrida would write on a responsibility and a decision "of the other". As Derrida explains in *The Gift of Death*, "Levinas wants to remind us that responsibility is not at first responsibility of myself for myself, that the sameness of myself is derived from the other, as if it were second to the other, coming to itself as responsible and mortal from the position of my responsibility before the other, for the other's death and in the face of it."[3] This sense of responsibility for the other expropriates the subject, deposed from its position of mastery and subject to the call of the other (Derrida 1992).

Levinas' thinking of responsibility arises out of a peculiar reversal of the modern Cartesian tradition in philosophy, from Descartes to Husserl, that is, a reversal of the primacy of egology and the predominance of the will, which he seeks to overturn. However, can the other only be said to lie beyond being, if being, as Heidegger would show, is itself the beyond, the transcendent pure and simple? Being might include a relation to the other, which explains why Heidegger thematizes being-with as a constitutive feature of existence. To that extent, one may seek to inquire into the ontological senses of responsibility. Responsibility for being would not be exclusive of an openness to the other: Levinas posits that responsibility for the other represents the essence of *subjectivity*. However, does responsibility as openness to the other not require a non-subjective experience? Heidegger's thought of being entails a profound philosophy of responsibility. But it is no longer developed in terms of subjectivity, even in its reversal. Rather, Heidegger shows that one is ultimately responsible for an inappropriable, a secret or mystery. This secret of being represents a sense of otherness that is not reduced, as in Levinas, to the "other *human being*," (Levinas 2005)[4] that is, within a subjectivist, anthropocentric *horizon*. I will explore in the following pages the terms of this debate.

---

[1] Emmanuel Levinas. *Entre Nous*, trans. Michael B. Smith and Barbara Harshav (NY: Columbia University Press, 1998), p. 105. Hereafter cited as EN, followed by page number.

[2] Emmanuel Levinas. *Autrement qu'être ou au-delà de l'essence* (Kluwer Academic, Le livre de poche, 1996), p. 252. Hereafter cited as AE, followed by page number. All translations mine.

[3] Jacques Derrida. *The Gift of Death* (Chicago and London: Chicago University Press, 1992), p.46. Hereafter cited as GD, followed by page number.

[4] See Emmanuel Levinas, *Humanisme de l'autre homme*. (Montpellier: Fata Morgana, 1972), rendered in an English translation as *Humanism of the Other* (University of Illinois Press, 2005).

1   Responsibility for the Other

Levinas' thought of ethics and responsibility developed out of a movement of exit out of ontology. As Levinas recounted in several autobiographical texts or interviews, (Levinas 1995, 2001)[5] he began his philosophical career as a commentator of Husserl's phenomenology and Heidegger's fundamental ontology, indeed introduced Husserl and Heidegger in France (Janicaud 2000).[6] These were references from which he broke decisively as he began to develop his own *ethical* thought. One of the key features of such a departure, in addition to the rupture with the paradigm of totality, was the break with ontology as such (and with a certain phenomenology of intentionality and consciousness). Far from being included within the horizon of being, ethics is situated in the relationship to the other person, in the "inter-subjective," a relation which for Levinas takes place beyond being: "A responsibility beyond being," as he writes in *Otherwise than Being or Beyond Essence* (AE, 31) (Levinas 1996). The inter-subjective relation is the original experience. This claim already places the ethical – the relation to the other – as prior to the order of knowledge, outside of the element of being, and situates Levinas in opposition to traditional ontology and the privilege of knowledge in Western philosophy. Levinas aims at reversing the traditional hierarchy in which ethics is reduced to being a branch of ontology and epistemology. Ethical responsibility will take place for beyond being, and knowledge.

This move beyond being and towards the other (the other human) constitutes the core of Levinas' thought and he indeed characterized this movement in a late interview as "the kernel of all I would say later" (Levinas 2001) (*Is it Righteous to be?*, p.46). One could in fact approach Levinas's thought as a whole from this effort to escape, exit, or go beyond, towards an other that does not return to a same, that does not come back, and in that sense is in-finite. His decisive early essay, *On Escape*,[7] thematizes and articulates a need to break with the "suffocating" horizon of being, the "there is" and with the isolation or solitude of existence. Ultimately, it was a matter of "escaping *from being*" (EI, 59) (Levinas 2003), an escape that takes place in my devotion to the other, that is to say, in my *responsibility* for the other (Levinas 1995). How does one escape from being, from oneself? By going beyond oneself towards the other. The exit from both the "there is" (impersonal being) and oneself (egology) are opening onto the other. In the end, for Levinas, the true exit out of being, out of the ego, lies in responsibility for the other (to the point, as we will see, of dying for the other).

This need to escape the horizon of being and the enclosure of the self accounts for Levinas' critique of totality and totalizing philosophies, although one should note that for him "it is in fact the whole trend of Western philosophy", culminating with Hegel, that has "this nostalgia for totality" and that seeks a "panoramic vision of the real"

---

[5] See for instance *Ethics and Infinity*, p. 37–38 (hereafter cited as EI), and *Is It Righteous to Be?*, edited by Jill Robbins (Stanford, CA: Stanford University Press, 2001), pp. 31–37.

[6] On Levinas' role in the early reception of Heidegger in France, see Dominique Janicaud's *Heidegger en France* (Paris: Albin Michel, 2000), in particular pp. 31–36.

[7] Emmanuel Levinas. *On Escape* (Stanford, CA: Stanford University Press, 2003).

(EI, 76) (Levinas 1995). Levinas found the sources of his critique of totality first in Frank Rosenzweig's critique of Hegel (but also in those moments in the history of Philosophy such as Plato's Good beyond being, Descartes' third meditation and the idea of God as infinite), and he conceives of it in terms of the inappropriability – or, as he terms it, exteriority and infinity – of the other. The encounter with such inappropriable other is the original experience: before knowledge, since knowledge presupposes such an encounter, and before ontology, since being as such presupposes the encounter with the other being. Ethics breaks totality, opening onto an irreducible exteriority, and inappropriability. The face to face is transcendence, and "the face breaks the system" (EN, 34) (Levinas 1998). There is for Levinas a non-synthesizable, and that is the face to face ("The relationship between man is certainly the non-synthesizable par excellence", EI, 77) (Levinas 1995). There is simply no context (being, the world, and horizon) that would include the face to face with the other, as the face "originally signifies or commands outside the context of the world" (EN, 167) (Levinas 1998).

Levinas describes the original ethical experience as the face to face with the other, in which I am faced with the destitute and vulnerable nature of the other. Faced with such vulnerability (ultimately, the mortality or irremediable exposure to death of the other), I am called to responsibility for the other. This is why Levinas challenges Heideggerian egoistic solipsistic death, and opposes to it a death that would be more primordial, the death of the other. The death of the other, he asserts, is the first death. Reversing the Heideggerian mineness of death, Levinas claims that I would be concerned for the other's death before my own death. In his effort to give thought to an experience of alterity that cannot to be reduced to the Same, Levinas rejects the Heideggerian primacy of mineness based on death. He explains, in "Dying for…" that for him it is a matter of a genuine "alternative between, on the one hand, the identical in its authenticity, in its *own right* or its unalterable *mine* of the human, in its *Eigentlichkeit*, independence and freedom, and on the other hand being as human devotion to the other." (EN, 211, my emphasis) (Levinas 1998). Levinas opposes to "solitary mineness" a being-for-the-other that would be more authentic, a being-for-the-other *that is defined in terms of responsibility*. This will be achieved by another conception of the self, no longer a subject or even a Dasein, but a hostage to the other. This being-hostage, that is, a non-chosen responsibility for the other ("Condition of hostage – not chosen", AE, 214) testifies to the radical dispossession or ex-propriation of the subject in Levinas's work (Levinas 1996). The figure of this expropriation is what Levinas calls the face.

What does Levinas mean by the face (*visage*)? In one word: vulnerability. More precisely, a *human* vulnerability, or vulnerability itself as the meaning of humanity.[8] More precisely, the face signifies the vulnerability of the *other human*, as for Levinas humanity is the humanity of the other human. In *Ethics and Infinity*, Levinas begins by noting that the face is not an object of perception, a perceptual phenomenon, indeed perhaps not even a phenomenon, if a phenomenon is what appears and becomes pres-

---

[8] The French word "*visage*" immediately gives a human character to the face as thematized by Levinas, as *visage* refers exclusively to the human face, whereas the term "*gueule*" refers to the animal's "face". The humanism of Levinas' thought is thus already inscribed linguistically, in the French language.

ent. The face, seen as it were from *beyond the visible*, has a proximity, but it is not a present phenomenon. In *Otherwise than Being*, Levinas specifies in this respect that the face escapes presentation and representation, and that it is indeed "the very defection of phenomenality" (AE, 141) (Levinas 1996). The face exceeds presentation, not because it would be too much as an appearance, but on the contrary due to its poverty, its weakness: "a non-phenomenon because 'less' than the phenomenon" (AE, 141) (Levinas 2005). Phenomenology is here exceeded, and Levinas does state in *Otherwise than Being* that his work exceeds the confines of appearance in being (*l'apparoir de l'être*), and therefore "ventures beyond phenomenology" (AE, 281) (Levinas 1996). It is in this sense that Levinas states: "one can say that the face is not 'seen'" (EI, 86), not the object of a thematic gaze (Levinas 1995). What is being seen in the face is its own invisibility, that is, its absolute alterity, what Derrida would call the secret of the other. This break with a phenomenology of perception is apparent when Levinas states that the best way of encountering the face "is not even to notice the color of his eyes" (EI, 85) (Levinas 1995). In fact, this way of looking at the face would be a kind of defacement, and the face seen in this perceptual way would then be "defaced," as in the French *devisagé*. To *de-visager* or scrutinize someone is tantamount to a defacing. This is why Levinas specifies that "Defacement occurs also as a way of looking, a way of knowing, for example, what color your eyes are. No, the face is not this". (*Is it Righteous?*, 144–145) (Levinas 2001). The face does not *present* a countenance or a form but exposes a nakedness and a passivity: "The disclosure of the face is nudity – non-form – abandon of oneself, aging, dying; more naked than nakedness: poverty, wrinkled skin" (AE, 141) (Levinas 1996). Levinas describes further the moral aspect of the face, in his analysis of the skin (*la peau* and not the flesh, *la chair*). Levinas undertakes an analysis of the skin, the "contact of a skin," emphasizing its thinness (*minceur*), thin surface, "almost transparent," already pointing to the face's poverty and lack of substantiality. The skin is thus thought of in terms of the exposure and poverty of the face (AE, 143) (Levinas 1996). The skin of the face, he tells us, "is the most naked" (EI, 86) (Levinas 1995), a nakedness that is described in its moral dimension. *That exposure is an originary honesty*, not an intentional honesty, but a honesty of exposure. It is straight because exposed, and vulnerable because exposed.

The face is thus exposure, an exposure to injury, that is, already, to death. *The face is above all exposure to death*. This radical exposure of the face is radically stripped of protection, defenseless: the face is defenselessness itself. The other's vulnerability, ultimately, reveals his or her mortality. For, if the face is what can be outraged, defaced, done violence to, if it can be injured, it is because the other is mortal, already exposed to death. What is an injury is not the announcement of death? Levinas speaks of the exposure of the face to death, to "an invisible death and mysterious forsaking" (EN, 145) (Levinas 1998). What is laid bare in the face? Death. The face *expresses* the death of the other, behind all the masks and defenses: "Face of the other – *underlying* all the particular forms of expression in which he or she, already right 'in character,' plays a role – is no less *pure expression*, extradition with neither defense nor cover, precisely the extreme rectitude of a *facing*, which in this nakedness *is an exposure unto death*: nakedness, destitution, passivity, and pure vulnerability. *Face as the very mortality of the human being*" (EN, 167, my emphasis) (Levinas 1998). Therein lies the origin of ethics, of responsibility for the other. "The face is exposed, menaced, as if inviting us to an act of violence. *At the same time*, the face is what forbids us to kill" (EI, 86, my emphasis) (Levinas 1995). Thou shalt not kill, a command that Levinas significantly specifies as a "Thou Shalt not leave me alone in my dying!" *At the same time*: in a dangerous proximity, threatening its very purity, if not possibility, ethics is rooted in an experience that also constitutes the possibility of violence. Paradoxically, it is that inviolable character of the other that can give rise to the desire to kill, as the "other is the only being I can want to kill" (EN, 9) (Levinas 1998). This impure origin of ethics, the intertwining between ethics and violence (ethics is the suspension of violence; violence is the negation of ethics) will always represent a continual threat to the integrity of ethics.

What is responsibility? It is *fearing for the other*: I fear for the death of the other. That is *my* fear, although it is not, Levinas clarifies, a fear *for oneself* ("Fear for the other, fear for the death of the other man is my fear, but it is in no way a fear for *oneself*," EN, 146) (Levinas 1998). Rather, it is *my* fear *for another*, following the structure of subjectivity as "for-the-other." I fear for the other's suffering, but also for my own potential violence as a being-in-the-world who can establish a home expulsing and excluding all others in some third (or fourth!) world, in other words, a fear "for all the violence and murder my existing… can bring about" (EN, 144) (Levinas 1998). Levinas goes so far as to raise this suffering of the other to the level of the "supreme principle of ethics" (EN, 94) (Levinas 1998)!

That responsibility for the other leads to, indeed arises out, of my de-posing as masterful ego, my expropriation as subject. Levinas's radicalization of this responsibility for another follows and registers the expropriation of the subject. The being of the subject is no longer for-itself but for-the-other. I have not done anything and yet I am responsible. I am assigned to the other before any engagement on my part, a relationship before the act, which Levinas calls obsession or persecution: radical expropriation of the self that is at once an obligation to the other! I have done nothing and yet I have always been accused, thus persecuted. This is, not the human condition, but the *human incondition (l'incondition humaine)*, as Levinas stresses the destitute insubstantiality of the expropriated I hostage of the other. It is indeed an expropriation that is at the basis of the de-posing of the I. "Is the human I first? Is it not he who, in place of being posed, ought to be de-posed?" (*Is it Righteous?*, 97) (Levinas 2003). This logic of expropriation allows us to account for Levinas's fundamental categories. The notions of "hostage," of as subject as subjected, of obsession, persecution, accusation, of the "other as infinite," all these can be traced back to a logic of expropriation that reveals the radical *dispossession* and *destitution* of the subject, the *ex-propriation* of any sense of "home," of "ownership," of egohood. Responsibility registers for Levinas the expropriation of the subject, expropriated towards the other for whom it is now responsible.

A question nonetheless needs to be raised with respect to the role of subjectivity in this thought of responsibility. Perhaps the most determinative assumption in Levinas' discourse is his paradoxical reliance on the motif of subjectivity. We recall how he rejected the neutrality and impersonality of being, of the "there is, "to return to the subjective. Responsibility for the other, he insists, is the very structure of subjectivity. This emphasis on the subjective is accompanied by a focus on the human.

Therein lies Levinas's undeconstructed, indeed assumed and proclaimed humanism, a humanism... of the other human being, and Levinas states: "I advocate, as in the title of one of my books, the humanism of the other human being" (EN, 112, tr. modified) (Levinas 1998). Levinas is not interested in deconstructing humanism, and in fact he is critical of the contemporary critiques of humanism and of the subject. It should therefore not come as a surprise if Levinas actually declares, in *Totality and Infinity*, that his work is "a defense of subjectivity" (TI, 11)! A *defense* of subjectivity, even as it takes the paradoxical form of a subjection of the subject to the other: but precisely *as* destitute, expropriated, the subject is maintained and becomes what Levinas calls the elected or chosen one. Levinas goes so far as to designate this destitute, expropriated ego as the true *subjectum*. Subjectivity means for Levinas such a being subjected, "as subjection to all, as a supporting all (*un tout supporter*) and supporting of the whole (*un supporter le tout*)" (AE, 255) (Levinas 1996). Levinas thus reinforces the position of ground of the *subjectum*, now rethought in terms of the accusation and passivity of the subject, as persecuted subject of responsibility.

Ultimately this hermeneutical situation reveals, paradoxically, the Cartesian-Husserlian heritage of Levinas and the limits of his thought of responsibility, tributary of an undeconstructed subjectivism and humanism. Levinas' critique of Heidegger paradoxically arises out of a site that Heidegger had already deconstructed, that of subjectivity and humanism. The analysis begins with the I, with the ego (as we recall, for Levinas the origin of meaning is the intersubjective relation, "the original experience," therefore within the horizon of subjectivity), which Levinas *then* attempts to exceed towards the other. Indeed, this accounts for the excess proper to Levinas' thinking and vocabulary: a *reactive* thought, a thought "of rupture," of "excess," of "hyperbole" leading to the paroxistic formulations of *Otherwise than Being or Beyond Essence*, a kind of symmetrical reversal of the Cartesian and Husserlian tradition in philosophy, opposing it but never really questioning its foundations. Levinas betrays this reactive dimension of his thought. He writes that the responsibility for the other "*goes against the grain* (*à rebours*) of intentionality and the will" (AE, 221) (Levinas 1996), or that the persecution of the subject "goes against the grain (*à rebours*) of intentionality" (AE, 177) (Levinas 1996). Levinas explicitly presents his understanding of subjectivity as a reversal of the traditional subject. For instance: "Subjectivity as hostage. This notion *inverts* (*renverse*) the position from which the presence of the ego to itself appears as the beginning or the accomplishment of philosophy" (AE, 202, my emphasis) (Levinas 1996). Among many instances of this reversal of the modern tradition in philosophy, let us mention but the following list: first, the subject is not a "for-itself," but a "for-the-other"; second, the subject is not a freedom, but a passivity; third, the subject does not posit or constitute the meaning of the other, but is "affected" by the other. The I is not a nominative, but an accusative; the subject does not initiate, but can only respond. The subject is not a spontaneity, but a receptivity. Responsibility no longer designates an activity of the subject, but is reversed into a symmetrical passivity. The subject does not thematize, but is exposed to the transcendence of the infinite. The subject, finally, is precisely not a active subject, a spontaneity, but is subject*ed*, as an hostage, to the other. Responsibility for the other is "the defeat of the I think", the defeat of "the originary *activity* of all *acting*, source of the *spontaneity of the subject*, or of the subject as spontaneity" (AE, 220) (Levinas 1996). As one can see, all the features of the Levinasian concept of responsibility as subjection of the subject to the other amount to a peculiar reversal of its traditional sense as accountability of the free acting spontaneous subject. But to that extent, they maintain the horizon of subjectivity. We may ask: Does responsibility need to be tied to the figure of the subject? Reversing egological responsibility still leaves the question of the *being-responsible* still open. What does it mean to *be* responsible? One will see how responsibility is tied to a non-subjective experience of being, and ultimately is an exposure to a secret, an inappropriable.

2   Responsibility for a Secret

Heidegger's corpus, it is perhaps not stressed enough, entails a major thought of responsibility (Raffoul 2010).[9] Being is an event for which each Dasein is responsible, responding and corresponding to its call. In fact, Dasein is defined in terms of responsibility: it designates that being in which being is at issue, called by being to respond and correspond to its givenness. Being is indeed not a generic universality but has a singularizing reach. Thus is why Dasein is "each time mine": being happens to Dasein, who must make it its own. In this sense, being cannot be distinguished from the singular event of an existence which is in each case delivered over to itself, and which is to that very extent responsible for itself. This is what the expression of Care (*Sorge*) seeks to express, namely, the primordial responsibility that Dasein is. Dasein is that entity that does not "simply occur among other being;" but "is concerned *about* its very being" (Heidegger 1927).[10] In such original responsibility, the notion of the human being as subject is abandoned.

Original responsibility is indeed not simply the reversal of accountability. Rather, Heidegger situates the question of responsibility outside of a problematic of the ego, outside of the accountability of the free acting subject, and arising out of the very openness of being where the human being dwells as Dasein. Heidegger's thinking of Dasein breaks decisively with the tradition of subjectivity (Raffoul 1999).[11] Heidegger's understanding of ethics and responsibility develops in terms of being itself, and no longer in terms of subjectivity, will or agency. This is the decisive difference with Levinas: responsibility is not about the subject, even as reversed into the subjected one or the hostage; responsibility is about being. Ethics is desubjectified, and the realm of ethical responsibility severed from the predominance of subjectivity.

---

[9] See my *The Origins of Responsibility* (Bloomington, IN: Indiana U. Press, 2010).

[10] Martin Heidegger. *Sein und Zeit* (1927), ed. Friedrich Wilhelm von Herrmann (Frankfurt am Main: Vittorio Klostermann, 1977), GA 2, p. 12. English translations used: *Being and Time*, trans. John Macquarrie and Edward Robinson (New York: Harper, 1962). *Being and Time*, trans. Joan Stambaugh. Revised and with a Foreword by Dennis J. Schmidt (Albany: SUNY Press, 2010). Hereafter cited as SZ, followed by original pagination.

[11] On this point, I take the liberty of referring the reader to my *Heidegger and the Subject* (Amherst, NY: Prometheus Books, 1999).

This can be seen in the treatment of decision as it intervenes in Heidegger's later thought, which develops a radically non-subjectivistic approach to ethical responsibility. In *Introduction to Metaphysics*, Heidegger stresses that "de-cision *(Ent-scheidung)* here does not mean the judgment and choice of human beings but rather a division *(Scheidung)* in the... togetherness of Being, unconcealment, seeming and not-Being" (Heidegger 2000).[12] The measure of decision, of responsibility, is no longer the subject but the event of being itself. This is further developed in the *Contributions to Philosophy*. In paragraph 43, Heidegger states clearly that ordinarily, when "we speak here of de-cision *(Ent-scheidung)*, we think of an activity of man, of an enactment, of a process." However, decision for Heidegger is not a human power or faculty: "But here neither the human character in an activity nor the process-dimension is essential" (Heidegger 1999).[13] This is why he clarifies that "Decision [is] related to the truth of being, not only related but determined only from within it" *(Contributions*, 69) (Heidegger 1999). Decision is not to be taken in its "morally-anthropologically" sense, but pertains to being itself. We can even wonder whether such an original responsibility can be characterized at all as a *human* responsibility, following Heidegger's claim that in the determination of the humanity of human beings as ek-sistence what is essential is not the human being but Being (Heidegger 1993).[14] In fact, for Heidegger responsibility is not a human characteristic, but instead is a phenomenon that belongs to being itself (insofar as humans are called by being). The entirety of ethics is thus to be recast in terms of being itself, responsibility instead naming the co-belonging of being and Dasein (a co-belonging not posited by the human being but rather one in which we are thrown).

Responsibility is no longer attached to the subject, but to the event or enactment of being. Such an enactment is thus not the act of a subjectivity, because, as Heidegger says of project or projection *(Entwurf)*, it is always thrown *(Geworfen)*. Any projecting-open is thrown, and in the *Contributions*, thrownness is understood as belongingness to be-ing (that is, *not* as the project of the subject!), so that to be thrown now means: to be en-owned. Thus, "the projecting-open of the essential sway of be-ing is merely a response to the call" *(Contributions*, 39) (Heidegger 1999), and one sees here how the realm of responsibility – of originary responsibility – is located in the space of a certain call, a call to which a response always corresponds.

This correspondence nonetheless always implies otherness, withdrawal and expropriation. First, the phenomenon of the call of conscience in *Being and Time* reveals a singular inscription of otherness within the selfhood of Dasein. As we saw, the very concept of Dasein means: to be a responsibility for being, as being is given in such a way that I have to take it over and be responsible for it. Care, concern, solicitude, anxiety, authenticity, being-guilty, all are different names for such origi-

---

[12] Martin Heidegger. *Introduction to Metaphysics*, trans Gregory Fried and Richard Polt (New Haven, CT: Yale University Press, 2000), p.116.

[13] Martin Heidegger. *Contributions to Philosophy (From Enowning)*, trans. Parvis Emad and Kenneth Maly (Bloomington and Indianapolis: Indiana University Press, 1999), p. 60. Hereafter cited as *Contributions*, followed by page number.

[14] See Martin Heidegger. *Basic Writings*, rev. and exp., ed. David Farrell Krell (San Francisco: Harper, 1993), p. 237.

nary responsibility. Dasein is concerned about its own being, or about being as each time its own. However, this "own" is not the sphere of ownness of an ego. Responsibility is the taking on of such an "own" in a way that reveals an otherness at its heart. Certainly, the call is said to come from the being "which I am each time." But since I am this being only in the mode of a *zu-sein*, a having-to-be, it does not therefore "belong to me," if what is meant by this is projected by me. When Heidegger writes that Dasein "calls itself," it does not mean that the "I," as author, is the origin of the call (as we will see, he on the contrary insists that there is *no author* of the call), or even that there is a strict identity between the caller and the called one. In the context of the passage, this statement intervenes when Heidegger is attempting to stress that the call does come from an entity other than Dasein, whether an ontic other, or a transcendent theological other. Heidegger rejects the theological notion of a call coming from God, *and*, *in fact*, *from any entity*. The theological representation of the call is an ontic representation of the call. Rather, to "call oneself" means that the call resonates in the dimension of selfhood, not projected by a self-identical subject, but to take on and respond to. One already notes here the presence of an otherness in the phenomenon, which Heidegger approaches in terms of the "uncanniness" of the call of conscience. There is no self at the basis of the call, because *the self itself arises out of the call*. It is the very movement of the call that brings a self-to-come, the impersonal or pre-personal event of being that precedes and exceeds the one who will have to assume it as its own. The fact that the I arises out a non-subjective call allows us to understand why the 'author' of the call, in a certain sense, escapes all attempts at identification (SZ, 274–275). The caller remains "in a striking indefiniteness," it "fails to answer questions about name, status, origin, and repute" (SZ, 274) (Heidegger 1927). The author of the call remains *other*, *foreign*, and "absolutely distances any kind of becoming familiar" (SZ, 275) (Heidegger 1927). The "caller" evades any attempt at identification simply because there is no "author" of the call. This agent is "other" as uncanny. The "caller" in fact is identified with the calling itself: *the caller is the calling*.

A dissymmetry and otherness within the self is becoming apparent: "When Dasein is summoned, *is* it not 'there' in another way from that in which it does the calling?", asks Heidegger (SZ, 275) (Heidegger 1927). The call comes from the being that I am (that is, *not* from another entity, an ontic other), but as something that *falls upon me*, thus in a sense, *as something that does not come from me*. This is why Heidegger clearly states that the "call is precisely something that *we ourselves* have neither planned nor prepared for nor willfully brought about" (SZ, 275). The call sur-prises me: "'It' calls, against our expectations and even against our will" (SZ, 275). Nonetheless, it calls *me* ("*es ruft micht*," writes Heidegger, SZ, 277) (Heidegger 1927), as if the self arose from the impersonal event of the call. The "caller" is an "it" because it cannot be referred to any entity, be it divine, as it is the event and advent of presence itself. It happens, before me, without me, but nonetheless "it" happens only to me, because it calls me: *Es ruft mich*. There lies what we could call the verticality of the call, calling me from a height that is nonetheless not foreign to the self. This dissymmetry interrupts any autonomous self-relation, and introduces heteronomy in auto-nomy. Hence this passage from Heidegger: "The call comes *from* me and yet from *above and beyond* me (*Der Ruf kommt* aus *mir und doch* über *mich*)." (SZ, 275) (Heidegger 1927).

One thus needs to recognize in conscience a certain dissymmetry, a gap within identity, a transcendence within the self, allowing for the call to be heard. This verticality, or dissymmetry, prevents all autonomous closure of the self and in fact represents the irruption or the "breach" of otherness within Dasein itself. Autonomy is hetero-nomy, and the call of conscience is a hetero-auto-affection, manifesting the otherness at the heart of Dasein's selfhood. Because of this inscription of otherness in the coming to itself of the self, responsibility can no longer be for Heidegger a responsibility for oneself, if that means the responsibility of a self-enclosed ego for itself. As we saw, Levinas opposes a responsibility for the other to self-responsibility. However, unlike Levinas, who situates the other outside of the ego (as exteriority), Heidegger inscribes otherness in the structure of the self as hetero-affection, *rendering the opposition between a responsibility for the other and a responsibility-for-oneself moot.*

It is thus incorrect to claim that Heidegger privileged the "pole" of the self over the other, or that he conceives of responsibility as being primarily for oneself, existence unfolding (an)ethically as an infamous "struggle for existence". Heidegger explicitly rejected this social Darwinism, as early as a 1921–1922 course, where he explained that "Caring is not a factually occurring *struggle for existence*, understood as elapsing and 'taking place' within so-called Objective unities of life" (Heidegger 2001a).[15] On the contrary, care includes a care for others because of the hetero-affection of Dasein and due to the fundamental constitution of Dasein as being-with. Heidegger consistently stressed the constitutive openness to the other of Dasein, from his early courses all the way to his last seminars, as this passage from the *Zollikon Seminars* reveals. Answering a question by Medard Boss, regarding the signification of that proposition from *Being and Time*, "Dasein is that being for which, in its being, that being is an issue", Heidegger clarifies: "Da-sein must always be seen as being-in-the-world, as concern for things, and as caring for other [Da-seins], as the being-with the human beings it encounters, and never as a self-contained subject" (Heidegger 2001b).[16] To that extent, responsibility will always include a responsibility for others.

Once understood apart from the tradition of egology, responsibility signifies an essential exposure to the other, and cannot simply be reduced to the responsibility of the "self-contained subject" of which the *Zollikon Seminars* spoke. Now, insofar as an otherness is inscribed at the heart of responsibility, there will always be an inappropriable in the motion of our responsible being. What weighs in the weight of responsibility is a certain inappropriability remaining other to Dasein. This is why Heidegger understands responsibility as exposure for an inappropriable, for a "secret".

---

[15] Martin Heidegger. *Phenomenological Interpretations of Aristotle* (Bloomington, In: Indiana University Press, 2001), p. 100.
[16] Martin Heidegger, *The Zollikon Seminars*, trans. Franz Mayr and Richard Askay (Evanston, Ill.: Northwestern University Press, 2001), p. 159.

For what, in the end, does the call of conscience, later renamed call of being, reveal? An inappropriable. *Schuldigsein* or *Nichtigkeit* in *Being and Time*, withdrawal of being in later writings, in each case Heidegger shows that an inappropriable inhabits the motion of responsible being, indeed, that such an inappropriable is the very possibility of responsibility. Derrida has stressed this aporetic structure of responsibility, situating an impossible at its heart (Raffoul 2008).[17] Far from being identified to the position of a good conscience, "the concepts of responsibility, of decision, or of duty, are condemned a priori to paradox, scandal, and aporia" (GD, 68) (Derrida 1992). Responsibility becomes less about the establishment of a sphere of control and power, less about the establishment of a sovereign subject, and more about an exposure to an inappropriable event that does not come from us and yet calls us. The call of conscience calls Dasein back from its disburdened, irresponsible existence in the everyday back to its own being-guilty. Existing authentically, far from overcoming such being-guilty, is projecting oneself resolutely towards it. It means taking over or making oneself responsible for this "not". Heidegger states this quite clearly: by choosing itself, Dasein chooses its being-guilty and its finitude: "in so choosing, Dasein makes possible its ownmost being-guilty" (SZ, 288) (Heidegger 1927). Being-guilty, the call of conscience, throwness, the taking on of the inappropriable, all these motifs point to *facticity* as the site of ontological responsibility. Facticity is not what faces the position of a consciousness, but the "throw" of an existence that is called from such a throw to appropriate what will always remain inappropriable for it: responsibility for a "not," for a "secret."

This negativity or "nullity" lies in the fact of *not* being the basis of one's own being, of being *thrown* into existence; the "guilt" lies in the fact that I must make myself the origin or basis of this existence of which *I am not* the origin. Dasein exists as thrown, that is to say, it did not bring *itself* into existence by first projecting itself on the basis of a pre-existing self. There lies the fundamental and irreducible impotence or powerlessness of Dasein. *Dasein can never overcome the finitude of throwness*. Heidegger would speak of such powerlessness in the course entitled *Introduction to Philosophy* (*Einleitung in die Philosophie*), claiming that "Dasein exists always in an essential exposure to the darkness and impotence of its origin, even if only in the prevailing form of a habitual deep forgetting in the face of this essential determination of its facticity" (Heidegger 1996).[18] This throwness constitutes the "nullity" of Dasein, as well as its paradoxical responsibility: the dispossession or expropriation that comes to light in my incapacity to make myself the author or master of my existence is precisely what opens this existence to itself, what frees it for itself. In this sense, by resolutely projecting being-guilty, Dasein appropriates the inappropriable *as* inappropriable. *I must be the improper* (*inauthenticity*) *properly* (*authentically*). Ultimately, one is responsible *from* out of the facticity of exis-

---

[17] On this question, see my "Derrida and the Ethics of the Im-possible," *Research in Phenomenology*, 38, Spring 2008.

[18] Martin Heidegger. *Einleitung in die Philosophie*, ed. O. Saame et I. Saame-Speidel, 2nd edn, 2001 (Wintersemester 1928/29), vol. 27 of Gesamtausgabe (Frankfurt am Main: Klostermann, 1996), p. 340. Hereafter cited as GA 27, followed by page number.

tence, and *for* it. Responsibility then manifests the essential exposure of human beings to an inappropriable that always remains "other" for them.

The "inappropriable" may be in fact the secret resource of appropriation (responsibility as properly being one's own). For Heidegger to be thrown is to be thrown into a responsibility. *This immediately means that responsibility will be for this very thrownness*, that is, for the inappropriability of Dasein's being. In *Introduction to Philosophy*, Heidegger thus explains that precisely that over which Dasein is not master must be "worked through" and "survived". He writes: "Also that which does not arise of one's own express decision, as most things for Dasein, must be in such or such a way retrievingly appropriated, even if only in the modes of putting up with or shirking something; that which for us is entirely not under the control of freedom in the narrow sense… is something that is in such or such a manner taken up or rejected in the How of Dasein" (GA 27, 337) (Heidegger 1996). If thrownness does not designate some fall from a higher realm, but the very facticity from which Dasein becomes a care and a responsibility for itself, then the weight of existence is from the outset an original responsibility. The inappropriable in existence (facticity), as we see in the phenomena of moods, is primarily felt as a weight or a burden. Facticity is given to be read in the phenomena of moods. Thrownness is *felt* in the mood, a mood that manifests an ontological truth of Dasein. What is most striking in those descriptions is how Heidegger describes moods in terms of the opacity and withdrawal of our factical origins, as an expropriation of our being that seems to break and foreclose any possibility of responsible appropriation. What weighs is the inappropriable. Heidegger speaks of a "burden" (*Last*). The being of the there, Heidegger writes, "become[s] manifest as a burden" (SZ, 134) (Heidegger 1927). But, interestingly, the very concept of weight and burden reintroduces, as it were, the problematic of responsibility. In a marginal note added to this passage, Heidegger later clarified: "Burden: what weighs (*das Zu-tragende*); human being is charged with the responsibility (*überantwortet*) of Dasein, appropriated by it (*übereignet*). To carry: to take over one's belonging to being itself" (SZ, 134) (Heidegger 1927). The burden is described as "what weighs," as what has to be carried (*das Zu-tragende*). The weight of facticity, i.e., the burden, is to be carried, Heidegger indicating the taking on of facticity as the carrying of the weight. The weight is facticity; the carrying is the taking on of facticity: such is the "facticity of responsibility." The sentence continues thus: "man is charged with the responsibility (*überantwortet*) of Dasein, appropriated by it (*übereignet*)".

Being withdraws in the very "throw" that brings Dasein into existence. But it is this withdrawal itself that *calls* Dasein, which summons it to be this being-thrown as its ownmost. In its very eventfulness, being withdraws, is the mystery: such a withdrawal, as Heidegger stresses in the first lecture of *What is Called Thinking*, *calls us*.[19] The origin of responsibility is the withdrawal of being in its givenness as this withdrawal calls us. For as Heidegger explains, this "withdrawing is not nothing. Withdrawing is an event. In fact, what withdraws may even concern and claim

---

[19] Martin Heidegger. *What is Called Thinking?* English translation by J. Glenn Gray (New York: Harper & Row, 1968), pp. 7–10, 17–18. Hereafter cited as WCT, followed by page number.

man more essentially than anything present that strikes and touches him" (WCT, 9) (Heidegger 1968). This withdrawal touches us, and calls us to take it on as a weight to carry. Dasein's belongingness to being, to *Ereignis*, happens from a certain expropriative motion, which Heidegger calls *Enteignis*. One notes the presence of such expropriation in all the characterizations of Heidegger's responsibility, of our being-responsible: from the "ruinance" of factical life in the early writings and lecture courses to the *Uneigentlichkeit* of existence in *Being and Time* and the being-guilty of conscience; from the thrownness felt in moods and the weight of a responsibility assigned to an inappropriable to the withdrawal of being as origin of the call (what calls to responsibility is a withdrawal) and the *Enteignis* within *Ereignis* of the later writings, one finds that responsibility in Heidegger is each time described as the exposure to and experience of an inappropriable, an inappropriable that is not opposed to appropriation, but "plays" in it and lets it be, in a motion named by Derrida, in one word, "ex-appropriation." Original responsibility is hence a responsibility for such withdrawal, responsibility for a secret. It is indeed around this motif of the secret that Heidegger may be closest to Levinas, if it is the case, as Derrida wrote, that "the other is secret insofar as it is other" (Derrida 2001).[20]

References

Derrida, Jacques. 1992. *The gift of death*. Chicago/London: Chicago University Press.
Derrida, Jacques. 2001. "Autrui est secret parce qu'il est autre" interview by Antoine Spire, *Le Monde de l'Education* (July–August 2001). www.lemonde.fr/mde/ete2001/derrida.html.
Heidegger, Martin. 1927. *Sein und Zeit,* ed. Friedrich Wilhelm von Herrmann, Frankfurt am Main: Vittorio Klostermann, 1977. Trans. Macquarrie, John and Edward Robinson. *Being and Time*, New York: Harper, 1962.
Heidegger, Martin. 1968. *What is called thinking?* English translation by J. Glenn Gray. New York: Harper & Row.
Heidegger, Martin. 1993. *Basic writings*. ed. Krell, David Farrell. San Francisco: Harper.
Heidegger, Martin. 1996. *Einleitung in die Philosophie*, ed. O. Saame et I. Saame-Speidel, 2nd edn, 2001 (Wintersemester 1928/29), vol. 27 of Gesamtausgabe. Frankfurt am Main: Klostermann, p. 340.
Heidegger, Martin. 1999. *Contributions to philosophy (From Enowning)*, Trans. Emad, Parvis and Kenneth Maly. Bloomington/Indianapolis: Indiana University Press.
Heidegger, Martin. 2000. *Introduction to Metaphysics*. Trans Gregory Fried and Richard Polt. New Haven: Yale University Press.
Heidegger, Martin. 2001a. *Phenomenological interpretations of Aristotle*. Bloomington: Indiana University Press.
Heidegger, Martin. 2001b. *The Zollikon seminars*. Trans. Mayr, Franz and Richard Askay. Evanston: Northwestern University Press.
Janicaud, Dominique. 2000. *Heidegger en France*. Paris: Albin Michel.
Levinas, Emmanuel. 1995. *Ethics and infinity*. Trans. Richard A. Cohen. Pittsburgh: Duquesne University Press.

---

[20] Jacques Derrida. "Autrui est secret parce qu'il est autre" [*Autrui* is secret because it is other], interview by Antoine Spire, *Le Monde de l'Education* (July–August 2001), www.lemonde.fr/mde/ete2001/derrida.html.

Levinas, Emmanuel. 1996. *Autrement qu'être ou au-delà de l'essence*. Kluwer Academic, Le livre de poche.

Levinas, Emmanuel. 1998. *Entre Nous*. Trans. Smith, Michael B., and Barbara Harshav: Columbia University Press.

Levinas, Emmanuel. 2001. *Is it righteous to be?* ed. Robbins, Jill. Stanford: Stanford University Press.

Levinas, Emmanuel. 2003. *On escape*. Stanford: Stanford University Press.

Levinas, Emmanuel. 2005. *Humanisme de l'autre homme*. Montpellier: Fata Morgana, 1972. Trans. Nidra Poller, *Humanism of the other*. University of Illinois Press, 2005.

Raffoul, Francois. 1999. *Heidegger and the subject*. Amherst: Prometheus Books.

Raffoul, Francois. 2010. *The origins of responsibility*. Bloomington: Indiana University Press.

Raffoul, Francois. 2008. Derrida and the ethics of the im-possible. *Research in Phenomenology*, 38, Spring.

The 1924 Lecture "The Concept of Time" as the Step Beyond *Being and Time* (1927) and After Deconstruction

Rajesh Sampath

Abstract This paper argues that Heidegger's 1924 lecture on "The Concept of Time" can be appropriated and reinterpreted to surpass some of the inherent limits of *Being and Time*. Furthermore, it tries to demonstrate the passage beyond deconstruction, which also attempts to critique the unity, stability, and systematic nature of fundamental ontology in Being and Time and the latter's attempts to destroy the history of metaphysical conceptions of time. The paper concludes with speculative metaphysical ruminations on future directions for continental philosophy.

Keywords Metaphysics • Deconstruction • Fundamental ontology • Phenomenology of religion • Heidegger, • Derrida

Perhaps patient mediation and painstaking investigation on and around what is provisionally called writing, far from falling short of a science of writing or of hastily dismissing it by some obscurantist reactions, letting it rather develop its positivity as far as possible, are the wanderings of a way of thinking that is faithful and attentive to an ineluctable world of the future which proclaims itself at present, beyond the closure of knowledge. The future can only be anticipated in the form of an absolute danger. It is that which breaks absolutely with constituted normality and can only be proclaimed, *presented*, as a sort of monstrosity. For that future world and for that within it which will have put into question the values of sign, word, and writing, for that which guides our future anterior, there is as yet no exergue.[1]
    Are we ourselves time? or Am I my time?[2]

---

[1] Derrida (1974, p. 4).

[2] Heidegger (1992, p. 22E).

R. Sampath (✉)
Heller School for Social Policy and Management, Brandeis University, Waltham, MA, USA
e-mail: rsampath@brandeis.edu

© Springer International Publishing Switzerland 2016   149
L. Foran, R. Uljée (eds.), *Heidegger, Levinas, Derrida: The Question of Difference*, Contributions To Phenomenology 86,
DOI 10.1007/978-3-319-39232-5_11

1   Introduction

The startling fact about the 1924 lecture "The Concept of Time" is not just its fore-shadowing of difficult and hard-to-understand concepts that would emerge in the 1927 masterpiece *Being and Time*: namely Dasein, Care, Being-in-the-World, Historicality, Temporality, Resoluteness, Within-Time-Ness etc. That great work of 1927, which changed continental European philosophy as it had been developed up to that point (i.e. from the Pre-Socratics onwards), had to invent a whole new set of terms within a flexible German language. Its philosophical resources are immense as so many sympathetic commentators have attested. Yet in the 1924 lecture we get a straightforward presentation by arguably the most significant figure in twentieth century philosophy, which certainly puts him in the canon of the history of Western philosophy with other greats who pondered the mystery of time, namely Heraclitus, Parmenides, Plato, Aristotle, Descartes, Leibniz, Kant, Hegel and Nietzsche. But unlike favorable judgments on most of his predecessors, Heidegger's critics condemn his corpus for inexcusable obscurities, if not an intentional obfuscation or will to deceive. The 1924 lecture, however, escapes this criticism. Heidegger speaks like a pastor to his flock.[3]

Heidegger for his part says he is not revolutionizing philosophy by providing a revolutionary answer to the age-old question- "What is time?" Rather, his undeniable and breath taking originality comes from the simple fact that he changed the very structure of the question by restructuring our relation to it so that it is no longer like any other question- say a question in science like 'what is an atom?' or a question in the social sciences like 'how do social movements arise and occur?' Rather, we humans become the question in so far as the question of time inhabits our very essence in as much as we inhabit the question. Being-there (Dasein) has everything to do with the mystery that surrounds the ontological status of the question of the meaning of itself (of the questioner), which means inhabiting the question of one's timing and not being a certain point in time or space, i.e. a point on a graph or a minute on a clock. (Only human subjects who pursue objects, including themselves or the human sciences, are in space and time.) And so pursuing the question of time separates philosophy from any other branch of human inquiry, say the natural and social sciences. By asking about time, we are asking about ourselves, but without solutions from the history of metaphysics (a concept or notion like Spirit or the Absolute) or theology (the revelation of God as kairologically-fulfilled time) as an available answer to the question. Hence revolutionary interrogations begin to flow such as 'Are we ourselves time?' or 'Am I my time?' in the 1924 lecture. The great shift that Heidegger's thought catalyzes (at least in the history of Western thought) is the creation of this distinction, namely the being of time as we inhabit its question AND time as an object (scientific, psychological, philosophical or theological) pur-

---

[3] Interestingly enough, the lecture was delivered to a group of theologians at Marburg and not a room full of technical specialists in academic philosophy. I use the metaphor of the pastor assuming that most pastors try to speak clearly to ordinary people and presumably act in a manner not to deceive. Most think they are attesting to the truth—at least from the standpoint of their faith.

sued by an inquiring subject. The history of metaphysics (Plato to Hegel) separated the human subject from the question and thought of time as an object to be probed,[4] and therefore 'what' becomes the proper subject of the question's object, namely time. Whereas in Heidegger, 'who' is substituted for 'what,' and so by asking about the very 'who' of time it forces a reorientation in the way philosophy must proceed with its greatest question (what will become the question of the meaning of being in *Being and Time*) and a way for this project to ground itself with its own rationale for turning away from the history of metaphysics. By examining the works of the early Derrida, particularly *Of Grammatology*, I will unpack Derrida's critique of Heidegger. But then I will reopen the early Heidegger's "The Concept of Time" to mount a rebuttal to Derrida's attempt at a separation of his novel deconstruction from Heidegger's destruction of metaphysics and the latter's justification for the project of fundamental ontology.[5]

Before I attempt an appropriative reading of "The Concept of Time" to preempt any attacks on *Being and Time* by Derrida,[6] I must bracket a few assumptions here so we do not get confused in a morass of typical assumptions about time and the way it is interrogated in much of the history of Western philosophy. If Derrida says there is as yet no 'exergue' (time and place of the minting of a coin) for his 'monstrous' science of writing as the encroachment of a 'dangerous' future (beyond the closure of the history of metaphysics), then one must be particularly sensitive to relating Derrida's 'faithful and attentive' thought to Heidegger's philosophical destruction of the history of metaphysical conceptions of time. Such an encroachment and its temporalization are irreducible to any normal or intuitive understand-

---

[4] Plato and Hegel come to mind. Hegel (1977, p. 487) says in the *Phenomenology of Spirit* that 'Time is the Concept that is there, but Spirit as conscious of itself as the Notion will only appear when Spirit no longer appears in time.' Although Plato and Hegel represent two of the most sophisticated dialectical minds in the history of human thought, albeit in different modes of reasoning, they both offer predications. Of course Heidegger would confront both of these along with every other major figure in the history of Western philosophy up to his day in an ambitious attempt to separate himself from that history: he does so both in terms of the way the question of time is structured and how the questioner of the meaning of Being orients its Being (Dasein) to the question so time is not metaphysicalized as an object but becomes the horizon for any understanding of Being whatsoever. And anyone who has studied *Being and Time* with any seriousness knows we are not dealing with a simple hermeneutic circle—questioner of time seeks an understanding of time whose horizon is nothing but time, whereby the questioner becomes subject and object and time becomes subject and object. The subject (questioner) becomes the object (time), which moves into the subject and vice versa. I shall return to this topic later in the paper.

[5] In different ways the *unfinished* project of fundamental ontology came under attack by the later Heidegger, Levinas and Derrida. If anything, I want to re-appropriate the early Heidegger in a fundamental critique and supersession of the limits of the later Heidegger, Levinas and Derrida and their respective critiques of the entire project of *Being and Time*. My unrelenting goal is to advance a position beyond the extant, published divisions of *Being and Time* and the critics of fundamental ontology that followed, i.e. pretty much everything that has appeared since *Being and Time*.

[6] Although *Being and Time* pervades most, if not all, of Derrida's immensely diversified corpus, three of the most sustained mediations on it are in *Of Grammatology*, "Note on a Note from *Being and Time*" from *Margins of Philosophy* and Derrida's lectures on death in *Being and Time* in *Aporias*.

ing of past, present, or future, and any mathematical or geometrical infinitization of their interrelations. Rather, the timing of a critical dialogue between Derrida's critique of Heidegger and the early Heidegger's retrieval must be bracketed for its subtlety, complexity and nuance as to not minimize the force of Derrida's critique but also not foreclose the possibility of a genuine re-appropriation of Heidegger after Derrida. A return to the 1924 lecture "The Concept of Time" is the passage between Heidegger's Division II ("Dasein and Temporality") published in *Being and Time* to the missing division III ("time and Being"), allegedly on time itself, which never came to light. If something is missing, then it might as well not exist; and if it does not exist, then even its possibility as something extant has never been an object of attack by anything that followed *Being and Time*.[7] For sure, something that Derrida does not consider in his critique of Heidegger's fundamental ontology and its metaphysical ambition to discover the meaning of Being in terms of time is the following verisimilitude: there is an uncanny resemblance between Heidegger's ending questions in *The Concept of Time* and the possibility of a unique phenomenological destruction and clearing of a proper way to philosophize about time in the New Testament Gospels.[8]

The 1924 lecture—"The Concept of Time"—must be appropriated to reconstruct the missing division III ("time and Being" of *Being and Time*) through a philosophically heterodox set of 'wanderings' that are 'faithful and attentive' but also 'monstrous and dangerous' in the non-phonemes of the New Testament Greek written texts. This is a strange movement, which defers its own identity, precisely to surpass the limits of *Being and Time* once and for all and therefore overcome all those who have challenged Heidegger's fundamental ontology with their own radical agenda, such as Derrida's deconstruction.[9] This is about radical heterodoxy to the

---

[7] And this includes the thought of the post-*Being and Time* Heidegger on *Being and Time* itself.

[8] Even the most average of theologians recognizes a glorious, complex set of articulations about the relation between Jesus's Being and His 'time.' Great examples are: 'My time has not yet come' (John 2:4) and 'It is for this reason that I have come to this hour' (John 12:27). And the most mysterious of all in which no one is privy to the mystery of the eschaton or the end—"But of that day and hour no one knows, neither the angels of heaven, nor the Son, but the Father alone" Matthew 24: 36. For these famous biblical phrases, see *The New American Bible* (1987). This paper is by no means a work of theology. It is not even an attempted heterodox theology, which would use philosophy in an intentionally evil way or a milder, a-theistic way outside the scope of the good-evil distinction to challenge mainstream Christian dogma. Rather, this is an entirely philosophical, even speculative-metaphysical exercise, which takes the form of an appropriation to achieve a supersession of limits, i.e. Derrida's deconstruction. How this work impacts matters of theology, let alone the general relation between theology and philosophy, as pertinent for the needs of *either* systematic and fundamental theologians *or* non-theological, non-faith oriented philosophers of religion (whether negative theologians at heart or not) must be deferred to a separate reflection. Perhaps this will be taken up after the completion of this paper. It would require a return to Heidegger's *Phenomenology of Religious Life* lectures, which occurred many years before *Being and Time* and the 1927 lecture on "Phenomenology and Theology," which appeared right after *Being and Time*.

[9] Derrida says in the exergue: "By alluding to a science of writing reined in by metaphor, metaphysics and theology, this exergue must not only announce that the science of writing—*grammatology*—shows signs of liberation all over the world, as a result of decisive efforts. These efforts are necessarily discreet, dispersed, almost imperceptible; that is a quality of their meaning and of the

(continental) philosophical landscape in all its plurality today and not theological orthodoxy or heterodoxy for that matter. Before anything 'proclaims its own dislocation' (which for Derrida is the entire 'historical-metaphysical epoch' to think science, logic, writing, philosophy, everything under the sun) we must take a step back to locate what has not been located and then relocate it in the space that has not been written, namely the missing Division III of *Being and Time*. This would be the true meaning of 'liberation,' which one can argue got its false start with the stammering of Derrida's exergue: the latter does not and cannot decide between 'closure' and 'ending,' nor can it produce anything definitive with regard to establishing this renegade 'science of writing,' 'its unity, object, discourse, method and the limits of its field.'

Derrida's world is phantasmagorical: it admits the impossibility of escape from any metaphysical residue of presence, logos, concept, truth, sense and sensibility while pronouncing with revolutionary bravado that it is at least self-conscious of this impossibility. The (unbounded) system is closed but will not end as it hollows itself out in which what is exterior or other is traced within, lurking beneath the surface, and what is within opens itself up to risk and exposure to an unknown as if its ground is abyssal. The so-called radicalism of deconstruction justifies itself without naively resuming the project of metaphysics (to discover truth as an object of any kind) and its history of concepts and notions or simply announcing that we can depart human language and the world's origin like a space traveller who can leave the earth and suddenly inhabit the planet of a whole new alien species. (If truly 'alien,' then such a species would lack human speech and writing). Derrida is caught within an exergue, which can never happen, between the inscription that is the domination of the sign and the space between it and its border that should suggest the origin and place of the inscription's birth. In this intermundia, deconstruction must live and die.

In order to aufheben (i.e. in reference to Hegel's notion of supersession, raising and lifting a ban) Derrida's intermundia, I will begin with a brief musing in and through the Prologue of the Gospel of John. I will interlace such a reading with

---

milieu within which they produce their operation. I would like to suggest above all that, however fecund and necessary the undertaking might be, and even if, given the most favorable hypothesis, it did overcome all technical and epistemological obstacles as well as all the theological and metaphysical impediments that have limited it hitherto, such a science of writing runs the risk of never being established as such and with that name. Of never being able to define the unity of its project or its object. Of not being able either to write its discourse or method or to describe the limits of its field. For essential reasons: the unity of all that allows itself to be attempted today through the most diverse concepts of science and of writing, is, in principle, more or less covertly yet always, determined by an historical-metaphysical epoch of which we merely glimpse the *closure*. I do not say *end*. The idea of science and the idea of writing—therefore also of the science of writing—is meaningful for us only in terms of an origin and within a world to which a certain concept of the sign (later I shall call it *the* concept of the sign) and a certain concept of the relationships between speech and writing, have *already* been assigned. A most determined relationship, in spite of its privilege, its necessity, and the field of vision that it has controlled for a few millennia, especially in the West, to the point of being now able to produce its own dislocation and itself proclaim its limits" (1974, p. 4).

attempts to respond to questions opened up by Heidegger's 1924 lecture while unfolding a creative vision of what the missing Division III of *Being and Time* could look like if it were not to repeat anything said in Division II of *Being and Time*: namely 'ecstatic, primordial, finite, unified, authentic time and the temporalizing of time' in contrast to the inauthentic sense of an infinite, linear flow of now-points ('present as now, past as no longer now and future as yet to be now'), 'within-time-ness,' time as presence, and Hegel's attempt to link time and Spirit (at least according to Heidegger's interpretation of Hegel). The content has to be new, the clearing is made possible through an appropriation of the 1924 lecture, what is being destroyed ontologically are the two divisions of *Being and Time*, and what is being exposed for its futility and ephemeral nature is Derrida's deconstruction.

Deconstruction never had its day, and that is what it would probably prefer, i.e. closure and not end. Undecidability is transvaluated within deferral so that no end as presence or no finality, security or appearance of concepts becomes its other: that is an occluded, endless value-chain even though no sign of eternity and all relations and distinctions with time (time vs. eternity, time as eternity, eternity as the negation of time and vice versa) is ever insinuated. Endlessness is not a spatial analogue to metaphysical eternity, and eternity is subjected to an indescribable finitude or impossibility to identify any meaning for itself. For deconstruction, its time can never come, which in deference to Heidegger's destruction of metaphysics, time is never a thing that can come or go, and Being (Dasein as the 'relation of Being as transcendence')[10] is never anything like beings within time. Both thinkers strain the ability of mortal beings to reckon the very mystery of their being in terms of the mystery of time/timing and vice-versa. But no end to this deferential thinking of deferral does not necessarily mean defaulting to an endless futility. For this overcoming, we must turn to the Prologue and infiltrate it with the full force of the 1924 lecture.

2   The New Testament Greek: Prologue to the Gospel of John[11]

For Derrida, the Word/Logos is precisely the foundation of the historico-metaphysical concept, which has dominated and suppressed writing from time immemorial. Writing was always forced to become phoneticized in its history, and the barren assumption is that it, writing, is simply an inferior representation of lived speech whose full presence occurs between living human subjects. Real sounds can always be heard by living ears, whereas written texts are merely soundless echoes from a dead source that can never be identified as an original sound from an original

---

[10] Phrase that links Being to transcendence is taken from the introduction to *Being and Time*. See Heidegger (1962, p. 62).

[11] I am referring to the Greek text of the Prologue to the Gospel of John in *The New GREEK_ENGLISH Interlinear New Testament* (1990).

voice. Hence writing is always about deferring the presence of its voice and its origin and what appears as text is really traces of traces, which has no origin or non-
origin, a beginning or an eternity that would erase any site in which either an origin
or end would sit. There is *neither* an origin or end *nor* non-origin or non-end to any
written text, which is replete with infinite possibilities of meaning. The paradox of
this is that the text is still finite: it is not omnipresent or omnitemporal as if the
unbounded, expanding physical universe and everything in it was just one big open
book. Yet what if the Prologue to the *Gospel of John* completely overruns these
Derridean assumptions about speech and writing, about the subjugation of the latter
by the former, and the alleged, delusional attempts by metaphysics and its history to
locate the origin of the truth in the logos and then have science take over the project
to dominate all of humanity? Heidegger's "The Concept of Time" can be retraced
within the Gospel to reveal that time is not of three axes in a single dimension ('past
as no longer now, present as now, and future as yet to be now'). Furthermore, the
Word/Logos transcends Derrida's idea of the specious nature of the traditional distinction of speech and writing (the marginalization and secondary quality of writing
in the history of metaphysics which prioritizes lived presence), whereby closure and
end are completely engulfed in something entirely Other. Time is nothing but the
'Who' that is answered when we inquire into the meaning of the very Being of
God.[12]

So let us read the Gospel of John. The 'who' of the being described in relational
terms- Word, God, beginning, relationality, existence and subjectification-have to
do with concealment and revelation in which an Event of indescribable complexity
occurs. This is the Event of the Being of Truth itself. In the New Testament Greek,
one can make a distinction between 'in the' beginning and just 'in' beginning. 'In
the beginning' usually connotes a specific moment in time: for example, 'in the
beginning of this story, Tom went to the store.' But if we go with 'in beginning' we
can substitute the point in time with a trace, distended and stretched—by beginning,
by happening, by occurring something else occurs, the occurrence is an effect by a
decision to begin and not that of a cause- or 'by touching the hot pan, my hand is in
pain.' Beginning happens concealing any type of when as in asking 'when did the
story begin?' If anything, the origin withdraws into a void so that the beginning of
any origin is not the origin that is called the beginning, i.e. someone's birthday. With
a decision to begin comes an enormous act of signification; beginning is stretched
within itself to an outer core on one extreme pointing to the unimaginable density of
a motion that does not identify itself and to another outer core that splits apart any
immediate sense of 'beginning and end and everything in between.' Taken as a total
event—a motion and its two poles each split within themselves (the possibility and
impossibility of saying what is beginning, what happens after the beginning, and
what is ending)—is the very being called the 'Word.' The Word is not the beginning,
the Word does not cause the beginning, and the Word is not there in terms of any
kind of presence or absence. Rather, the Word is the event of the motion-the-decision

---

[12] Contrast this statement with the traditional notion that God is an eternal object subject to eternal
laws, which are divined by the eternal and universal qualities of Reason.

as 'in beginning', in happening, everything else happens. Put another way, the Word is not in the beginning but rather the Word is 'in beginning' itself; what the latter is remains to be explicated. The Word is the Event of a momentous decision.

This Word is a strange being, and the next line of the Gospel says that this Word-Being-Motion-Decision was towards or with God. So the next line in Koine Greek raises the issue of a *relation*—being towards God means facing and heading towards Him but also an intimate relation- the Word is with or Being-with God in which what is prior is the notion of relationality of being-with and of sharing. Something that moves is towards God, and not just moving along space like a dot on a line towards a goal. Motion itself 'is' towards something. Moving is an occurrence that is bearing on God, an uncanny movement itself which is not happening along a predetermined sense of time or motion in geometric space. First the Word was an Event of Motion, and now the Word is of Relation, which means motion and relation partake of some deeper event. The Word is motion or 'in beginning' something decides to take place, the exteriorization of this motion is not caught between two poles, like a birth date and a death event. But the very being of this motion is also a being-with or sharing and hence a partaking of one with another. If that is the case, then *neither* an origin or non-origin *nor* an end or non-end suffice to describe the being of motion (the Word) and the sheltering, dwelling and communing that it has with the Being called 'God' (Theos). Logos and Theos have to do with motion as a relational occurrence. And if the history of metaphysics only has a recourse to ideas of origin and end and non-origin and non-end, and anything Other to those four terms, then obviously we cannot have recourse to those intuitive and logical ideas that have been deduced in the history of (human) reason. Now comes the hard part.

The relational-motion-event of the decision to occur, the process of sharing with in being with as to not be oneself without an-other, and motion itself towards something other than itself (not just something moving along a line towards a goal) now requires the relation of equality without assuming a simple identity. For example, these predications are too simple—'Word is God or Logos is Theos.' These are empty identities that need to be raised to a higher level of conceptualizing by negating what is concealed within them and un-concealing what should be revealed beyond them. Hence the next question is what is the 'who' of this 'is' that binds Word and God? Who 'is' the Being of the 'is' so to speak so that Logos as Event/Decision/Movement and Theos as Being-with and sharing with oneself as another actually admits to equality so that Event-Motion and Relation-Sharing are 'One.' Neither the non-Christian Pre-Socratics nor the post-Christian Heidegger during and after *Being and Time* can help us with these meditations.[13] To deconstruct these initial propositions requires that we re-inhabit Heidegger's "The Concept of Time" as we respond to Derrida's initial declarations in *Of Grammatology*: the latter dismissed the history of the metaphysical concepts of logos, which presumably includes the theological rendition of Word/Logos in the Gospel of John. Ironically

---

[13] I say this with all due respect to Plato's *Parmenides* and Aristotle's *Metaphysics* both of which are acknowledged with the utmost reverence in Hegel's Preface to the *Phenomenology of Spirit* and Heidegger's Introduction to *Being and Time*.

the early Heidegger meets the Heidegger of *Being and Time* and thereafter and therefore the early to late Derrida in a confrontation-encounter, a genuine philosophical Auseinandersetzung to use a German phrase.[14]

2.1   The Concept of Time by Way of Being and Time and The Phenomenology of Religious Life

> *Being is transcendens pure and simple.* And the transcendence of Dasein's Being is distinctive in that it implies the possibility and necessity of the most *radical individuation.* Every disclosure of Being as the *transcendens* is the *transcendental* knowledge. *Phenomenological truth (disclosedness of Being) is veritas transcendentalis.*[15]
>
> The modern history of religion accomplishes much for phenomenology, if it is subjected to a phenomenological destruction [*Destruktion.*] Only then can the history of religion be considered for phenomenology.[16]

What is at stake here is the question of phenomenological truth for Heidegger. In the first quote-'phenomenological truth' has the 'disclosedness of Being' as its parenthetical shadow identity and that is equated with 'transcendental truth.' But from the second quote, we learn that phenomenology—regardless if one sees it as a method, a mode of research, an epistemological justification for a type of knowledge, an a priori or empirical science, or a theory of consciousness—can consider something like the history of religion. The history of religion has value for phenomenology but only it if is destroyed. Destruction is not negative at all but perhaps even related to some kind of authentic grace encoded with its own unique alterity. We must inquire into the meaning of the history of religion being destroyed so that it can have value for phenomenology. Religious content may have its own independent value for phenomenology and not for itself. And phenomenogical truth as disclosedness of Being is ultimate—it is the transcendental truth. Phenomenological-disclosedness-transcendental occurs in relation to truth, Being and truth. One can say that phenomenon of truth relates to the disclosedness of Being, which by nature is transcendental in that it transcends anything that 'is.' This truth transcends all other truths (empirically derived by human senses or experience about humans or the world), but how it relates to the *truth of transcendence* becomes a question. The fact of the matter is that there is a truth of transcendence: transcendence is true but what it means is obscured in the history of metaphysics and religion. This takes us back to the first quote from *Being and Time* because Being is linked with transcendence. Dasein's Being is unique and 'distinctive' because it 'implies the possibility and necessity of the most radical individuation.' The uniqueness of Dasein's Being assumes the 'possibility and necessity' (strong words by Heidegger) of a most radically irreducible

---

[14] It connotes the idea of a 'dealing, conflict and dispute' all at once. A genuine confrontation and reckoning is an appropriate translation.

[15] Heidegger (1962, p. 62).

[16] Heidegger (2004, p. 56).

and incomparably specific, non-relational, infinitely Other, a borrowing and deep-
ening to a point of singularity in which individuation is a radically cutting off from
anything else including the most unique individuals—living or dead. But this is not
about inflation of a single self or ego. There is no bounded subject, ego, self, soul,
or person in space-time when it comes to fundamental ontology. Being 'is' transcendence, and Dasein's Being is a most 'radical individuation.' Let us bracket off any
immediate sense or intuition of what these statements mean, particularly from a
human perspective.[17] At stake is a primordial relation between the 'who' of transcendence, or transcendence relating to itself as Other, and the relation itself as
Other than any form, kind or category of subjectivity.

This is where we can begin our reading of "The Concept of Time". My hypothesis is that what the disclosedness of Being means is time itself and so phenomenological truth is time itself. Truth is time, but what that means no recorded (written)
material has ever shown in a conclusive manner. Thus we need to provide evidence
to establish the credibility for formulating this rather grandiose hypothesis. And
writing lacks living presence, according to the dominant history of metaphysics that
prioritizes speech over writing, and hence any present or origin within writing is
subjected to deferral and internal differentiation for deconstruction. But one does
not have to operate by this register. Dasein's Being as the 'possibility and necessity
of the most radical individuation' is that the transcendental truth, which is the relation of Dasein's Being as a relation of Being as transcendence, and this relation is
time. Time indeed is a relation but not between two poles (say a beginning or end or
no beginning and no end, namely infinite linear flow). This whole construction of
the non-Euclidean relation remains to be explicated in systematic and deductive
moves. By time I do not mean anything in the history of (human) intuitions, concepts, records, symbols (i.e. lines, circles), or experiences of time. Rather, I speak of
the very Being of God's Time in which God is constructed exclusively from the
'data'—the written word—available in the Hebrew Bible and the New Testament
Greek: this is the Word that for Derrida has been subdued by living speech and its
priority of the metaphysics of presence. What has closed but not ended has to be
overcome, and this is/remains undecided, unaccomplished and undesired by
Derridean deconstruction and its contemporaries. Derridean deconstruction must be
destroyed.

Let us look at the constructions in the two quoted passages more carefully as we
begin to imagine certain relations. We can ask ourselves—what being would say
something like "Am I my time?" This is the great question posed at the end of "The
Concept of Time". That 'I am' at all is a sheer mystery, which is the mystery of the
very being that underpins not only the 'I am' (which is no simple object in physical
time and space) announcing itself: Someone can ask- "who are you?" and you say-
"I am the President of the United States." These are false questions and answers

---

[17]This is an allusion to what Heidegger means by inauthentic, average, everyday interpretations
that tend to level-off Dasein's primordial and authentic possibility to be.

when it comes to the meaning of Being in general. Akin to the great encounter between Moses and God in Exodus 3:14, we have in Heidegger's lecture an explicit linkage between the mystery of the being of the 'I am' (since we do not know what that 'is' in advance), the relation between that mystery and question of the meaning of being in general and the meaning of the question in relation to what we think it is posing when it announces the 'question of the meaning of being,' and finally the relation between all of those relations on the one hand the question of time on the other. To that we can add the question of the meaning of time and the meaning of the question, which means the meaning of the one who poses the question- "Am I my time?"

"Am I my time?" The question lingers with us. And by this Heidegger does not mean a subject seeking a predicate as if "I am" is the subject and "my time" is the predicate. My time is not something private: something I do when I am alone or not in my public responsibility as a teacher which is owed to some public or private institution. My time is not something that is concrete or objective like a quantity such as a bushel of rice that I choose to share or not to share with someone. My time is not the transposition of my entire life into a singularly pre-designed frame, which can account empirically for every moment of my life from birth to death, which someone else can then memorialize, i.e. through personal or public history. My time is not analogous to anything else's time say when a fruit is ripe and ready to be plucked for its sensuous consumption. My time is not an internal sense that I have psychologically when I am anxious about a future exam; nor is it an internal organ in my body that initiates the deterioration of all other organs until the body finally collapses and dies. Certainly my time is not that of a seconds, minutes and hours ticking away on my watch, or days and months in the calendar year. My time is not metaphysical or theological—"neither here nor there" or "not of this world" or "my time has not yet come." (Reference to the mystery of the kairological time of Jesus's sayings in the New Testament Gospels.) My time and the time of anything else (cosmos, earth, human history, events, other individuals on earth) are dis-analogous. The relation between this "my time" and the "I am" of course has correlates in both the God of the Hebrew Bible (Exodus 3:14: "I will become") and Jesus Christ in relation to His Father in the New Testament Greek. However, they are by no means the same thing. But if we move into *The Phenomenology of Religious Life* and *Being and Time* and the quotes just offered, then we create a sort of tension, polarity, and field of resistances that compromise any easy dialectical synthesis when comparing the following items: (A) the resources of the Hebrew Bible and the New Testament Greek with (B) what is being stated about 'destruction' of the history of religion as appropriate for phenomenology to be put into action. Then we can frame a pre-understanding (that is true to the spirit of fundamental ontology) of what later is revealed in *Being and Time* as the link between the following phrases: phenomenological truth, disclosedness of Being, transcendental truth, Being as transcendence, and the uniqueness of Dasein's Being (as a relation of transcendence) as the 'most radical individuation' with regard to time. "Am I my time" has its twin poles in both these moments of *The Phenomenology of Religious Life* and *Being and Time*.[18]

So in conclusion I am not working with theology even though I will appropriate the inscriptive data from the Hebrew Bible and the New Testament Greek. I have been explicit about my creative intention to construct the missing division III independently of any extant hypotheses of a missing text and hence not doing philosophy in the Heideggerean sense of destruction or Derridean sense of deconstruction. And lastly this is not an activation of theology to defend some definable form of faith within Christianity.[19] All we have to go on is the "Am I my time?"

---

[18]Although Heidegger addresses a group of theologians during 1924 lecture he goes to great lengths in the beginning moments to show how he is not doing traditional philosophy even though what he is doing is closer to theology's greatest concerns—namely the mystery of being and time and eternity for God—without subscribing to any religion or faith. And hence he is not doing theology either. What is he up to? Heidegger (1992, pp. 1E–2E) states:

"Philosophy can never be relieved of this perplexity. The theologian, then, is the legitimate expert on time; and if recollection serves us correctly, theology is concerned with time in several respects.

Firstly, theology is concerned with human existence before God. It is concerned with the temporal Being of such existence in relation to eternity. God himself needs no theology; his existence is not grounded through faith.

Secondly, Christian faith is in itself supposed to stand in relation to something that happened in time—at a time, we are told, of which it is said: It was the time 'when time was fulfilled.' (footnote 3- Galatians 4:4. Mark 1:15; also Ephesians 1:9).

The philosopher does not believe. If the philosopher asks about time, then he has resolved *to understand time in terms of time* or in terms of the aei, which looks like eternity but proves to be a mere derivative of being temporal.

The following considerations are not theological. In a theological sense—and you are at liberty to understand it in this way—a consideration of time can only mean making the question concerning eternity more difficult, preparing it in the correct manner and posing it properly. Nor, however, is the treatise philosophical, in so far as it makes no claim to provide a universally valid, systematic determination of time, a determination which would have to inquire back beyond time into its connection with other categories." At the end of the paragraph that follows this statement Heidegger (1992, p. 3E) concludes his introductory remarks with this statement: "the following reflections have only this much in common with philosophy: the fact that they are not theology." I will not go into this complex passage on how Heidegger weaves back and forth in relating to both philosophy and theology, relating and un-relating them to each other, and not relating his project to either one. What this movement means has everything to do with the stakes of Heidegger's fundamental ontology as whole, which was to appear more fully in *Being and Time*. But in *Being and Time* we have an explicit statement that Heidegger (1962, p. 30) is not doing theology at all. All human sciences (anthropology, psychology, etc.) and even the human science of God, or theology, is ontic in nature. Whereas, he will set up the possibility for an authentic fundamental ontology whose question is the meaning of Being in general. But this negative distancing from theology by Heidegger is not my concern. I am pointing to the possibility of constructing the missing Division III independently of any extant notes of a missing text and not to advance either thinking or scholarship about Heidegger's project (either as a critique or defense of mainstream theology) or to extend Heidegger's project based on some continuity with what Heidegger does offer in the written record before and after *Being and Time*.

[19]That means staying within traditional doctrines of Christology, Trinity and Eschatology, albeit in creative and fascinating ways. Barth, Rahner, Tillich, Pannenberg, Moltmann, N.T. Wright and Zizulous fall under this camp.

and its utter mystery and a metaphysical complexity yet to be explicated given the anchoring poles of *The Phenomenology of Religious Life* and *Being and Time* passages.[20]

References

1987. *The new American Bible*. Canada: World Bible Publishers.

1990. *The New GREEK_ENGLISH Interlinear New Testament*, translation of the *Greek New Testament* United Bible Societies' Fourth, Corrected Edition with the New Revised Standard Version, New Testament. Trans. Robert K. Brown and Philip W. Comfort. ed. J.D. Douglas. Wheaton: Tyndale House Publishers.

Derrida, Jacques. 1974. *Of Grammatology*. Trans. G.C. Spivak. Baltimore: Johns Hopkins University Press.

Hegel, G.W.F. 1977. *Phenomenology of Spirit*. Trans. A.V. Miller. Oxford: Oxford University Press.

Heidegger, Martin. 1962. *Being and Time*. Trans. J. Macquarrie and E. Robinson. New York: Harper & Row.

Heidegger, Martin. 1992. *The Concept of Time*. Trans. W. McNeill. Oxford: Blackwell.

Heidegger, Martin. 2004. *The Phenomenology of Religious Life*. Trans. M. Fritsch and A. Gosetti-Ferencei. Bloomington: Indiana University Press.

---

[20] Some many argue that my endeavor merely repeats great insights in negative theology that descend from the Western medieval tradition of philosophical theologies of time and being in their explorations of the mystery of the Godhead. Careful and extensive study, such as the early work of John Caputo, has tried to explore Heidegger's resonation with such negative theologies. Furthermore, *The Phenomenology of Religious Life* offers several lectures on the mysticism of Eckhart for example. However, I state in my thesis I am not looking to do philosophical theology or use philosophy to explore theological mysteries as confined in the history of scriptural dogmatics of the Hebrew Bible or New Testatment. If that were the case, then the claim of retrieving the tradition to 'go beyond' Heidegger would be specious without first addressing the relationship of Heidegger's philosophy in its entirety with the history of theology and negative theology. But this is not my project, i.e. 'negative theology' or even a 'philosophy of religion.' I am seeking to articulate new speculative-metaphysical categorical distinctions that are irreducible to what is offered in major twentieth century figures of Protestant, Catholic and Orthodox theology (see footnote 19), which of course appropriates and responds to the entire history of the theology. In parallel, I do not want to 'interpret' what is present in the first two divisions of *Being and Time*—Being and beings, Dasein, being-in-the-world, guilt, conscience, care, being-towards-death, resoluteness, ecstatic temporality, etc.—as isolated objects in themselves and everything before and after that is available in Heidegger's corpus, particularly the *Beiträge* (1936) and the 1962 lecture "On Time and Being"

Syntax Is the Metal Itself. Derrida on the Usure of the Metaphor

Mauro Senatore

> *How can we make this sensible except by metaphor? which is here the word usure. In effect, there is no access to the usure of a linguistic phenomenon without giving it some figurative representation. What could be the properly named usure of a word, a statement, a meaning, a text? (Jacques Derrida, "White Mythology")*

Abstract The following pages can be read as a preliminary study on Derrida's thought of the usure. The point of departure is the reading of Levinas' treatment of the spatial metaphor (such as "the Most-High" and "absolute exteriority") that Derrida mobilizes in "Violence and Metaphysics. An Essay on the Thought of Emmanuel Levinas" (1964). What is at stake in this reading, I suggest, is not only the interpretation of Levinas' metaphysics but also the formulation of another thought of the metaphor (of the metaphoricity of the metaphor) as the originary spatialization and inscription of language (and, as we shall see, of life in general). In tracing the metaphor of the usure across Derrida's early writings, I aim to shed light on a path of thought that goes from the reading of Levinas' spatial metaphors to that of Freud's scene of writing.

Keywords Metaphor • Space • Derrida • Levinas • Inscription

The following pages can be read as a preliminary study on Derrida's thought of the usure. The point of departure is the reading of Levinas' treatment of the spatial metaphor (such as "the Most-High" and "absolute exteriority") that Derrida mobilizes in "Violence and Metaphysics. An Essay on the Thought of Emmanuel Levinas" (1964). What is at stake in this reading, I suggest, is not only the interpretation of Levinas' metaphysics but also the formulation of another thought of the metaphor (of the metaphoricity of the metaphor) as the originary spatialization and

M. Senatore (✉)
Instituto de Humanidades, Universidad Diego Portales, Santiago, Chile
e-mail: mauro.senatore0@gmail.com

© Springer International Publishing Switzerland 2016   163
L. Foran, R. Uljée (eds.), *Heidegger, Levinas, Derrida: The Question of Difference*, Contributions To Phenomenology 86,
DOI 10.1007/978-3-319-39232-5_12

inscription of language (and, as we shall see, of life in general). In tracing out the metaphor of the usure across Derrida's early writings I aim to shed light on a path of thought that goes from the reading of Levinas' spatial metaphors to that of Freud's scene of writing.[1]

1 Inhabiting the Metaphor in Ruins

When commenting on the opening section of Levinas' *Totality and Infinity* (1961), in "Violence and Metaphysics" Part II, Derrida lingers on the expression "the Most-High [*le très-haut*]" that, for Levinas, stands for the dimension of the height opened up by the metaphysical desire and, thus, for the Invisible (namely, the absolutely other).[2] On Derrida's reading, the expression betrays a specific treatment of the metaphor, which consists in obliterating its originary spatiality through the recourse to the superlative. He writes:

> Inaccessible, the invisible is the most high. This violence and metaphysics expression—perhaps inhabited by the Platonic resonances Levinas evokes, but more so by others more readily recognizable—tears apart, by the superlative excess, the spatial literality of the metaphor. No matter how high it is, height is always accessible; the most high, however, is higher than height. No addition of more height will ever measure it. It does not belong to space, is not of this world. But what necessity compels this inscription of language in space at the very moment when it exceeds space? And if the pole of metaphysical transcendence is a spatial non-height, what, in the last analysis, legitimates the expression of trans-ascendance, borrowed from Jean Wahl? (Derrida 1978, 115–116)

Derrida wonders why Levinas resorts to a spatial metaphor that he must obliter-ate in order to account for a height that belongs neither to space nor to the world; why Levinas inscribes language into space (or, more simply, writes) if he refers to what exceeds space (and, thus, the spatialization of language, namely, writing). In reading the Most-High as a spatial non-height, Derrida seems to understand this expression as the double operation of reverting to a spatial metaphor (to inscribe language into space or to write) and, at the same time, of negating this spatiality (or inscription). In other words, this expression accounts for the excess of space by obliterating or negating the spatiality that it bears within itself. Derrida suggests that a certain necessity has imposed itself on Levinas' recourse to a spatial metaphor and, thus, on the spatial inscription of language. It has to do with the fact that the metaphor is originarily spatial and, therefore, that language is originarily inscribed

---

[1] This article is a result of the research project CONICYT/FONDECYT INICIACION n.11140145, hosted by the Instituto de Humanidades, Universidad Diego Portales (Santiago, Chile).

[2] See Levinas 1969, 34–35: "Desire is desire for the absolutely other. [...] A desire without satisfac-tion which, precisely, understands [*entends*] the remoteness, the alterity, and the exteriority of the other. For Desire, this alterity, non-adequate to the idea, has a meaning. It is understood as the alterity of the Other or the Most-High. The very dimension of height is opened up by metaphysical Desire. That this height is no longer the heavens but the Invisible is the very elevation of height and its nobility. To die for the invisible—this is metaphysics."

into space or inscribed tout court (it is writing). Hence, one can account for what exceeds space only by presupposing the spatiality of the metaphor and the inscription of language, and, therefore, as Levinas does, by obliterating or negating these spatiality and inscription. Obliteration and negation are in turn inscriptions (perhaps, inscriptions over inscriptions, overprinting), that require space, take place in the latter and, thus, leave the possibility of more writing open. I propose to understand the evoked necessity as the impossibility of thinking any linguistic sign outside the world qua space of inscription and, then, outside the regulated play of differences and differences of differences among signs.[3] Although here Derrida does not speak of the trace, the irreducible spatiality and inscription of language imply the structure of reference of the trace, "where difference appears as such and thus permits a certain liberty of variations among the full terms" (Derrida 1974, 46–47).

The reading of Levinas' treatment of the spatial metaphor is further developed in the following part of "Violence and Metaphysics", where Derrida comments on Levinas' notion of absolute exteriority, that is, of an outside that does not stand against an inside, yet exceeds space.[4] Derrida finds in the use of the concept of exteriority the already described operation of obliterating and negating the spatiality and thus inscription of language, in order to refer to the excess of space.

> Now not only does *Totality and Infinity*, which is subtitled *Essay on Exteriority*, extensively recur to the notion of exteriority. Levinas also intends to show that *true* exteriority is not spatial, for space is the Site of the Same. Which means that the Site is always a site of the Same. Why is it necessary still to use the word "exteriority" (which, if it has a meaning, if it is not an algebraic *X*, obstinately beckons toward space and light) in order to signify a violence and metaphysics nonspatial relationship? And if every "relationship" is spatial, why is it necessary still to designate as a (nonspatial) "relationship" the respect which absolves the other? Why is it necessary to *obliterate* this notion of exteriority without erasing it, without making it illegible, by stating that its truth is its untruth, that *true* exteriority is not spatial, that is, is not exteriority? That it is necessary to state infinity's *excess* over totality *in* the language of totality; that it is necessary to state the other in the language of the Same; that it is necessary to think *true* exteriority as *nonexteriority*, that is, still by means of the Inside-Outside structure and by spatial metaphor ... (Derrida 1978, 139–140)

Derrida understands Levinas' treatment of exteriority as a certain operation of usure. "…and that it is necessary still to inhabit the metaphor in ruins", he continues, "to dress oneself in tradition's shreds and the devil's patches—all this means, perhaps, that there is no philosophical logos which must not *first* let itself be expatriated into

---

[3] For the elaboration of this impossibility, with reference to Saussure's concept of sign, see Derrida 1974, 44: "The very idea of institution—hence of the arbitrariness of the sign-is unthinkable before the possibility of writing and outside of its horizon. Quite simply, that is, outside of the horizon itself, outside the world as space of inscription, as the opening to the emission and to the spatial *distribution* of signs, to the *regulated play* of their differences, even if they are 'phonic'".

[4] For the use of exteriority, see, for instance, Levinas 1969, 35: "This absolute exteriority of the metaphysical term, the irreducibility of movement to an inward play, to a simple presence of self to self, is, if not demonstrated, claimed by the word transcendent". In the same section, entitled "The Breach of Totality", see also the treatment of the concept of site [*lieu*] (Levinas 1969, 37–38).

the structure Inside-Outside." (Derrida 1978, 140) In remarking the difference between obliteration and erasure, Derrida recalls the irreducibility of the spatial inscription of language. There can only be an obliteration of that inscription, namely, one more inscription, a trace. In other words, erasure demands the space of writing and, thus, is already obliteration. Derrida conceives of the metaphor itself as the originary inscription of language, its spatial and worldly genesis (or birth), and, thus, as the movement and essence of the metaphor in general (namely, the meta-phoricity of the metaphor). More generally, the metaphor qua originary inscription (writing, the trace, etc.) accounts for the minimal structure of any genesis. "Space being the wound and finitude of birth (of *the* birth)" (Derrida 1978, 140), Derrida emphasizes.

At this point, Derrida evokes in an explicit fashion the metaphor of the usure, in order to describe the treatment of the spatial metaphor that is at work in Levinas' use of exteriority. Recalling a tradition that he takes into account later, in the exergue of "White Mythology" (1971), Derrida compares the operation of obliterating and negating the originary inscription of the word to that of consuming the archaic inscription of a coin.

> Therefore, one can, by using them, *use up* tradition's words, rub them like a rusty and deval-ued old coin; one can say that true exteriority is nonexteriority without being interiority, and one can write by crossing out, by crossing out what already has been crossed out: for cross-ing out writes, still draws in space. The syntax of the Site whose archaic description [*inscription*] is not legible *on* the metal of language cannot be erased: it is this metal itself, its too somber solidity and its too shining brilliance. Language, son of earth and sun: writ-ing. (Derrida 1978, 140)

In Derrida's reformulation of the traditional metaphor of the usure, obliterating, negating, crossing out the inscription are still inscribed and, thus, consist in more writing.[5] Therefore the originary metaphor, that permits these operations (and writ-ing in general), is not an inscription among others, that can be erased or made unreadable, but amounts to the very space of writing, to space tout court (to the metal itself, in the case of the coin). Derrida refers to it as to syntax, that is, to the regulated play of differences according to which each inscription does not close upon itself but is, somehow, broken by the space for more inscriptions and thus by the reference to another inscription. It becomes more and more evident that what is at stake in addressing Levinas' use of exteriority is the impossibility of detaching any inscribed element from the space of its inscription (namely, from space) and of taking it as absolute, and, at the same time, the necessity that any attempt to do it solves into more writing. One can find here, for instance, the premises of the law of

---

[5] For a *philosophical* version of this metaphor, see the passage from Nietzsche's *Wortbuch* that is quoted in Derrida 1982, 217: "What then is truth? A mobile army of metaphors, metonymics, anthropomorphisms: in short, a sum of human relations which became poetically and rhetorically intensified, metamorphosed, adorned, and after long usage, seem to a nation fixed, canonic and binding; truths are illusions of which one has forgotten that they *are* illusions; worn out metaphors which have become powerless to affect the senses (*die abgenutzt und sinnlich kraftlos geworden sind*), coins which have their obverse (*Bild*) effaced and now are no longer of account as coins but merely as metal."

remarking that Derrida formalizes in the reading of Mallarmé developed in "The Double Session" (1970).

> One would attempt in vain, in order to wean language from exteriority and interiority, in order to wean language from weaning, to forget the words "inside," "outside," "exterior," "interior," etc., and to banish them [*mettre hors jeu*] by decree; for one would never come across a language without the rupture of space, an aerial or aquatic language in which, moreover, alterity would be lost more surely than ever. For the meanings which radiate from Inside-Outside, from Light-Night, etc., do not only inhabit the proscribed words; they are embedded, in person or vicariously, at the very heart of conceptuality itself. (Derrida 1978, 140)

Putting out of play is still playing, proscribing is still writing. The play is metaphoricity itself, the originary inscription, syntax, the space of writing, space tout court, the metal of the coin, etc. The implications of these remarks for conceptuality itself are enormous: there would be no absolute and self-referential term, inscription, text, that has not already retained the play as such and, thus, has not already referred to another term, inscription, text.

2   The History of the Philosophical Metaphor

In the exergue of "White Mythology" Derrida tracks the metaphor of the usure from the perspective and tradition of the philosophical metaphor, which is seen to admit the usure as its own process and essence. In fact, in declaring his interest "in a certain usure of metaphorical force in philosophical exchange", he points out that "usure does not overtake a tropic energy otherwise destined to remain intact", but "constitutes the very history and structure of the philosophical metaphor" (Derrida 1978, 209).

Derrida takes up Anatole France's *Garden of Epicurus* as an exemplary treatment of this metaphor of the structural usure of the metaphor. We are almost at the end of the work, where Aristos and Polyphilos wage a short dialogue that is subtitled "or the language of metaphysics". What is at stake in this dialogue, that is, the effacement of the sensible figure in the metaphysical concept and, thus, this effacement as the very history of the metaphysical language, is called by Derrida *usure*. Commenting on Polyphilos' reverie, in which the metaphysicians are assimilated to the knife-grinders that efface the inscriptions on the coin, Derrida conceives of the usure in a fashion that resonates with the operation evoked in the reading of Levinas' treatment of exteriority:

> And the history of metaphysical language is said to be confused with the erasure of the efficacity of the sensory figure and of its effigy. The word itself is not pronounced, but one may decipher the double import of usure: erasure by rubbing, exhaustion, crumbling away, certainly; but also the supplementary product of a capital, the exchange which far from losing the original investment would fructify its initial wealth, would increase its return in the

form of revenue, additional interest, linguistic surplus value, the two histories of the meaning of the word remaining indistinguishable. (Derrida 1978, 209).[6]

Derrida identifies Polyphilos' concept of the usure and, thus, of the history of the
philosophical language with an etymologism that stands between the two following
limit points: "the original virtue of the sensory image [the etymon of a primitive
sense], which is deflowered and deteriorated by the history of the concept" (Derrida
1978, 209) and "degradation as the passage from the physical to the metaphysical"
(210). From the perspective of this etymologism, Derrida explains, the usure as the
very process of metaphorization (namely, the metaphoricity of the philosophical
metaphor) consists in the double effacement of the primitive sense (that is displaced
and turned into a metaphor) and of the metaphor itself (that turns into the proper
sense). He explains:

> It [the primitive meaning] becomes a metaphor when philosophical discourse puts it into
> circulation. Simultaneously the first meaning and the first displacement are then forgotten.
> The metaphor is no longer noticed, and it is taken for the proper meaning. A double efface-
> ment. Philosophy would be this process of metaphorization which gets carried away in and
> of itself. (Derrida 1978, 210)

As Derrida points out, "Polyphilos cannot avoid the extreme case [*le passage à la
limite*]" for the process of metaphorization and, thus, for philosophy itself, that consists in "the absolute usure of a sign" (Derrida 1978, 211). It is the case in which the
primitive sense is *negated* and, thus, the negative metaphor is taken as the proper
sense. Is this not what the metaphysician precisely aims to, Derrida suggests, when
choosing "concepts in the negative" [*les concepts en forme negative*], such as "absolute", "in-finite", "in-tangible" (Derrida 1978, 211)?[7] Derrida alludes to
Polyphilos' observation on the disproportion between negative and positive terms in
Hegel's *Phenomenology of Spirit*. Here Polyphilos raises the question of negativity
that Derrida develops later in the text, in his remarks of Hegel's reading of the process of metaphorization.[8] One may wonder whether Levinas' treatment of the spa-

---

[6] For Polyphilos' reverie, see Derrida 1978, 250: "Polyphilos: It was just a reverie. I was thinking
how the Metaphysicians, when they make a language for themselves, are like [image, comparison,
a figure in order to signify figuration] knife-grinders, who instead of knives and scissors, should
put medals and coins to the grindstone to efface the exergue, the value and the head. When they
have worked away till nothing is visible in their crown-pieces, neither King Edward, the Emperor
William, nor the Republic, they say: 'These pieces have nothing either English, German or French
about them; we have freed them from all limits of time and space; they are not worth five shillings
any more; they are of an inestimable value, and their exchange value is extended indefinitely.' They
are right in speaking thus. By this needy knife-grinder's activity words are changed from a physical
to a metaphysical acceptation. It is obvious that they lose in the process; what they gain by it is not
so immediately apparent."

[7] Derrida formalizes the absolute usure of a sign—that stands for metaphorization and philosophy
at their limits—in the following terms: "For in dissolving any finite determination, negative concepts break the tie that binds them to the meaning of any particular being, that is, to the totality of
what is. Thereby they suspend their apparent metaphoricity" (Derrida 1978, 212).

[8] See the following remark between parentheses in Derrida 1978, 211: "Later we will give a better
definition of the problem of negativity, when we can recognize the connivance between the
Hegelian *relève*—the *Aufhebung* which is also the unity of loss and profit—and the philosophical

tial metaphor, as it is discussed in "Violence and Metaphysics", does not fall back into the extreme case of usure, namely, the absolute usure of the sign, represented by negative concepts. However, there Levinas is seen to use (that is, to obliterate, negate, cross out, etc.) not the primitive sense of the metaphor but the very space for any metaphor in general.

Finally, in the conclusive remarks of the exergue, Derrida recalls that "the usure implies a continuist presupposition" insofar as it accounts for the history of the metaphor "not as displacement with breaks, as system, mutations, separations without origin, but rather as a progressive erosion [...] of the primitive meaning" (Derrida 1978, 215).

3 Tearing Apart the Proscription of the Originary Inscription[9]

The thought of the usure of the originary inscription, as it is developed in the reading of Levinas' spatial metaphors, offers the key to decipher the concatenation of violences that Derrida brings to the stage in his reading of Levi-Strauss' account of the war of the proper names among the Nambikwara young girls (*Of Grammatology*, 1967). I propose to find in this concept of the usure, to which Derrida seems to refer only implicitly in the aforementioned reading, the scheme that articulates and ties together one violence with another.

Derrida aims to investigate the conditions of possibility (or the a priori) of a fact concerning the life of the Nambikwara that Levi-Strauss limits himself to registering in the following terms: "they are not allowed ... to use proper names" (Derrida 1974, 109). This fact has to do with writing since, according to Derrida, the latter brings about the originary obliteration of proper names. Therefore, as he puts it, the originary inscription (namely, the regulated play of differences, syntax, the space of writing, space itself, etc.) is, at the same time, an originary obliteration. He observes:

> This fact bears on what we have proposed about the essence or the energy of the *graphein* as the originary effacement of the proper name. From the moment that the proper name is erased in a system, there is writing, there is a "subject" from the moment that this obliteration of the proper is produced, that is to say from the first appearing of the proper and from the first dawn of language. This proposition is universal in essence and can be produced a priori. (Derrida 1974, 108)

The fact of the prohibition is not the obliteration of the proper name that is originary and structural—there would be no name without that obliteration, no name could be detached from it—but a further obliteration, a crossing out of the originary and

---

concept of metaphor." For the reading of Hegel's text on the history of the concept of concept, see Derrida 1978, 224–226.

[9] This section was provoked by the lecture that Rodolphe Gasché dedicated to *Of Grammatology* at the *Collegium Phenomenologicum 2014* (in Città di Castello, Italy), and by the subsequent discussion.

structural crossing out, an inscription over the originary and structural inscription. The prohibition presupposes the originary inscription and obliterates it.

> It does not involve the structural effacement of what we believe to be our proper names; it does not involve the obliteration that, paradoxically, constitutes the originary legibility of the very thing it erases, but of a prohibition heavily superimposed, in certain societies, upon the use of the proper name. (Derrida 1974, 109)

The proscription is derived precisely as it obliterates the originary obliteration and inscription of names. Somehow, it can *only* obliterate the originary inscription. In fact, how would it be possible to proscribe, to obliterate, to inscribe tout court, without the very space of writing (and for more writing) that the originary obliteration and inscription open up? To this extent, Derrida explains that it is because of this obliteration that the proscription, namely, the derived obliteration, is possible. In other words, this so called originary obliteration is the condition of possibility, the a priori, or, rather, the space for any inscription in general.

> Before we consider this, let us note that this prohibition is necessarily derivative with regard to the constitutive erasure of the proper name in what I have called arche-writing, within, that is, the play of difference. It is because the proper names are already no longer proper names, because their production is their obliteration, because the erasure and the imposition of the letter are originary, because they do not supervene upon a proper inscription; it is because the proper name has never been, as the unique appellation reserved for the presence of a unique being, anything but the original myth of a transparent legibility present under the obliteration; it is because the proper name was never possible except through its functioning within a classification and therefore within a system of differences, within a writing retaining the traces of difference, that the interdict was possible, could come in to play… (Derrida 1974, 109)

Because of their irreducible relation, the derived obliteration (or, the proscription) can obliterate but not erase the originary one (the inscription of the name). Proscribing is more writing, which leaves the space of writing intact. Therefore, the possibility of the prohibition bears within itself the possibility of its transgression, the possibility of tearing apart the derived obliteration and to shed light on the originary one. "… and, when the time came, as we shall see,", Derrida continues, "could be transgressed; transgressed, that is to say restored to the obliteration and the non-self-sameness [*non-propriété*] at the origin" (Derrida 1974, 109). At this point, Derrida formalizes the concatenation of the three violences on the basis of the relation among obliterations (or inscriptions). There is a first violence "to be named", which precisely consists in the obliteration and inscription of the name: arche-writing and arche-violence, "inscribing within a difference", "classifying", "suspending the vocative absolute". As pointed out above, this writing/violence is what permits a second violence, which amounts to the obliteration and proscription of the originary obliteration and inscription and, thus, of the arche-violence. Indeed, Derrida recalls that the first violence is "forbidden and therefore confirmed by a second violence […] prescribing the concealment of writing and the effacement and obliteration of the so-called proper name which was already dividing the proper". In this concatenation, the third violence represents a purely "empirical possibility", to the extent that the derived obliteration and violence can neither erase the originary obliteration and violence nor make them unreadable. They can only proscribe and hide them, that is, prescribe their erasure or unreadability. To this extent, the possibility remains open—and this possibility represents precisely arche-violence and arche-writing—that a third violence comes about, "which consists of revealing by effraction the so-called proper name, the originary violence which has severed the proper from its property and its self-sameness [*propriété*]" (Derrida 1974, 112).

4   The Space That Writing Has Always Claimed for Itself

The thought of the usure of the metaphoricity and inscription of language, which I have attempted to take into account throughout my reading, asks us to imagine a writing surface, namely, the metal of a coin, in which "a perpetually available innocence" and "an infinite reserve of traces" are reconciled (Derrida 1978, 280). But these are the constitutive requisites of memory as they are laid out by Freud in his *Project* (1895) and, finally, are found satisfied in the writing machine described in the *Note on the Mystic Pad* (1925). Derrida recalls them in the last part of the essay "Freud and the Scene of Writing" (1966), in which he comments on Freud's later text. He observes that the aim of the *Note* is describing the writing surface and, therefore, the concept of space that allow Freud to think the work of memory. Here I can only limit myself to advancing the following hypothesis: the syntax that Derrida conceived of as the metal of the coin has already responded to the specific task announced in the following passage from "Freud and the Scene of Writing", the task of bringing to light what has always been the space of writing. Derrida writes:

> Freud's theme here is not the absence of memory or the primal and normal finitude of the powers of memory; even less is it the structure of the temporalization which grounds that finitude, or this structure's essential relation to censorship and repression; nor is it the possibility and the necessity of the *Ergänzung*, the *hypomnemic supplement* which the psychical must project "into the world"; nor is it that which is called for, as concerns the nature of the psyche, in order for this supplementation to be possible. At first, it is simply a question of considering the conditions which customary writing surfaces impose on the operation of mnemic supplementation. Those conditions fail to satisfy the double requirement defined since the *Project:* a potential for indefinite preservation and an unlimited capacity for reception. A sheet of paper preserves indefinitely but is quickly saturated. A slate, whose virginity may always be reconstituted by erasing the imprints on it, does not conserve its traces. All the classical writing surfaces offer only one of the two advantages and always present the complementary difficulty. Such is the *res extensa* and the intelligible surface of classical writing apparatuses. In the processes which they substitute for our memory, an unlimited receptive capacity and a retention of permanent traces seem to be mutually exclusive" (XIX, 227). Their extension belongs to classical geometry and is intelligible in its terms as pure exterior without relation to itself. A different writing space must be found, *a space which writing has always claimed for itself* [my emphasis]. (Derrida 1978, 279–280)

References

Derrida, Jacques. 1974. *Of Grammatology*. Trans. G.C. Spivak. Baltimore: The John Hopkins University Press.

Derrida, Jacques. 1978. *Writing and Difference*. Trans. A. Bass. London: Routledge and Keagan Paul Ltd.

Derrida, Jacques. 1982. *Margins of Philosophy*. Trans. A. Bass. Brighton: The Harvester Press.

Levinas, Emmanuel. 1969. *Totality and Infinity*. Trans. A. Lingis. The Hague: Martinus Nijhoff Publisher.

Between the Singular and the Proper: On Deconstructive Personhood

Simon Skempton

Abstract The notion of personhood initially appears to be something that is put into question by Derridean deconstruction. This is due to this notion implying the self-presence of an autonomous consciousness and the narcissism of an exclusionary qualitative identity. Yet Derrida's later works emphasize the connection between deconstructive difference and the concept of singularity, a singularity which Derrida associates with the "who" of personhood as opposed to the generic "what". This article advocates a rethinking of personhood as itself a deconstructive dislocation of the realm of presence and identity. Proto-deconstructive conceptions of personhood that are enlisted to support this rethinking include Hegel's notion of the subject as the 'disparity of substance with itself', Heidegger's notion of the transcendent finitude of being 'held out into the nothing' as a precondition of personhood, and Levinas's avowedly personalist notion of the singular other that transcends and 'undoes' its phenomenal presentation.

Keywords Derrida • Hegel • Heidegger • Levinas • Personhood • Singularity

The phrase 'deconstructive personhood' presents a jarring juxtaposition of incongruous terms. There once was a time in which a metaphysically-tainted term like 'personhood' might well have found itself preceded by the aggressive gerund 'deconstructing', promising that personhood was to be submitted to deconstruction. In more recent times, Derrida reception has responded to the dead-end of deconstruction by making of it an affirmative adjective, more often than not prefixed by 'post', as in 'post-deconstructive subjectivity' or 'post-deconstructive realism', implying the reconstruction of an old conception in the light of its deconstruction. However, the concern here is with an understanding of personhood that would itself be deconstructive, a personhood that manifests itself as a dismantling from within of the proper identity in which it is presented.

S. Skempton (✉)
National Research University – Higher School of Economics, Moscow, Russia
e-mail: simonskempton@gmail.com

© Springer International Publishing Switzerland 2016
L. Foran, R. Uljée (eds.), *Heidegger, Levinas, Derrida: The Question of Difference*, Contributions To Phenomenology 86,
DOI 10.1007/978-3-319-39232-5_13

An understanding of personhood as the unity of consciousness of a Cartesian subject is one of the principal targets of Derridean deconstructive critique. It is to be argued here that Derrida's elaboration of the theme of singularity opens up the possibility for a re-conceptualization of personhood, not as something to be submitted to deconstruction, but as itself deconstructive. This argument will involve placing Derrida within a tradition of thinkers, including ones as diverse as Hegel, Heidegger, and Levinas, who, despite their considerable differences, share a concern with the non-objectifiability of personhood into a present and proper identity.

1 The Singular as the Dislocation of the Proper

Derridean deconstruction is pitched against so-called 'metaphysical' notions of 'presence' and 'the proper', notions that underlie a traditional 'humanist' understanding of personhood as involving an 'autonomous' and unified consciousness. While the 'metaphysics of presence', the understanding of being on the basis of entities that are present, supposedly goes back to Plato, the 'metaphysics of the proper', the interiorized self-presence of an uncontaminated identity, allegedly goes back to the Cartesian internalizing inflection of the 'metaphysics of presence' in the form of the inauguration of the philosophy of the modern subject. For Derrida, Husserl's philosophy of phenomenological consciousness provides one of the most powerful exemplifications of this modern Cartesian tendency in which the 'metaphysics of presence' manifests itself as the 'metaphysics' of the presence to itself of a proper subjectivity. In *Voice and Phenomenon*, Derrida characterizes the Husserlian conception of consciousness as a case of 'hearing-oneself-speak [*s'entendre parler*]', a kind of internal monologue that involves 'an auto-affection of an absolutely unique type' in which the speaker and the hearer are immediately identical (Derrida 2011: 67). Immanently utilizing the conceptual resources provided by Husserl's text, Derrida argues that this supposed immediacy and unity of consciousness is actually marked by temporal mediations and disunifying differentiations. The 'living present' of consciousness may be put forward as an immediate and given unity, but it is in fact the effect of an interplay of perception, repetition, retention, and protention, of traces referring to other traces in a process that never comes to rest in a moment of presence. The unity of consciousness, and thus of personhood conceived on this basis, is merely an illusory effect of this interplay of unconscious and impersonal marks and traces, an epiphenomenal effacement of non-phenomenal processes.

While the earlier works of Derrida suggest that the proprietorial self-presence underlying a certain traditional conception of personhood is an illusory effect and effacement of the impersonal movement of *différance* and the trace, his later works display a concern with what he calls 'singularity', an irreplaceable uniqueness often associated with personhood in the form of a 'who-ness' irreducible to 'what-ness'. According to Derrida, the 'singular "who"' is irreducible to the 'general "what"' (Derrida 2001: 41). It must be noted here that personhood as singularity is very different, even antithetical, to personhood conceived in terms of the egological self-presence of an 'autonomous' consciousness. The quality of being a 'what' is general, because it is the quality of being an assemblage of qualities, attributes and identifications that are far from unique, being 'universals' that are shared by numerous entities. For this reason, the singular 'who' that is not a general 'what' is utterly empty in a qualitative sense. This is an undetermined, non-conceptualizable singularity, which can only be referred to indexically, by pronouns or the meaninglessness of a proper name. It is what the followers of Duns Scotus would call a haecceity, a contentless non-qualitative thisness. This concurs with a feature of the notion of the personal contained in the term 'personal identity' as used in analytic philosophy of mind. This feature is the fact that 'personal identity' refers to a merely numerical identity and not to a qualitative identity. In this sense, numerical identity refers to the idea that someone is this person and not another, whereas qualitative identity refers to the characteristics attributed to a person, and not to the person's personhood itself. There is a difference then between personal identity *qua* singularity and qualitative social identity *qua* 'the proper' (to use Derrida's preferred term). It is the latter kind of identity which embodies the identitarian thinking critically targeted by deconstruction.

Singularity is always other to any qualitative identification, hence its proximity to the Derridean notion of *différance*, the endless differentiating process that constitutes determinate identity while simultaneously undermining it, exposing it to a non-identity that is essential to its very constitution as an identity. Singular personhood evades and exceeds its qualitative phenomenal presentation, any attempt at conceptually grasping it. Thus personhood as uniqueness infinitely differs from its presentation as a 'personality', a personality that is always an exemplification of a generic 'personality-type'. Personality, in this sense, is a mask, an objectification that effaces singular personhood. As personhood is a singular indeterminacy irreducible to the determinations of personality, it is the locus of determinability or possibility. Richard Kearney describes unique personhood (which he, somewhat obtusely, calls '*persona*') as an 'aura of "possibility" which eludes but informs a person's actual presence' (Kearney 2001: 10), and contrasts it with personality (which he refers to by the word 'person'), which is a 'token of sameness… comparable in the order of like-with-like' (Kearney 2001: 14).

Singularity exceeds and dislocates the proper identity in which it is presented. It manifests itself within the proper as excess and dislocation, as that which within the proper prevents it from forming a fully coherent totality. Unique personhood transcends and disrupts the presence of a unified and coherent personality.

2 The Disparity of Substance to Itself

The notion of personhood as involving the self-determinability of a free subjectivity which disrupts its presentation as an objectified identity ultimately stems from German Idealism. According to Hegel, the occurrence of such subjectivity is an immanent irruption within objective substance. In the *Phenomenology of Spirit*, Hegel argues that the personal 'subject' is characterized by the negativity that is defined as 'the disparity of substance to itself' (Hegel 1977: 21). The non-pre-givenness and self-positing determinability that characterize the subjectivity at the basis of personhood occur as a productive negativity that prevents the givenness and qualitative identity of a substantial thing from cohering as a static unity. Personhood is the immanent self-dislocation of thinghood, and in this manner it transcends the given or the merely natural. The merely natural, when animated by the restless negativity of the subject, becomes what Hegel calls 'living Substance'. He writes (1977: 10): '[This] living Substance is being which is in truth *Subject*, or, what is the same, is in truth actual only in so far as it is the movement of positing itself, or is the mediation of its self-othering with itself. This Substance is, as Subject, pure, *simple negativity*'. The undetermined subject is the negating of all determinations. This negativity that 'constitutes' the subject is the precondition of the freedom and self-determination of personhood. The link between negativity, subjectivity, and person-hood is made clear in the *Science of Logic*, where Hegel (1989: 835–836) writes: '[T]he negative of the negative... [is] the *innermost, most objective moment* of life and spirit, through which a *subject*, a *person*, a *free being*, exists. ... [A]s absolute negativity the negative moment of absolute mediation is the unity which is subjectivity'. The paradox of this conception of personhood is that the negativity that dissolves all determinations nevertheless *is*, existing as an absolute qualitative identity which dissolves all qualitative identifications.

Thus the Hegelian subject's very lack of qualitative determination is the precondition of its absolute determination, the qualitative emptiness of its singular numerical identity. For Hegel, the evasion and transcendence of qualitative determination is the precondition not only of the subject's irreducible singularity, but also of its genuine universality. The latter is the negative universality that evades any particularization into a determinate qualitative content. Singularity is similarly evasive, as its qualification would submit it to a generalized typological classification that would reduce singularity to generality. As they both overcome qualitative particularity, singularity and universality are two sides of the same coin of the contentless negativity of the subject. Hegel (1989: 583) writes:

> [T]he *I* is... pure self-related unity... only as making abstraction from all determinateness and content and withdrawing into the freedom of unrestricted equality with itself. As such it is *universality*; a unity that is unity with itself only through its *negative* attitude... [T]he *I* as self-related negativity is no less immediately *singularity* [Einzelheit] or is *absolutely determined*... This absolute *universality* which is also immediately an absolute *singularization* [Vereinzelung]... constitutes the nature of the *I*[.][1]

The Hegelian conception of the freedom of personhood is that it rests on the subject's self-othering elusion of any identification or determination. This othering is, in its empty numerical identity, singularity, singularity as the evasion of being reduced to a typological qualitative determination. It is simultaneously universality, universality as the evasion of being defined by, or restricted to, any particular

---

[1] Translation modified.

qualitative determination or identity. It is this negativity and elusiveness that distinguishes personhood from the pre-given positivity and determinacy of thinghood.

The Hegelian subject should not then be confused with the so-called 'metaphysical' notion of the subject as a self-present substantiality. This goes against Derrida's claim, in *Of Grammatology* (1976: 68–69), that the philosophical notion of the subject has always, at least since Descartes, referred to the interiority and self-presence of a substantial exclusionary qualitative identity. Such an exclusionary egological identity, which Derrida refers to by the term 'the proper [*le propre*]', is actually an objectification and reification of what Hegel means by the 'subject', the subject as the negativity within substance that disables its self-identity. The subject as pure negative activity is very different from the notion of the subject as a substantial self-thing. Jean-Luc Nancy (2002: 5) argues that the Hegelian subject should not be confused with the substantial interiority of an ego. He writes: 'The Hegelian *subject* is not to be confused with … subjectivity as the exclusive interiority of a personality… It is, to the contrary, … what… dissolves all substance – every instance already given, supposed first or last, founding or final, capable of coming to rest in itself'. Rather than exemplifying 'the proper', Hegel's subject defies and undermines it.

Derrida's understanding of what the term 'subject' has traditionally meant derives from Heidegger, who similarly assumes that the term has always, since Descartes, referred to the reduction of human existence [*Dasein*] to a present-at-hand [*vorhanden*] object. Such a subject is the Cartesian subject of contemplation who observes present-at-hand objects that present themselves to its consciousness. Being a substantial 'thinking thing [*res cogitans*]', the Cartesian subject is itself a present-at-hand object. It is thus an inappropriate objectification of *Dasein*, an entity which cannot be rendered present-at-hand without ceasing to be what it is. The Hegelian conception of the subject as the practical negativity of self-determination and self-positing has more in common with Heidegger's notion of non-objectifiable *Dasein* than it has with Descartes' substantial thinking thing.

3   Ownmost Nullity

Heidegger's notion of *Dasein*, as elaborated in *Being and Time*, is an attempt at conceiving of authentic personhood in terms of the radical singularity of being. He explicitly identifies being with singularity in his posthumously published book *Mindfulness*. There he writes: 'Being's singularity and uniqueness are not qualities attributed to being. … Rather, being itself is uniqueness, is singularity' (Heidegger 2006: 108). *Dasein* has a unique relationship with uniqueness, because *Dasein* is that entity to whom being is an issue (Heidegger 1962: 32). *Dasein* is confronted by being through the lived experience of its own finitude, the possibility and ultimate inevitability of non-being. This is its 'being-towards-death', the mode of existence it enters into when it ceases to be lost in the everyday anonymous sociality of the realm of 'anyone [*das Man*]'. 'Being-towards-death' is a radical singularization, as death is inalienable, 'in each case mine' (Heidegger 1962: 284). Only the singular individual dies; the social realm in which it participates in its 'inauthentic' every-dayness does not die.

Heidegger's use of the term 'authenticity [*Eigentlichkeit*]' to refer to this singularization implies that he conflates the singular and the proper. However, the authentic or the proper in question here is not the qualitative identity that can always be submitted to a generalizing typology. For Heidegger, what is most one's own is not a set of gathered together identifying properties, but the qualityless emptiness of one's sheer being. Being as such is empty because it is not an entity that *is*; it is the is-ness itself. One's own being is revealed to oneself through one's lived finitude, one's confrontation with one's ultimate non-being, one's death. Someone's rich qualitative social identity is inauthentic, not her own, not what makes her irreducibly unique. Heideggerian ownness, or 'authenticity', is concerned with singularity rather than identity. What is most one's own is the emptiness of one's sheer being faced with ultimate death, what Heidegger (1962: 379) calls one's 'ownmost nullity'.

This awareness of death enables *Dasein* to transcend the realm of entities which *are*, and to be concerned with *being* as such, *being* which is in each case singular. In his article 'What is Metaphysics?' Heidegger (1993: 105) describes *Dasein*'s finitude, its 'being-towards-death', as a life 'held out into the nothing'. *Dasein*'s concern with its own nothingness is a precondition of its ability to transcend the ontical realm of given entities, and to apprehend the ontological realm of pure being. This is its ability to transcend the naturalistic realm of things that *are*, that are available to scientific objectification. Heidegger (1993: 103) relates nothingness to the essential freedom of personhood when he writes: 'Without the original revelation of the nothing, no selfhood and no freedom.' The freedom of personhood can only occur if the universe is not reducible to the ontical positivity and immanence of the totality of substance. The determinism of the latter is not only a characteristic of the traditional pre-Critical metaphysics of substance, but also of a scientific worldview that reduces the world to the 'what' of 'what is', ignoring the 'is' itself. This ignoring is an ignorance of the difference between entities that *are* and being as such, what Heidegger calls the 'ontico-ontological difference'. Ontological being transcends ontical entities-that-are in that it makes possible such entities and is not itself an entity-that-is. As it is not an entity, being is in ontical terms nothing. In ontological terms this nothing is positivized as '*the* nothing', a negative activity that prevents the objectified ontical totality of what-is from ossifying into an untranscendable absolute. For the Heidegger of 'What is Metaphysics?', it is the nothinging of the nothing that opens up the closure of the ontical realm, of the immanence of what Hegel calls 'substance', to the experience of the being that transcends entities, an opening which alone enables the occurrence of the personhood of *Dasein*.

While Heidegger is at pains to differentiate his phenomenological ontology from Scheler's personalism, and implicitly from Lukács's theory of reification, this is not because *Being and Time* is unconcerned with personhood, but because personhood must be understood in terms of the relationship to being. As with Hegel's notion of the subject as the 'disparity of substance to itself', Heidegger's notion of human existence [*Dasein*] as the entity that transcends the totality of entities through being concerned with its own being and non-being constitutes a conception of personhood as a dislocation from within of the ontical totality of substance.

4   Undoing the Form Presented

As with Heideggerian *Dasein*, Levinas's understanding of human subjectivity is that it involves a breach, dislocation, and transcendence of the totality of what-is. The difference is that Levinasian transcendence does not enable the relationship to one's ownmost being, but to the singularity of the other person. Levinas's notion of the subject is not the ego of an enclosed narcissistic identity repressing all otherness, but is rather itself the breach of totality and the exposure to the other. He writes: 'It is in order that alterity be produced *in being* that … an I is needed. … "Thought" and "interiority" are the very break-up of being and the production… of transcendence' (1969: 39–40). The 'break-up of being' here refers to the rupture from within of the given totality of objectified substance, of what-is, by the irreducible subjectivity of a personhood that lies beyond objecthood.

While the infinite alterity of personhood transcends objecthood, the other nevertheless has to present itself in the objectified form of a phenomenon. Singular alterity can only shine through in this presentation by means of a kind of disassembling from within of the form presented, through some expressive quirk. Levinas (1969: 66) writes: 'Form… alienates the exteriority of the other. … The life of expression consists in undoing the form in which the existent, exposed as a theme, is thereby dissimulated. The face speaks. … He who manifests himself… at each instant undoes the form he presents.' The other person is 'alienated' by the form in which she is presented, reified and objectified as a 'theme [*thème*]', a theoretical object of observation. This form is immanently 'undone' in the face-to-face act of intersubjective communication.

It should be noted that Levinas's use of the term 'alienates' to mean 'objectify' is a usage derived from Hegel's notion of '*Entäußerung*', which means externalization, alienation, and objectification. Levinas claims that theoretical knowledge reifies the other in this manner when he writes: 'Philosophy itself is identified with the substitution of ideas for persons, the theme for the interlocutor' (1969: 88). Such reification is a de-personalization of the other through an effacement of the face-to-face relation inherent to the act of communication. It is only the other as a person that can transcend and rupture the closure of the phenomenal world of objects. This is a world of typological classification and general equivalence that effaces irreducible singularity. Levinas (1969: 73) writes: '[I]t is only man who could be absolutely foreign to me – refractory to every typology, to every genus, to every characterology, to every classification – and consequently the term of a "knowledge" finally penetrating beyond the object.' The person who is effaced by this alienated objectivity is non-phenomenalizable and not an object. The closed totality of the phenomenal realm of objects is immanently disrupted and dislocated through the life of expression of the singularity of the always-other person.

5   Derridean Formalism

Derrida, in his essay on Levinas, 'Violence and Metaphysics', objects to the emphasis on speech and the face-to-face encounter. Despite this, he adheres to what he sees as Levinas's proto-deconstructive critique of the enclosure of logocentric identity when he writes: '[Levinas's] thought summons us to a dislocation of the Greek logos, to a dislocation of our identity, and perhaps of identity in general' (Derrida 1978: 82). Derrida's objection is that the phonocentric privileging of speech coupled with the phenomenological privileging of the face embroils Levinas in a metaphysics of presence. As the closed phenomenal totality is itself based on such a metaphysics, it cannot be effectively breached by the face-to-face relation of the speech act. Rather than on the empirical basis of the face-to-face act of communication, the deconstruction of identity should be approached in a formal manner. Derrida writes:

> [T]he attempt to achieve an opening toward the beyond of philosophical discourse, by means of philosophical discourse, ...cannot possibly succeed *within language*... except by *formally* and *thematically* posing *the question of the relations between belonging and the opening*, the *question of closure*. Formally - ...not in a *logic*... but in an inscribed description, in an inscription of the relations between the philosophical and the nonphilosophical, in a kind of unheard of *graphics*, within which philosophical conceptuality would be no more than a *function* (1978: 110–111).

The most effective way to dislocate and rupture the substantial and phenomenal totality is by means of a deconstructive and grammatological formalism. Here the 'inscribed' and written form would be shown to dislocate and exceed the univocal closure of the form of presence and identity. The movement of *différance*, the 'unheard of graphics' that supposedly places philosophical conceptuality within a field it does not master, can itself be said to be a formalization of the Levinasian transcendence of totality through the encounter with the other person. The deconstructive operation demonstrates that the act of this encounter takes the form of a disruptive and irresolvable aporia within that conceptuality. The question is whether such a deconstructive formalism might itself efface the singularity of personhood.

6   Singularity in the Early Derrida

Throughout his work Derrida refers critically to the notion of 'the subject' as involving the narcissistic enclosure of a proper identity. For example he writes: 'the unity of the proper [is] the nonpollution of the subject absolutely close to himself' (1978: 183). The question of whether singular personhood needs to be conceived in such a manner has been answered in the negative in the foregoing analyses of personhood in Hegel, Heidegger, and Levinas. While Heidegger conceives of singularity in terms, at least rhetorically, of the proper (the 'authentic'), albeit not as a qualitative identity, Levinas conversely conceives of singularity in terms of alterity or otherness. Indeed, Levinas pitches his philosophy against what he regards as Heidegger's ontological egoism. As for Derrida, singularity and the proper are clearly antithetical in his later writings, but this is not always the case in his earlier work. In *Of Grammatology*, singularity is an impossible myth, due to a fundamental duplicability or iterability. It is thus something to be submitted to deconstruction. Derrida (1976: 91) writes:

> A signifier is from the very beginning the possibility of its own repetition… It is the condition of its ideality, what identifies it as a signifier, and makes it function as such, relating it to a signified which, for the same reasons, could never be a "unique and singular reality." From the moment the sign appears, that is to say from the very beginning, there is no chance of encountering anywhere the purity of "reality," "unicity," "singularity."

There can be no singularity, right from the beginning, as soon as there is language and meaning. Signified 'reality' can never be singular 'for the same reasons' that signifiers are repeatable. In his essay 'La Parole Soufflée' Derrida criticizes Artaud's notion of the 'unique'. He describes this concept as that which 'eludes discourse and always will elude it' (1978: 173). Language, being a universalizing medium, cannot capture uniqueness. What Derrida appears to object to in Artaud is the idea that there can even be such a uniqueness, a uniqueness that cannot be talked about. Derrida (1978: 174) writes: '[W]hen we appear to regret a silence or defeat before the unique, it is because we believe in the necessity of reducing the unique, of analyzing it and decomposing it by shattering it even further.' Here Derrida wishes to reduce the irreducibly singular and submit it to deconstruction.

Derrida at this point initially appears to be asserting that the generalizing nature of discourse and language is inescapable and all-powerful, and that there is 'no chance of encountering' anything that is not appropriated or colonized by it. However, the point of Derrida's notion of *différance* is that it undermines discourse, rather than confirming its all-encompassing power. In his essay '*Différance*' (1982: 19) he claims that *différance* produces a 'general economy' that eludes the 'restricted economy' of discourse. In dislocating the closure of discourse, *différance* opens it out onto non-discourse and non-meaning. Within discourse, the radical alterity of irreducible singularity can only take on the form of non-meaning. So for Derrida, singularity cannot be encountered in an absolute outside of the restricted economy of discourse, but only through an immanent dislocation of the functioning of discourse, only through some kind of deconstruction. The deconstructive operation disables the closure of qualitative identity, an identity that eludes singularity and is always universalized, recognizable in a typological classification, equivalent to all cases with the same defining qualities. Singularity is non-identity, the deconstructive dislocation of identity, eluding any universalizing ideality. For Derrida, the unique can only elude discourse within discourse, not as something subsisting in an absolute outside.

7   Singularity in the Later Derrida

A singularity antithetical to the proper becomes a recurrent theme of Derrida's later writings. For example, in *Spectres of Marx* he claims that singularity is always the singularity of the other and that it can only occur as a disruption of systematicity. He writes: 'The lack of a system is not a fault... On the contrary, heterogeneity opens things up, lets itself be opened up by the very effraction of that which unfurls, comes, and remains to come – singularly from the other' (Derrida 1994: 33). This disruption enables the unassimilable singularity of the radically other to intrude within the identity of the present, an 'event' that prevents the reduction of the 'now' to the 'present'. While *différance* is the endless deferral of presence, its disjuncture is the precondition of the event of the 'now'. Derrida writes:

> In the incoercible differ*a*nce the here-now unfurls. Without lateness, without delay, but without presence, it is the precipitation of an absolute singularity, singular because differing, precisely [*justement*], and always other, binding itself to the form of the instant... No differ*a*nce without alterity, no alterity without singularity, no singularity without here-now (1994: 31).

This passage explicitly places singularity at the heart of Derridean concern, almost identifying it with *différance* itself.

The later Derrida links singularity to personhood by contrasting it with what he considers to be the generality of thinghood, referring to the 'singular "who"' and the 'general "what"'. He also argues for the irreducibility of singular personhood to substantial thinghood, to what-is, referring explicitly to 'the irreducibility of *who* to *what*' (Derrida 2001: 41). Here deconstruction becomes a critique of the reification of the personal 'who', signifying the singularity of radical alterity, into the impersonal 'what', signifying an objectified entity taking the form of the substantial identity of presence.

The emergence of personhood in the thought of the later Derrida does not necessarily mean that he abandoned his earlier suspicion of theoretical humanism. The personhood of the 'who' is a singularity irreducible to any general category such as the 'human'. The word 'human' answers the question 'what?' rather than 'who?' The meaninglessness of a proper name is the only answer to the question 'who?' As has been mentioned, irreducible singularity can only take the form of non-meaning within meaning. The term 'human' could be theoretically redefined paradoxically as that being which is in each case irreducibly singular. In that case, the human would be a being whose proper nature is not to have a proper nature.

The indeterminacy of singular personhood means that it involves not being confined to a given qualitative identity. This lack of givenness entails that all the qualities a person has are the result of a process of identification and are open to an endless process of revision and re-identification. Derrida (1998: 28) writes: 'an identity is never given, received, or attained; only the interminable... process of identification endures.' *Différance* and identification both involve an endlessly destructive and productive process that simultaneously makes possible and undermines difference and identity. Singularity evades all forms of proper identity, whether collective or individual. In *The Politics of Friendship* Derrida refers to 'anonymous and irreducible singularities, infinitely different and thereby indifferent to particular difference, to the raging quest for identity' (2005: 106). This indicates that the emphasis on singularity does not entail an individualism in which the subject asserts its own identity. Even individual identity effaces the radical singularity of a personhood which is always other. Rather than referring to an identifiable phenomenal substantiality, singularity is unidentifiable, indeterminate, and meaningless. It occurs as a deconstructive disjuncture within identity, determinacy, and meaning.

8 Deconstructive Anti-naturalism

Derrida's notion of an originary technicity which is effaced by the myth of self-presence may seem to set him apart from Heidegger and Levinas and their attempts at the radicalization of the notion of personhood. His early works involve a critique of phenomenology and its dependence on the notion of presence, a critique that utilizes the resources of anti-humanist structuralism and its functionalist account of the 'death of the subject', in which the subject is reduced to being an effect of differential relations and structural systems.

The debunking of the myths of self-presence and the unity of consciousness at one level appears to ally grammatology with philosophical naturalism. Even arch-naturalist Daniel C. Dennett tacitly concedes the proximity of his own ideas with those of Derrida in his book *Consciousness Explained* (1993: 410–411). Tacitly, because the comparison is actually made to the ideas expressed in a satirical portrayal of a Derridean in a novel by David Lodge. Dennett identifies his idea of the 'Self as the Center of Narrative Gravity' with what is 'apparently a hot theme among the deconstructionists', the theme of the 'self' being a fiction that is really nothing more than a 'subject position' within a 'web of discourses' rather than a unique self-present originator of meaning.

Henry Staten, in his article 'Derrida, Dennett, and the Ethico-Political Project of Naturalism' (2008), makes the comparison between Dennett and Derrida clearer and vigorously advocates the placing of the latter in the pantheon of 'strong naturalists'. Staten pitches what he calls Derrida's 'deconstructive naturalism' (2008: 32) against the 'analytic' brethren of the phenomenologists, the so-called 'weak naturalists', such as Nagel, Searle, and Chalmers, who insist on the irreducibility of the 'first-person ontology' of consciousness. Staten accuses such philosophers of adhering to a 'metaphysical' line of demarcation between consciousness and physicality that Derrida's work problematizes. He writes that 'they still insist on the metaphysical distinctness of consciousness, as though something infinitely momentous depended on continuing to draw this boundary' (Staten 2008: 31).

However, contrary to what Staten suggests, the deconstructive troubling of boundaries does not entail the homogeneous continuum of a naturalism bereft of 'infinitely momentous' ruptures. The deconstructive unraveling of the fixity of instituted and established distinctions does not mean the abolition of distinctiveness as such. Derrida (2008: 30) writes that his work has always involved an 'attention to difference… to heterogeneities and abyssal ruptures as against the homogeneous and the continuous. I have thus never believed in some homogeneous continuity between what calls *itself* man and what *he* calls the animal.' The philosophy of *différance* is itself a philosophy of 'infinitely momentous' discontinuities.

Staten's article also symptomatically ignores the themes of singularity and alterity that permeate Derrida's writings. The structuralism that was employed against phenomenology was itself famously submitted to a deconstruction which undermined the all-encompassing hegemony of linguistic systems. It is the aporetic disjunctures that dislocate these structures that can enable an opening to the asystemic singularity of the other. As early as in the 1968 'Original Discussion of *Différance*', Derrida makes the eminently Levinasian proclamation: '*Différance* marks the separation and the relation to the entirely other' (1988: 85). The singularity of personhood inhabits the space opened up by the disjunctive inadequacy to itself of any configuration of presence. The concern with the irreducibility of the singular 'who' to the general 'what', the irreducibility of personhood to that which can be seen as an object, puts Derrida squarely within the anti-naturalist tradition, alongside Heidegger and Levinas, inaugurated by a German Idealism whose principal theme is the thinking of human freedom on the basis of the non-objectifiability of the person.

9 Conclusion

The thinking of personhood on the basis of the unified consciousness of a Cartesian subject is untenable in the light of Derrida's deconstruction of the metaphysical basis of the self-presence of a proper identity. However, this calls for a rethinking rather than an abandonment of the notion of personhood. This is partly because the idea of the phenomenal constancy of a fixed qualitative identity never sat comfortably with the idea of a person, a free being, anyway. Derrida's association of personhood with a singularity that is not reducible to the generality of thinghood suggests the possibility of a deconstructive reconceptualization of personhood. This singularity occurs as excess and dislocation of the qualitative identity of the proper, suggesting that personhood is itself deconstructive rather than something to be submitted to deconstruction. Such a deconstructive personhood has precedents in the works of Hegel, Heidegger, and Levinas. For Hegel, the 'free being' of personhood occurs as irruptive negativity within the objectivity of thinghood, disabling the latter's qualitative cohesion, a 'disparity of substance to itself'. Such disparity can be observed in Heidegger's understanding of the freedom of authentic *Dasein* as a person's 'ownmost nullity', meaning that a person, through the experience of mortality as the possibility of non-being, is that entity which involves a dislocation, opening-up, and transcendence of the ontical totality of entities (of 'substance') by means of an essential concern with the *being* of entities. For Levinas, such disparity takes the form of the singularity of the other person manifesting itself through the immanent undoing of the objectified phenomenal form in which it is presented. Derrida describes his deconstructive grammatology as a formalization of the Levinasian 'dislocation of... identity'. While grammatological formalism may appear at first glance in Derrida's earlier works to efface both singularity and the personalistic dimension of the dislocation of identity, even in the terms of these works a singularity properly construed, as that which eludes even the most fundamental forms of 'the proper', can constitute the unassimilable remains that can be opened onto through the deconstructive dislocation of the closed system of discourse. This is what makes possible the later Derrida's emphasis on and concern with questions of singularity and alterity, questions framed in personalistic terms when he speaks of the singular 'who' as against the general 'what'. A non-naturalistic interpretation of deconstruction enables personhood to be conceived in terms of the singular dislocation of a proper identity.

References

Dennett, D.C. 1993. *Consciousness explained*. London: Penguin.
Derrida, J. 1976. *Of Grammatology*. Trans. G.C. Spivak. Baltimore: John Hopkins University Press.
Derrida, J. 1978. *Writing and Difference*. Trans. A. Bass. London: Routledge.
Derrida, J. 1982. *Margins of Philosophy*. Trans. A. Bass. Hemel Hempstead: Harvester Wheatsheaf.
Derrida, J. 1988. The original discussion of *Différance* (1968) (trans: Wood, D., Richmond, S., and Bernard, M.). In *Derrida and Différance*, ed. Wood, D. and Bernasconi, R. Evanston: Northwestern University Press.
Derrida, J. 1994. *Specters of Marx: The State of the Debt, the Work of Mourning, and the New International*. Trans. P. Kamuf. London: Routledge.
Derrida, J. 1998. *Monolingualism of the Other: Or, the Prosthesis of Origin*. Trans. P. Mensah. Stanford: Stanford University Press.
Derrida, J. 2001. I have a taste for the secret (trans: Donis, G.). In *A Taste for the Secret*, ed. Derrida, J. and Ferraris, M. Cambridge: Polity.
Derrida, J. 2005. *The Politics of Friendship*. Trans. G. Collins. London: Verso.
Derrida, J. 2008. *The Animal That Therefore I Am*. Trans. D. Wills. New York: Fordham University Press.
Derrida, J. 2011. *Voice and Phenomenon* .Trans. L. Lawlor. Evanston: Northwestern University Press.
Hegel, G.W.F. 1977. *Phenomenology of Spirit*. Trans. A. V. Miller. Oxford: Oxford University Press.
Hegel, G.W.F. 1989. *Science of Logic*. Trans. A.V. Miller. Atlantic Highlands: Humanities Press International.
Heidegger, M. 1962. *Being and Time*. Trans. J. Macquarrie and E. Robinson. Oxford: Blackwell.
Heidegger, M. 1993. What is metaphysics? (trans: Krell, D. F.). In *Basic Writings: Martin Heidegger*, ed. Krell, D.F.. London: Routledge.
Heidegger, M. 2006. *Mindfulness*. Trans. P. Emad and T. Kalary. London: Continuum.
Kearney, R. 2001. *The God who may be: A hermeneutics of religion*. Bloomington: Indiana University Press.

Levinas, E. 1969. *Totality and Infinity: An Essay on Exteriority*. Trans. A. Lingis. Pittsburgh: Duquesne University Press.

Nancy, J.-L. 2002. *Hegel: The Restlessness of the Negative*. Trans. J. Smith and S. Miller. Minneapolis: University of Minnesota Press.

Staten, H. 2008. Derrida, Dennett, and the ethico-political project of naturalism. *Derrida Today* 1(1): 19–41.

Metaphysics and Its Other

Rozemund Uljée

Abstract In this paper I seek to point out both the proximity and distance between Heidegger's and Derrida's understanding of time in their attempts to think difference. By showing how close Différance is to Heidegger's structure of temporality of nearness, I argue how Heidegger's understanding of truth in relation to time leads to an understanding of the history of metaphysics to a structure of possible revelation. However, if we are to understand Derrida's Différance as a perpetually corruptive force, then how is it possible to ever conceive of Offenbarkeit in Being? The focus here will be set on the possibility of revelation as 'event' in Heidegger, and Derrida's counterargument that the event is always impossible.

Keywords Heidegger • Derrida • Difference • Ereignis • Différance • Truth

It is in both Heidegger's and Derrida's thought that we find a most fundamental and profound challenge put to thought, to language and to philosophy itself. This does not imply that their respective philosophical projects share the same orgin nor that they are aimed towards the same goal. It is rather an acknowledgement of a certain belonging in their attempts to think difference. This paper seeks to trace this belonging by investigating Heidegger's later thought as explicated in his lecture 'Zeit und Sein' ['On Time and Being'] and Derrida's essays 'Finis' and 'Foi et savoir'['Faith and Knowledge'] with the aim of shedding light on the problematic of difference in its relation to thinking.

We shall first investigate Heidegger's articulation of the relation between truth and Being as put forward in his lecture 'Zeit und Sein'. This text can be read as an attempt to think the truth of Being without being grounded in terms of beings. It is thus here that we see Heidegger's *Kehre* in a very explicit manner. In *Sein und Zeit* Heidegger engaged in a questioning of Being from the transcendental horizon of time, where the transcendental horizon is the realm in which the determination of Being is projected as presencing, as deployed from the standpoint of Dasein and as such, bringing the truth of beings into view. However, the truth of Being itself remained unthought, unsaid, and thus concealed. As Alfred Guzzoni writes: '[t]he

R. Uljée (✉)
Institute for Philosophy, Universiteit Leiden, Leiden, The Netherlands
e-mail: rozemund@gmail.com

© Springer International Publishing Switzerland 2016
L. Foran, R. Uljée (eds.), *Heidegger, Levinas, Derrida: The Question of Difference*, Contributions To Phenomenology 86,
DOI 10.1007/978-3-319-39232-5_14

fundamental experience of *Being and Time* is thus that of the oblivion of Being.'[1] This however is not an error in the common understanding of the term, since, for Heidegger concealment of Being belongs to the opening up of Being, as I will seek to clarify. In 'Zeit und Sein', Heidegger seeks to point out the truth of Being itself, a truth which undermines the primacy of presence that Heidegger sees affirmed in the history of metaphysics in favour of a thinking that thinks this very history and what remains unthought within it.

Heidegger opens this text with the claim that it is impossible to say that Being *is*, or that time *is*. Both Being and time are not a thing. However, Being understood as presencing is determined by time. Also time, in its passing, remains as time and can as such be named as presence. This means for Heidegger that Being and time are determined by each other, but it is impossible to determine Being as something temporal, and it is equally impossible to determine time as a being. According to Heidegger, it is the task of thinking to think this relation. The first task of this thinking is, finds Heidegger, to reflect on the fact that we do not say 'Being is and time is,' but rather, there is 'there is Being and there is time.'[2] What is needed is an explanation of the 'It' and what is given in the 'There is' or 'It gives,' claims Heidegger, as it will clarify how:

> There is, It gives Being and there is, It gives time. In this giving, it becomes apparent how that giving is to be determined which, as a relation, first holds the two toward each other and brings them into being. Being, by which all beings as such are marked, Being means presencing. Thought with regard to what presences, presencing shows itself as letting-presence. But now we must try to thing this letting presence explicitly insofar presencing is admitted. Letting shows its character in bringing into unconcealment. To let presence means: to unconceal, to bring to openness. In unconcealing prevails a giving, the giving that gives presencing, that is, Being, in letting-presence.[3]

For Heidegger to think Being in an explicit manner means to think that which is shown in letting-presence. From this unconcealing speaks a giving. For Heidegger, Being as a gift allows for presence and as such belongs to unconcealing. Thinking Being in terms of presencing derives from the beginning of the unconcealment of Being as something that can be said and thought. Heidegger claims that: 'ever since the beginning of Western thinking with the Greeks, all saying of "Being" and "Is" is held in remembrance of the determination of Being as presencing which is binding for thinking.'[4]

---

[1] Alfred Guzzoni, 'Summary of a Seminar' on the Lecture 'Time and Being' in *On Time and Being*, p. 29. Also Werner Marx notes that in the early Heidegger: 'The unveiling of Being is always the truth of the Being *of* being.' Werner Marx, *Heidegger and the Tradition*, trans. Theodore Kisiel (Evanston: Northwestern University Press, 1971), p. 125.

[2] 'There is' is a translation from the German 'Es gibt,' which literally means: 'it gives,' but with the idiomatic meaning 'there is.'

[3] ZS, p./trans, p. 5 From the time of *Vom Wesen der Warheit* [*On the Essence of Truth*] (1930), Heidegger describes the rapport between *aletheia* and unconcealment in an explicit manner. A translation of the Greek *aletheia* as unconcealment indicates for Heidegger that the early Greeks experienced presenting as an occurrence of truth in the form of a relationship to concealment.

[4] ZS, p. 10/trans. p. 7.

In the history of metaphysics however, Heidegger suggests that Being as presencing has undergone different transformations in which presencing manifests itself as *the One*, as idea, *ousia*, *energeia*, *Spirit*. These different transformations can be read as the way in which 'It gives Being.' Heidegger points out that in the beginning of Western thinking, Being is thought, not however the 'It gives.' The 'It gives' has, according to Heidegger, withdrawn behind the gift that it gives, a gift which has been conceptualized and handed down exclusively as the Being of beings throughout the history of metaphysics. Heidegger states that:

> A giving which gives only its gift, but in the giving holds itself back and withdraws, such a giving we call sending. According to the meaning of giving, which is to be thought in this way – Being – that which It gives – is what is sent. Each of its transformations remains destined in this manner.[5]

What is sent forth in the history of Being is destined. From this it becomes clear that the history of Being means its destiny, in which its sending and the 'It' which it is sending, holds back its own manifestation. This movement is understood by Heidegger as different epochs of the destiny of Being. The notion of *epoche* thus is not to be understood in the Husserlian sense, but rather as a sending of Being in which its fundamental character is the holding back of itself 'in favour of the discernibility of the gift.'[6]

According to Heidegger, different epochs overlap each other in the history of Being, so that the sending of Being as presence has become more and more obscured. Only a removal of these different layers – a dismantling of the history of metaphysics – can allow for thinking in the direction of what reveals itself as the destiny of Being. Different terms used in the history of metaphysics, such as Plato's idea, Hegel's absolute concept or Nietzsche's will to power, are for Heidegger determinations of Being, and are understood as answers to a claim which is speaking from the sending in which the 'It gives' of Being itself is concealed. As such, thinking always remains attached to the different epochs; to the tradition of the epochs of the destiny of Being, even when it attempts to think the manner in which Being itself receives its determination from the 'It gives Being.'

How then is it possible think the 'It' of the 'It gives Being?' For Heidegger this task means a return to the thinking of time. Being includes: presence, letting-be-present, presencing, and as such there is a necessary rapport with time. Heidegger finds that according to the Aristotelian conception of time, time is present in terms of the 'now.'[7] This interpretation of time is however incapable of answering the

---

[5] ZS, p. 12/trans. p. 8.

[6] ZS, p. 13/trans. p. 9.

[7] Aristotle, *Physics*, 217 b 31w, trans. R.P. Hardie and R.K. Gaye in *The Complete Works of Aristotle: The Revised Oxford Translation*, Vol. 1, ed. Jonathan Barnes (Princeton New Jersey: Princeton University Press, 1995, rev. ed.), p. 369. It might be stated that Heidegger takes an oversimplified account of Aristotle's understanding of time. Although Aristotle views time as the calculable measure of motion with respect to a *before* and *after*, implying time to mean the duration that is experienced between the beginning and the conclusion of a movement, the duration of time can be broken down into numerical units. As such, time for Aristotle is not a succession of atomic

question whether time *is*, and furthermore, Heidegger finds that the present in the sense of presence is radically different from the present in the sense of the now, so that the present as presence can in no way be determined in terms of the present as the now. For Heidegger, present in the sense of presence means that presence determines Being in a unified manner, namely as presencing and allowing-to-presence, and therefore as unconcealing. Presencing however, requires that 'we perceive biding and abiding in lasting as lasting as present being.'[8] As such, what is present is that which comes towards human beings. Heidegger writes that:

> [M]an, who is concerned with and approached by presence, who, through being thus approached, is himself present in his own way for all present and absent beings. Man: standing within the approach of presence, but in such a way that he receives as a gift the presencing that It gives by perceiving what appears in letting-presence. If man were not the constant receiver of this gift given by the "It gives presence," if that which is extended in the gift did not reach man, then not only would Being remain concealed in the absence of this gift, not only closed off, but man would remain excluded from the scope of: It gives Being. Man would not be man.[9]

This however does not merely imply that man is only concerned with the presencing of something actually present, since man is also concerned with absence. And the same counts for the future, as in that what comes towards man, presencing is offered. As such, not every presencing is necessarily the present. The giving of presencing that prevails in past, present and future is to be understood as a reaching in that it reaches human beings. This reciprocal relation brings about the present.' Heidegger contends that the mutual giving of past, present and future is to be thought of as time. Time as such is to be understood as the unity of reaching out and giving. This means for Heidegger that past, present and future belong to one another in the way in which they offer themselves to one another in terms of the presencing that is given. According to Heidegger, this presencing opens what he calls 'time-space.' This implies that time no longer has the supposed Aristotelian meaning of a series of 'nows' and space by no means refers to the distance between two 'now'-points in this series. Rather, 'time-space' means the openness, which opens the 'mutual self-extending of futural approach, past and present.'[10]

---

now-points, because according to his account time is continuous and infinitely divisible. See *Physics* 217b30-218a10, 219b1-30. However, if the now is not a real part of time, it still serves to identify the beginning, end and intervening stages of a movement. For this reason, Heidegger can plausibly hold on to the assumption that Aristotle tacitly takes the 'now' as the *standard* for understanding time. In and since Aristotle, on this revised account, there is a tendency to take the smallest numerical units with which one works - the practical terminus of some actual process of division - as denoting what is 'currently-now', 'no-longer-now' and 'not-yet-now.'

[8] ZS, p. 16/trans. p. 12.

[9] ZS, p. 16/trans. p. 12.

[10] ZS, p. 19/trans. p. 14 This openness gives the space in which space can unfold itself, which implies that the opening up in terms of self-extending of future, past and present lies before space. We note that for Heidegger, man's spatiality is 'embraced' by temporality. Already in *Sein und Zeit* [*Being and Time*], the representation of space is a temporalization. This however does not mean that space can be reduced to time. Each has its own essence. But exploring the essence of each, we see that their essence is a unified time-space. In *Unterwegs zur Sprache* [*On the Way to Language*],

Heidegger claims that the common, putatively Aristotelian understanding of time is one-dimensional because it is only capable of thinking time in a linear manner, whereas Heidegger's thinking of time is derived from the time-space of what is called 'true time' and is, in its threefold giving, three-dimensional. This is so because 'dimensionality consists in a reaching out that opens up, in which futural approaching brings about what has been, what has been brings about futural approaching, and the reciprocal relation of both brings about the opening up of openness.'[11] Dimension, however, is not to be thought of as a realm that allows for or can be measured. Rather, it is a reaching, understood in terms of an opening and a giving, such that the given allows for dimensionality in terms of measurement.

It thus becomes clear that the unity of the threefold dimensionality is to be thought in terms of a kind of presencing as an approach and a bringing about, in the present as well as in the past and the future. As such, it is impossible to think presencing only in terms of the present. Rather, the unity of the different dimensions of time consists in the interplay between the different dimensions. This makes the interplay for Heidegger the fourth dimension of time, as it is a true extending playing within time itself. 'True time is four-dimensional.'[12] The fourth dimension however, is actually the first dimension, because it is the giving that determines the three other dimensions. 'In future, in past, in the present, that giving brings about to each its own presencing, holds them apart thus opened and so holds them toward one another in the nearness by which the three dimensions remain near one another.'[13] Thus this dimension brings past, future and present near one another by distancing them in the sense that what has been is kept open by denying its arriving as present.[14] Heidegger calls this dimension of time the dimension of 'nearing nearness' or 'nearhood.'[15] Nearing nearness is a denial and a withholding, as it keeps open the approach coming from the future as it withholds the present within this approach. This means that nearing nearness already in advance unifies the different ways the past, future and present are reaching out towards each other.

It is thus impossible to say that time *is*. Rather: 'It gives time,' as the giving in which time is given is a denying and a withholding. 'It grants the openness of time-space and preserves what remains denied in what has-been, what is withheld in approach.'[16] The giving which gives true time is called by Heidegger an opening and concealing extending and since extending is to be thought of as a giving in itself, the giving of the giving is concealed in true time. It is impossible to ask after the place

---

Heidegger states: 'But already thinking time through in this way [as ecstatic] brings it in its relatedness to the There of Da-sein, into essential relation with Da-sein's spatiality and hence with space.' *Unterwegs Zur Sprache*, p. 213/trans. p. 213.

[11] ZS, p. 19/trans. p. 14.

[12] ZS, p. 20/trans. p. 15.

[13] ZS, p. 20/trans. p. 15.

[14] ZS, p. 20/trans. p. 15.

[15] This is a translation from the early German term *Nahheit*, a word used by Kant, as Heidegger points out. ZS, p. 20/trans. p. 15.

[16] ZS, p. 20/trans. p. 16.

of time as time itself is the pre-spatial region 'which first gives any possible "where"'[17] since it is the realm of threefold extending as determined by nearing nearness.

Since the history of metaphysics always thought the supposedly Aristotelian conception of time in terms of a series of now-points, it needed the existence of the psyche, consciousness or *Spirit*, to measure these 'nows' against one another. This assumption however, does not yet explain how human beings themselves relate to time. Heidegger seems to reaffirm the history of metaphysics in the assumption that it is impossible to think time without the existence of human beings, but the question whether man is giving or receiving time is not adequate since, for Heidegger:

> True time is the nearness of presencing out of present, past and future – the nearness that unifies time's threefold opening extending. It has already reached man as such so that he can be man only by standing within the threefold extending, perduring the denying, and withholding nearness which determines that extending. Time is not the product of man, man is not the product of time. There is no production here. There is only giving in the sense of extending which opens up time-space.[18]

The manner of giving in which time is given however, does not yet explain the 'It' of the 'It gives time.' Examining the phrase 'It gives Being,' the giving consists in a sending and a destiny of presence in its epochal transformations. And the giving in 'It gives time' is understood as an extending and opening-up of the four-dimensional realm. Therefore, Heidegger claims that true time seems to be the 'It' that gives Being, in that it gives presence, because, as noted, absence also manifests itself as a mode of presence:

> What has-been which, by refusing the present, lets that become present which is no longer present; and the coming toward us of what is to come which, by withholding the present, lets that be present which is not yet present – both made manifest the manner of an extending opening up which gives all presencing into the open.[19]

The destiny in which 'It gives Being' appears to be found in the extending of time. This however is not the case, as Heidegger points out, as time itself remains a gift of an 'It gives,' in which its giving preserves the realm in which presence is extended. It is only possible to determine the 'It' which gives 'in terms of the giving as the 'the sending of Being, as time in the sense of an opening up which extends.'[20] It is therefore the case that 'It' gives, but is itself not there. As such, the 'It' names the presence of an absence, or, presence and the other of presence, and has to be thought in terms of the kind of giving belonging to it, namely giving as destiny and a giving as an opening up which reaches. Therefore, destiny and opening up are to be thought together, because destiny lies in opening up. Heidegger states that in the extending of time as the sending of destiny:

---

[17] ZS, p. 21/trans. p. 16.
[18] ZS, p. 21/trans. p. 16.
[19] ZS, p. 22/trans. p. 17.
[20] ZS, p. 22/trans. p. 17.

[t]here becomes manifest a dedication, a delivering over into what is their own, namely Being as presence and of time as the realm of the open. What determines both, time and Being, in their own, that is, in their belonging together, we shall call Ereignis, the event of Appropriation. Ereignis will be translated as Appropriation or event of Appropriation.[21]

It is important to note here that the term 'event' is not just an occurrence, but that which makes any occurrence possible. Thus, for Heidegger, the manner in which Being and time belong together while holding them to their own is the event of Appropriation or *Ereignis*. As such, this event precisely means to think the other of presence in the present, and as such, opens the possibility to think the difference in which is simultaneously thought presence and its other, because as noted, in giving as sending there is a certain withholding in that the withholding and denial of the present 'play within the giving of what has been and what will be.'[22] Heidegger notes that: 'The sending in the destiny of Being has been characterized as a giving in which the sending source keeps itself back and, thus, withdraws from unconcealment.'[23] And further:

> In true time and its time-space, the giving of what-has-been, that is, of what is no longer present, the denial of the present manifested itself. Denial and withholding exhibit the same trait as self-withholding in sending: namely, self-withdrawal.[24]

Withdrawal belongs to *Ereignis* in the manner that *Ereignis* withdraws what is 'most fully its own'[25] from unconcealment and as such, it expropriates itself of itself. It is here that we find Heidegger's radical undecidability between presence and absence: an undecidability that is keeping and giving while concealing and withdrawing. As such, *Ereignis* can be read as the event in which presence is given, that is thus, the event in which presence is not present. This movement is thought, as Heidegger points out, in the German term *Anwesen*.[26] The term *An-wesen* can be understood as the movement before *wesen*, which refers to the essence as presence, also found in the Greek *ousia*. *An-wesen*, emphasizing the *before* this presence,

---

[21] ZS, p.24/trans. p. 19 The term 'Ereignis' is commonly translated as 'Event.' Heidegger however thinks the word more fundamentally and in a literal sense in which the prefix 'Er'- designates an executional character and where '-eignis' refers to the adverb 'eigen,' meaning 'own.' As such, translating this term into Appropriation or propriation, as many translations of Heidegger's use of Ereignis read, has the connotation of a 'bringing into the own,' or 'enownment.' There is a visual reference to term, as the German *Auge* means eye. Until the eighteenth century, Ereignis was spelt as *Eräugnis, eräugnen*, which literally means: 'to place before the eye, to become visible.'

[22] ZS, p. 27/trans. p. 22.

[23] ZS, p. 27/trans. p. 22.

[24] ZS, p. 27/trans. p. 22.

[25] ZS, p. 28/trans. p. 22.

[26] Heidegger calls what is present *das Anwesende* [beings in their presence], and the Being of those beings *die Anwesenheit* [Being as what grants beings or what is present]. Heidegger finds that An-wesen, as well as the Greek *ousia* or *parousia*, is used both as 'coming into presence,' and a 'self-contained farm or homestead See *Einführung in die Metaphysik* [*Introduction to Metaphysics*], p. 47/trans. p. 64. Heidegger finds that the term *Wesen* does not mean *quidditas*, but refers to 'enduring as present,' or presencing and absencing.' (p. 55/trans. 76) Wesen as a noun, meaning 'essence,' is derived from the seldomly used verb *Wesen*, finds Heidegger.

marks the source from which presence is possible as such and refers to the continuity of presence as *Anwesenheit*.[27]

It is important to point out that for Heidegger, *Ereignis* is not a relation retroactively imposed upon both Being and time. Rather *Ereignis* first appropriates Being and time into their own in virtue of their relation, and does so by the appropriating that is concealed in destiny and in the gift of opening out. Accordingly, the It that gives in 'It gives Being,' and in 'It gives time,' proves to be *Ereignis*. Further, it is important to mark that naming this event is, in a certain manner, impossible. Naming this event would present *Ereignis* as some present being, whereas Heidegger is precisely attempting to think presence and its other as such. Asking the question 'What is *Ereignis*' is asking how *Ereignis* presences, becomes present; it is asking after the Being of *Ereignis*. However, since Heidegger has pointed out that Being itself belongs to *Ereignis* and from there receives its determination as presence, we are led back to the beginning of Heidegger's questioning. That this question demonstrates how *Ereignis* must not be thought, means for Heidegger that what this event names should not be understood in terms of occurrence and happening, but as the extending and sending which opens and preserves. Moreover, the suspicion might be raised that *Ereignis* is another name for Being and as such, would precisely affirm the history of metaphysics in Heidegger's understanding of it. If however Being is thought in terms of presencing and allowing-to-presence that are in destiny which in turn lies in the extending of true time which opens and conceals, then Being belongs to *Ereignis*. However, it is important to observe that *Ereignis* is most surely not to be thought as the most general concept that would encompass both Being and time, because, as Heidegger writes: 'Being proves to be destiny's gift of presence, the gift granted by the giving of time. The gift of presence is the property of Appropriating, Being vanishes in Appropriation.'[28] Therefore, in the phrase 'Being as Appropriation,' the word 'as' should be read as: 'Being, letting-presence sent in Appropriating, time extended in Appropriating. Time and Being appropriated in Appropriation.'[29]

To care for the ontological difference and to accept the concern of presence means to stand in the realm of giving and as such, four-dimensional time has reached human beings. Because both Being and time are only there in appropriating, Appropriation brings man into its own as 'the being who perceives Being by standing within true time.'[30] Being appropriated, man belongs to Appropriation. This belonging, as Heidegger points out, is an assimilation of man to *Ereignis* and this assimilation allows for man to be admitted to *Ereignis*. And here we have arrived at 'that ancient something which conceals itself in *a-letheia*.'[31] Because *Ereignis* in a certain manner does not designate anything other but Being's act of concealing

---

[27] A preservation and a continuity that is found in language.

[28] ZS, p. 27/trans. p. 22.

[29] ZS, p. 27/trans. p. 22.

[30] ZS, p. 28/trans. p. 23.

[31] ZS, p. 29/trans. p. 24 Here comes to light the nuanced meaning of the Greek term *aletheia*. Aletheia means truth as unhiddenness. The verb *aletheuein* means 'to speak truly.' These words are related to *lanthanein*, with an older form *lethein*, meaning 'to escape notice, to be unseen, unno-

itself as it is withdrawing behind the gift that it gives, it makes possible its revelation to man as *aletheia*: truth as unconcealment. Thus, *aletheia* can be read as a self-concealing clearing or as a self-clearing concealment, as pointed out by Werner Marx in *Heidegger and the Tradition*.[32] Here is found that *aletheia* is rethought in such a manner that it does not only designate an openness, but also a relation to concealment, and as such, every openness is an *un*concealment.[33]

Ereignis is thus not circumscribed by truth. On the contrary, *Ereignis* precedes truth and as such, makes it possible. In recalling Heidegger's task of thinking the truth of Being itself, thinking the truth of Being itself thus means to think *Ereignis* as that which gives the gift of truth while withdrawing from its manifestation. As such, thinking this event means to think presence in terms of a 'letting presence,' and simultaneously that which is radically other and irreducible to presence. In giving presence while withdrawing, *Ereignis* is the possibility to think the history of metaphysics and simultaneously it is its voiding or its otherness in terms of its irreducibility to presence which, as such, gives this very history. Thinking *Ereignis* thus means to think simultaneously the manner in which metaphysics becomes possible and its otherness and the manner in which they necessarily belong together.

Ereignis is not simply the affirmation of the ontological difference, as in this event what is thought by Heidegger is what is preceding this difference, because this event is the thinking of the place from where Being gives itself as irreducible to beings. It thus designates the *where* from which the ontological difference can be stated and thought. Therefore to think *Ereignis* means a thinking of difference itself as an event. This is the most primordial and essential task of thinking, which means a thinking of nearness in which man's responsibility to Being becomes manifest.

Let us now turn to Derrida in order to bring to light both his closeness to and distance from Heidegger. Heidegger's *Destruktion* of the history of metaphysics can be read as an attempt to point towards the unthought in thinking. Derrida reinscribes this attempt into the question of writing. This reinscription however does not seek to reveal that which has been revealed by Heidegger's *Destruktion*, but points towards an impossibility within the possibility of thinking itself. What does this mean? For Derrida, *Deconstruction* refers to an impossibility of revealing the origin of thought, by adding a supplement beyond the possibility of comprehension. As such, we can view *Deconstruction* as a strategy of affirmation which problematizes and oscillates classical oppositions within the philosophical tradition by introducing an element of absolute indecision within these oppositions which conditions and defers and allows and interrupts these oppositions themselves.

---

ticed, and *lethe*, 'forgetting, forgetfulness.' It thus becomes clear that a-letheia as unconcealment implies a necessary concealment as expressed in the withdrawal of Appropriation.

[32] Werner Marx, *Heidegger and the Tradition*, p. 148.

[33] It is important to note that the realm of concealment must most surely not be understood as a 'nothing' in terms of a negativity. That which withdraws itself and remains hidden, provides the origin for a clearing or unconcealment understood in terms of *aletheia*. As such, the opening of Being is a process of presencing 'as a creative relationship of concealment and clearing' as Werner Marx points out. See *Heidegger and the Tradition*, p. 150.

It is here that we find the signicification of Différance. Différance, as a homophone and an orthographic corruption of *différence* (difference), plays most specifically between the infinitive of *différer* (to defer) and the present participle of *différer* (to differ) – *différant* (different/differentiated).[34] This is thus a language that is at once verbal and nominal. It describes an immemorial and endless process by which identity differentiates itself from the oscillation or indecision of difference and asserts itself in presence, but wherein this identity is consistently subverted and made different from itself by a radically other difference, which escapes presentification as such. In this sense, we find Heidegger's 'letting presence' of temporality and thus the dimension of nearness reaffirmed within Derrida's thinking.

But it is within the nature of indecision of différance that, contrary to Heidegger, there is neither origin nor possibility of revelation for Derrida. Because of différance, the reading of any text (or context) can only lead to a point of aporia.

Derrida explains the difference between problem and aporia in 'Finis'. The word problem has its sources in the Greek *problema*, which signifies projection or protection (it also means shield or barrier) in the sense of projecting a telos upon the undecidability of différance and through this act creating a protected space in which a decision can be made. As such, the notion of problem indicates the mode of thought that we find throughout the history of metaphysics: it remains concerned with that which can be brought into presence. Aporia on the other hand blocks the way in the very place where '*it would no longer be possible to constitute a problem.*'[35] This for Derrida is the point where the task indicated by the problem becomes absolutely impossible and where one is 'exposed, abolsutely without protection, without problem, and without prosthesis, without possible substitution, singularlaly exposed in our absolute and absolutely naked uniqueness.'[36] Aporia is the experience of the interrupting and oscillating dynamic of différance and signifies an undecidablity that renders any decision absolutely impossible. A decision, for it to be a decision, must pass through the impossibiltiy, the without-passage of aporia: 'in order to be responsible and truly decisive, a decision should not limit itself to putting into operation a determinable or determining knowledge, the consequence of some pre-established order.'[37]

What then is is that takes place or comes to pass with the aporia? Derrida refers to the *arriving* of the *arrivant* which makes the event arrive.[38] The arrivant par excellence is not a who or a what; 'does not yet have a name or an identity.'[39] The arrivant arrives from outside conceptual borders and demarcations and thus cannot be named or identified. Thinking the arrivant requires thus a most radical disruption in thinking; the arrivant 'no more commands than is commanded by the memory of

---

[34] MP, p. 5/trans. p. 8.

[35] FA, p. 30/trans. p. 11.

[36] FA, p. 31/trans. p. 120.

[37] FA, p. 38/trans. p. 17.

[38] FA, p. 66/trans. p. 33.

[39] FA, p. 67/trans. p. 34.

some originary event where the archaic is bound with the *final* extremity, with the finality par excellence of the *telos* or of the *eskhaton*.'[40]

Différance thus does not have a hidden or forgotten origin; it is immemorial and thus infinitely other and does not allow for revelation. In this manner, the indecision of différance is always and already in oscillation. In 'Foi et savoir' Derrida describes the thought of chora, an 'utterly faceless other' which remains 'absolutely impassable and heterogenous' to all the processes of historical revelation.'[41] We cannot even formulate the thought of chora because it never presents itself as such since it is: 'neither Being, nor the Good, nor God, nor Man, nor history.'[42] Chora thus does not allow for a remembrance as possible remembrance nor for an origin that can be thought in terms of a beginning. Derrida writes:

> This Greek noun says in our memory that which is not reappropriable, even by our memory, even by our 'Greek' memory; it says the immemoriality of a desert in the desert of which it is neither a threshold nor a mourning.[43]

Plato introduced the thought of *chora* in the *Timaeus* to signify a space that is neither Being nor non-Being but rather the 'place of absolute exteriority' as an interval in between in which the forms were kept. Derrida finds that as such, *chora* does not designate a 'positive Infinity' of alterity in terms of a divine figure which remains transcendent to thought, but rather 'a certain desert, that which makes possible, opens, hollows, or infinitizes the other.'[44]

As such, a revelation in terms of an event – a surprise – must come as a surprise not only to man, but to God as well. This amounts to saying that an event, epiphany, revelation or decision can only be an event if it is singular and unexpected, arising from the dynamic of aporia and not from any structure of an originary openness. Derrida names this 'messianicity without messianism'[45] as a sense of immanence that is riveted to the coming of an other that cannot be seen as a becoming-present, that presences as other:

> 'the messianic, or messianicity without messianism. Thus would be the opening to the future or to the coming of the other as the advent of justice, but without the horizon of expectation and without prophetic prefiguration. The coming of the other can only emerge as a singular event when no anticipation sees it coming...[46]

It now becomes clear that this *arrivant* is radically different from Heidegger's understanding of revelation. Derrida thus thinks the relation in a different manner where no order is appropriate. Derrida attempts to remove the event as revelation from the scheme of the veil, light, horizon. Why? And how? Let us seek to clarify this further. We could say that Heidegger's treatment of the history of metaphysics

---

[40] FA, p. 68/trans. p. 34.
[41] FS, p. 33/trans. p. 58/59.
[42] FS, p. 33/trans. p. 58.
[43] FS, p. 34/trans. p. 59.
[44] FS, p. 30/trans. p. 55.
[45] FS, p. 31/trans p. 56.
[46] FS, p. 31/trans. p. 56.

involves forcing this history back ipon itself to reveal its other, its difference: its unthought and unsaid. This unsaid is precisely Being itself. There is a clear *telos* to Heidegger's *Destruktion*; that of the revelation (*Offenbarung*) of Being whose destiny, in being concealed, is to be revealed in the thought and language of man. This amounts to stating that the concealment of Being is that which opens its *originary possibility* for being revealed. As Derrida puts it in 'Foi et savoir': 'It would accordingly be necessary that a 'revealabiltiy (Offenbarkeit) be allowed to reaveal itself, with a light that would manifest (itself) more originarity than all revelation (Offenbarung). This means that in Heidegger's thinking, the idea of revelation implies that a possibility of revealability was already there (be it non-logical or non-chronological). For revelation to take place, human existence is open to revelation (as seen in the correspondence between the openness of man and the openness of Being), which makes revealability ontologically prior to revelation. Heidegger's reading of the history of philosophy is as such always and already leading towards the revelation of Being.

It is however important to note that this revelation is a peculiar revelation. To think the unthought of the history of metaphysics means to think both what reveals itself to thought and to think that which remains inaccessible to it. Because to think the revelation of Being for Heidegger is to think precisely both what gives itself as manifest – namely Being, and to think simultaneously Being's act of withdrawing behind the gift that it gives. Thinking Being thus means to think that which reveals itself as unconcealed and that which does not reveal itself and remains concealed, and as such, makes unconcealment possible. Or, in other words: to think Being is to think the radical undecidability and incessant play between that which is keeping and giving while concealing and withdrawing. This entails that since the thinking of unconcealment means the thinking of concealment simultaneously, this thinking always remains in an ambiguity between that which is thought and that which is unthought.

We could say however that this thinking still reveals the withdrawal of *Ereignis as* unrevealed. This means that, in thinking, the concealment of Being is thought *as* unthought, revealed *as* unrevealed. Further, the fact that Being is destiny, and therefore history, implies that this thinking is always historical – thinking is always thinking the tradition. The problem thus is that thinking itself – even thinking in terms of exposedness to Being – cannot allow for an event outside its conceptual borders. It is possible to say therefore that Heidegger's *Ereignis* cannot be a revelation in the true sense – a surprise – since for Heidegger, revelation confirms and fulfils revealability and so could be named as the neutralization of the event. Therefore, we could suggest that *Ereignis* as destinality negates the event as surprise. Revelation, for it to be a revelation, has to reveal revealability, and not the other way around.

Heidegger's philosophical task consists in turning the questioning of Being throughout the history of metaphysics back upon itself. Heidegger is guided by the question:

'What is the meaning of Being?' Derrida however, in introducing the oscillation of différance, questions the question itself. In its eagerness to discover, the question seems to have the desire to encompass the hitherto unknown within its realm of understanding; its *telos* seems to be one of bringing into presence before it is a letting presence. As such, the possibility of the question of the meaning of Being can be questioned in terms of Being's fundamental temporality. Viewed from the perspective of Derrida's aporia, the question seems to remain within the projection and protection of the *problem*: a force of thought that wishes to assimilate, to grasp, to understand within the limits of what is already understood. The question, integral to the dynamic of revelation and revealability, does not respect the constant oscillation of indecision for itself; it cannot think difference *as* the other in terms of the other. In always searching to bring near, the question can be read as a disruption of *nearness* itself.

For Heidegger, the notion of futurity is still linked to possibility of coming into presence, even in the double movement of concealment and unconcealment, which would reduce futurity itself. This makes *Ereignis* not an event, but the possibility of grasping. In this sense, it is precisely the thinking of the possibility of futurity that reduces the future to a possibility of presence and thus reducing the other to a structure of possible revelation.

Furthermore, we have found that for Derrida 'messianicity without messianism' designates the opening to the future as the arrival of the other as the advent of justice. In the aporia, the future is marked as impossible, as always to come. In this sense, the other remains resistant to all determination. This justice thus is not a function of the truth of Being, as it works according to another logic: it always remains of the other and is unjustifiable in the very event it will come to open.

References

Derrida, Jacques. Finis. In *Apories*. Paris: Galilée, 1992. Trans. Thomas Dutoit as Finis In *Aporias*. California: Stanford University Press, 1993.

Derrida, Jacques. *Foi et Savoir*. Paris: Éditions du Seuil, 1996. Trans. Gil Anidjar as Faith and Knowledge In *Acts of Religion*. New York, Routledge, 2002.

Derrida, Jacques. Différance. In *Marges de la Philosophie*. Paris: Les Editions de Minuit, 1972. Trans. Alan Bass as Différance In *Margins of Philosophy*. Chicago: University of Chicago Press, 1982.

Heidegger, Martin. *Sein und Zeit*. Tübingen: Max Niemeyer Verlag, 1927. Trans. John Macquarrie and Edward Robinson as *Being and Time*. Oxford: Blackwell Publishing, 1962.

Heidegger, Martin. Vom Wesen den Warheit (1930). In *Wegmarken*. GA Band 9, 177–202. Frankfurt am Main: Vittorio Klostermann, 1976. Trans. John Sallis as On the Essence of Truth. In *Pathmarks*, ed. William McNeill, 136–154. Cambridge: Cambridge University Press, 1998.

Heidegger, Martin. Zeit und Sein. (1962). GA Band 14. Frankfurt am Main: Vittorio Klostermann, 2007. Trans. Joan Stambaugh as *On Time and Being*. Chicago: Chicago University Press, 2002.

Marx, Werner. 1971. *Heidegger and the Tradition*. Trans. Theodore Kisiel. Evanston: Northwestern University Press.

Heidegger, Buber and Levinas: Must We Give Priority to Authenticity or Mutuality or Holiness?

Lawrence Vogel

Abstract After considering Buber's and Levinas's critiques of Heidegger and of each other, I propose that we should acknowledge authenticity (Heidegger), "essential relations" of love and friendship (Buber), and holiness (Levinas) as aspects of a good life, though they pull in different directions. We should resist the temptation to take sides in a battle between different approaches to the complex nature of our social being.

Keywords Heidegger • Buber • Levinas • Authenticity • Mutuality • Holiness

Martin Buber and Emmanuel Levinas have been called "Jewish co-existentialists": marking their shared critique of Heidegger's allegedly individualistic account of authenticity in *Being and Time*.[1] But their disagreement over the deepest meaning of human co-existence is at the root of their dispute with each other. This boils over when Levinas charges that Heidegger's description of "leaping in" and helping another in need is closer to "holiness" or sacrifice on behalf of "the Other" – and hence to Levinas's own Jewish sensibility – than Buber's mutual encounter between I and You.[2] Levinas throws down the gauntlet; the former Nazi, Heidegger, is friendlier to the spirit of Judaism than the icon of The Hebrew University!

What's going on here, and what's really at stake? Given the complex nature of our social being, we students of philosophy should be wary of rallying under the flag of Heideggerian authenticity or Buberian mutuality or Levinasian holiness, like sports fans rooting for their favorite team. I propose that each philosopher points us

---

Thanks to Prof. Dermot Moran for inviting this essay as a keynote address to the Dublin conference, "Discovering the 'We': the Phenomenology of Sociality" sponsored by the Irish Research Council (May, 2013). I delivered a later version at Vassar College in honor of the retirement of my beloved professor, Mitchell Miller (September, 2013).

[1] Paul Mendes-Flohr, "Jewish Co-Existentialism: Being with the Other," in Jonathan Judaken and Robert Bernasconi, eds., Situating Existentialism (New York: Columbia University Press, 2012).

[2] Emmanuel Levinas, "Martin Buber's Thought and Contemporary Judaism," Outside the Subject (Stanford, California: Stanford University Press, 1993), 18.

L. Vogel (✉)
Department of Philosophy, Connecticut College, New London, CT, USA
e-mail: lavog@conncoll.edu

© Springer International Publishing Switzerland 2016
L. Foran, R. Uljée (eds.), *Heidegger, Levinas, Derrida: The Question of Difference*, Contributions To Phenomenology 86,
DOI 10.1007/978-3-319-39232-5_15

towards an aspect of a good life. The problem is: they pull us in different directions, like life itself.

1 Buber's Critique of Heidegger

In the autumn of 1933 Buber was stripped of his professorship at the University of Frankfurt, just months after another Martin – Heidegger – assumed the Rectorship at Freiburg under the auspices of Hitler. Five years later, Buber emigrated to Palestine, joined the Sociology faculty of the Hebrew University of Jerusalem, and delivered his inaugural lecture series, "What is Man?"[3]

Buber uses the occasion to tell his story of Western philosophy and, given the unfolding political drama, surprises his audience by endorsing Heidegger's existential turn. This turn, Buber tells us, brings "the anthropological problem" into "maturity" by disclosing our "homelessness," for after the discoveries of Copernicus and Einstein the universe can no longer be imagined as a home. Furthermore, two social developments exacerbate this cosmic alienation: (a) the breakdown of traditional, organic communities and (b) the sense that technology controls us more than we master it.[4] Today, "in the ice of [cosmic] solitude [and social dislocation]," Buber observes, "man becomes a question to himself."[5] We can no longer rely on philosophical systems to save ourselves from the uncertainty of life or depend on fixed rules to avoid responsibility for decisions that bear upon an open future.

So far, so good for Heidegger.

Buber proceeds to launch his critique with the following assertion:

> Heidegger's 'existence' is monological… [Authentic man], who in Heidegger's view is the goal of all life, can no longer live with man. He knows a real life only in communication with himself.[6]

Buber has in mind Heidegger's authentic individual standing before himself alone: anxiously listening to "the silent call of conscience" in the face of being-towards-death. The call is silent because there is no universal directive for how I should lead my life, only the demand that I take responsibility for myself instead of conforming to roles that have been handed down to me.

Heidegger conveys the impression that ordinary interpersonal relationships are primarily refuges enabling the individual to harbor a false sense of security by sheltering the "I" in the "we."[7] Even moral imperatives shield one from the existential issue: who am I, the singular individual, to be?[8] The "silent call of conscience"

---

[3] Martin Buber, "What is Man?," Chapter 5 in Between Man and Man (London and New York: Routledge, 2002).
[4] Buber, "What is Man?," 186–188.
[5] Buber, "What is Man?," 150.
[6] Buber, "What is Man?," 168.
[7] Martin Heidegger, Being and Time (New York: Harper and Row, 1962), 163–168.
[8] Heidegger, Being and Time, 328.

demands, in Kierkegaardian terms, a "teleological suspension of the universal for the sake of the particular," but before oneself alone – with no appeal to God.

For Heidegger "existential guilt" means that I bear responsibility for my own life even though I didn't create the situation into which I am "thrown." For Buber, however, "primal guilt" stems from our tendency to "remain within ourselves": to close ourselves off from others, treating them, in the I-It mode, as objects of knowledge, experience or use. Conscience demands acknowledging that like myself, "[You] secretly and bashfully watch for a 'Yes' that allows [you] to be and that can come to you only from another human person."[9] Minimally, this Yes-saying means treating others as one would wish to be treated oneself. But *Begegnung* or "encounter" supersedes mere respect when:

> 'Making the personal present' and 'imagining the real'... in a living partnership... I stand in a common situation with the other and expose myself vitally to his share in the situation as really his share. It is true that my basic attitude can remain unanswered, and the dialogue can die in seed. But if mutuality stirs, then the interhuman blossoms into genuine dialogue.[10]

Buber is fair-minded enough to acknowledge that Heidegger's *Dasein* is always already "with-others," and that authenticity urges one back into solicitude: as Heidegger puts it, "making Dasein, as Being-with, have some understanding of the potentiality-for-Being of Others."[11] Yet Heidegger denies that his description of *Mitsein* carries any prescriptive or "moralizing" weight.[12]

At this point we might expect Buber to highlight how Heidegger's account of Being-with-Others remains deaf to the prophetic cry for justice. After all, Buber often says he's most interested in uncomfortable, adversarial relationships where forging a mutual bond between I and You requires a "breakthrough": where the task is, as he quaintly puts it, "finding the common in the non-common" – in "the shop, the factory, the office, the mine, on the tractor, at the printing press."[13] Rather than focusing on adversaries or strangers, however, Buber faults Heidegger for failing to capture the importance of loved ones and friends in an authentic life.

> [Heidegger's] relation of solicitude... cannot as such be an essential relation, since it does not set a man's life in direct relation with the life of another, but only one man's solicitous help in relation with another man's lack and need of it.[14]

Heidegger's examples of solicitude – "leaping in" (or taking over that which is of concern to the other) and "leaping ahead" (or helping the other be free for his own possibilities) – fail to qualify as "essential relations" because in neither case do I make my whole self available to the other, hope for mutuality, or experience the vulnerability of caring that "You" care for me in return. Heideggerian solicitude may be the effect a relation that is essential in itself, when, e.g., helping my daughter

---

[9] Martin Buber, "Elements of the Interhuman" in <u>The Knowledge of Man</u> (New York: Harper and Row, 1965), 69.

[10] Buber, "Elements of the Interhuman," 81.

[11] Heidegger, <u>Being and Time</u>, 309.

[12] Heidegger, <u>Being and Time</u>, 211.

[13] Buber, "Dialogue" in <u>Between Man and Man</u>," 35.

[14] Buber, "What is Man?," 169.

or son expresses our prior bond. Or solicitude may lead to an essential relation when, e.g., reaching out to a stranger proves to be the beginning of a friendship. Buber amplifies this distinction as follows:

> In **mere solicitude** man remains essentially with himself, even if he is moved with extreme pity… He is "concerned with the other," but **not anxious for the other to be concerned with him**.
>
> In an **essential relation**, on the other hand, the barriers of individual being are in fact breached and a new phenomenon appears which can appear only in this way: one life open to another – not steadily, but attaining its reality from point to point, yet also able to **acquire a form in the continuity of life**. The other becomes present not merely in the imagination or feeling, but in the depths of one's substance, so that one experiences the mystery of the other's being in the mystery of one's own.[15]

Maurice Natanson speaks in a Buberian voice when he describes the "we" of friendship:

> The irreplaceability of partners in friendship constitutes itself only from within a relationship that is unrepeatable because its temporality – its ongoing character – constructs, step by step in shared time, the recognition of person by person.[16]

Because our "essential relations" acquire what Buber calls "a form in the continuity of life," he finds in them an answer to the solitude of dying. "A great relation can be as strong as death," he writes, "because it breaches the barriers of a lofty solitude and throws a bridge from self-being to self-being across the abyss of dread of the universe."[17] It's as if Buber imagines Heidegger's authentic individual courageously facing death alone but without loved ones or friends who care about him or would grieve his absence. The heart of our *Mitsein* lies in cultivating and sustaining relationships that will last through time and, in the telling words of Jewish prayer, "make [one's] memory a blessing to all who mourn and a comfort to all the bereaved among us."

Buber is no doubt reacting to how Heidegger's stark distinction between *das Man* and the individual rides roughshod over the difference between the death of "just anyone" and the death of someone close to you. Drawing on Tolstoy's "The Death of Ivan Ilych," Heidegger is surely right that "the dying of Others is seen often enough as a social inconvenience, if not downright tactlessness, against which the public is to be guarded."[18] The death of a parent, partner, friend, or child, though, tends to have the effect not of "transforming anxiety into fear in the face of an oncoming event," thereby letting one flee from one's own mortality, as Heidegger describes it, but rather of making one appreciate the ties that bind as what make life most worth living in the fleeting, precious time one has.

Mourning involves the "embedment" of our identity in the web of "essential relations" that define us. In his work on filmmaker Ingmar Bergmann, Jesse Kalin notes:

---

[15] Buber, "What is Man?," 170.

[16] Maurice Natanson, The Journeying Self: A Study in Philosophy and Social Role (Reading, MA: Addison-Wesley, 1970), 64.

[17] Buber, "What is Man?," 202 and 207.

[18] Heidegger, Being and Time, 298.

> We are histories in which the parts accumulate, even though we can live the relationships they establish in isolation and separation, turning away from them... [Ultimately, though, I] cannot answer questions about [my] identity without interpolating into [my] story the lives of many others. Who [I am] is determined by who [I] have helped them to be. This is a fact that cannot be avoided; it can only be forgotten... [O]ur portraits as human beings cannot be drawn without also including portraits of the others with whom are lives are shared.[19]

It's important to talk about love of my "essential You" in light of the possibility of our becoming parents and forming the larger "we" of a family. I do not take this to be a hetero-normative claim. The mystery of parenting is that children are "ours" and yet "other." Raising them involves a balance of guidance and responsive "letting be." The aim is not to forge a life-long relationship, but to "launch" a child to live their own life independent of the family where they grew up. Yet good parents want more than independence for their adult children: hoping their progeny will respect others, form caring relationships, and perhaps create a family of their own, keeping the cycle going. Parents likely hope that their children want to sustain family ties: linking their children with grandparents and even helping in some measure their aging parents. Though this "return" cannot be commanded, having children of our own tends to make us appreciate (even forgive) our parents and understand the constraints and uncertainties they faced.

Once again I turn to Jesse Kalin:

> While paternity and maternity may be automatic as natural states, as spiritual relationships they are not. Spiritually, our most elemental condition is as orphans, and we must all be adopted. What is central is not the having of children but the acceptance of them as ours whoever they might be. Even as adults, we are subject to this same condition... The continuity of life, of generations and generation itself, must be restored, or at least reclaimed, in an attempt to annul "the light-years of distance" that can beset it.[20]

Not many of us, to be sure, know anything about our great-great grandparents and those who came before them. Most of us affect a few near and dear to us, and fade into oblivion more than two generations down the line, though we may hope that our influence ripples in a good way to our descendants, even if unbeknownst to them. This is why we tend to find meaning in life through the network of our "essential relations." Without them, we're inclined to feel invisible, forgotten and "no place." In a universe with no spatial or temporal center, our lives give us the chance to establish a center that answers our desire for confirmation: "I matter (at least partly) because I matter to you." But fidelity is not simply "natural," and it is unfair to write off the commitment to friends and loved ones as expressions of narrow selfishness or narcissism.

Having highlighted love and friendship, Buber still worries that Heidegger remains correct about less intimate social spheres where "the nameless, faceless crowd in which I am entangled is not a 'We' but the 'One.'"[21] Buber introduces "the

---

[19] Jesse Kalin, The Films of Ingmar Bergman (Cambridge, UK: Cambridge University Press, 2003), 80–81.

[20] Kalin, The Films of Ingmar Bergman, 71–72.

[21] Buber, "What is Man?," 208.

essential We" echoing, in relation to a group, "the essential Thou on the level of self-being": "a community of independent, self-responsible persons who are able to say "You" to one another and be bound up in genuine communion."[22] "The essential We" can exist in more or less constant forms: Buber's examples range from revolutionary and religious groups to more transient unions formed by members of a movement whose leader has died, to a community aroused to heroic solidarity by a catastrophe.

Buber's romantic formulations seem to exclude most "Others" who appear, after all, "non-essential" to one's identity. The darkest side is that an "essential We" may generate "inessential" Others who poses a threat to "us" and should be suppressed, if not eliminated. Buber's "Hebraic humanism" extends its reach to all humanity, however, for I-You derives from the idea that one can only love God, the Eternal You, by loving one's neighbor as one like oneself. And this must include the stranger, for, as it says at Exodus 23:9, "we [Israelites] were strangers once in the land of Egypt." What we find in Buber, I submit, is an image of ethical life as a set of **concentric circles**, **emanating outwards** from a strong core of presence within one's personal life. I discover "the we" from the inner circle out, from the neighborhood to unfamiliar places: from the intimate *Du* to the less personal *Sie*. This is consistent with Michael McConnell's thought that "[moral education's] source of strength lies in the affections which must begin close to home and radiate outward… We will not love those distant from us more by loving those close to us less."[23]

Here, I think, is where Levinas takes aim. Buber proclaims: "I welcome every philosophy of existence that leaves open the door to the essential presence of the other as other; but I know of none that opens it far enough."[24] And Levinas replies, in effect: "Yes, Buber – and you need to open the door even further."

2   Levinas's Critique of Buber

Like Buber, Levinas both appreciates Heidegger's existential turn and criticizes his image of authenticity for being "egological," discerning herein the root of Heidegger's hostility to liberal politics:

> Authenticity, based on the notion of "mineness," saves the unique individual from the banality of the impersonal "Anyone," but the contempt inspired by the mediocrity of *das Man* may quickly extend to the rightful portion of commonality present in the universality of democracy.[25]

[22] Buber, "What is Man?," 210.

[23] Michael McConnell, "Don't Neglect the Little Platoons" in Martha Nussbaum, ed., For Love of Country? (Boston, MA: Beacon Press, 2002), 82.

[24] "Interrogation of Martin Buber" in Sydney and Beatrice Rome, eds., Philosophical Interrogations (New York: Harper and Row, 1964), 23.

[25] Emmanuel Levinas, "The Other, Utopia and Justice" in Is It Righteous to Be?,"(Stanford, CA: Stanford University Press), 203.

Levinas applauds Buber's shift from monological "visions" of Being to dialogical relationships between persons and "the priority of justice elevated to the status of religious experience." Buber's assertion of the autonomy of the social relation (I-You) over what comes one's way in knowledge, use and experience (I-It) comprises, in Levinas' view, his "principle contribution to Western thought" and also places him "close to a certain aspect of Judaism": the primacy of speaking and listening over vision, of interpersonal relationships over the comprehension of Being.[26]

Levinas faults Buber, however, for not going far enough towards "love of the stranger: holier and higher than fraternity."[27] Buber accords ontological priority to the sphere of "the Between" where fraternity beckons, for I and You meet as equals in mutuality: "I know that I am saying "You" to someone who is an "I" like me, and that s/he says "You" to me"[28] What Levinas experiences in "the face" of the Other, however, is not a conversation-partner, much less a friend, but someone in need, symbolized by the Prophetic figures of marginality: "the orphan, the widow, the stranger, and the poor." Naked and defenseless, "the Other" does not stand before me as an equal to whom I owe respect, but approaches me – paradoxically, from a "height" in its "destitution" – usurping my self-centered world. For "the face" silently commands that I help – to the point of suffering for his or her suffering. Before I take possession of myself, my ethical subjectivity is constituted by being-for-the-Other. Because the Other is prior to the Same, "ethics precedes ontology."

On this basis, Levinas criticizes Buber's I/You encounter for betraying, as he puts it, "[a] slightly romantic formalism of an overly vague spiritualism." Overlooking Buber's discussion of "essential relations" of love and friendship, Levinas accuses Buber of privileging:

[t]he special case of the relation that takes place between beings who do not know each other. The Meeting [between I and You] is consequently, to Buber, pure act, transcendence without content that cannot be told, a pure spark, a dazzling instant without continuity or content.

By Levinas's lights, the incessant commandment to be a "first responder" in an emergency takes precedence over the "ethereal" meetings that "sometimes" take place in the "rarified atmosphere" of Buberian dialogue.[29]

Whereas Buber's I-You is mutual, Levinas' Same-Other is asymmetrical; for if I truly "welcome" you, then I say, "You first! (Aprez vous!)" "Once one is generous in the hope of reciprocity," Levinas states, "that relation no longer arises from generosity, but from the commercial or procedural relation."[30] The measure of responsibility is charity or "mad goodness": giving the Other more than s/he has any right

[26] Levinas, "Martin Buber's Thought and Contemporary Judaism," 16–17.

[27] Levinas, "The Other, Utopia and Justice" 108.

[28] Levinas, "The Proximity of the Other" in Is It Righteous to Be?,"(Stanford, CA: Stanford University Press), 213.

[29] Levinas,"Martin Buber's Thought and Contemporary Judaism," 18.

[30] Levinas, "The Proximity of the Other" in Is It Righteous to Be?,"(Stanford, CA: Stanford University Press), 213.

to expect.[31] To be sure, sacrifice is "unnatural," but it is the mark of human dignity that we can transcend the *conatus essendi* - the natural desire to persevere in being - in a movement that is "otherwise than Being."

Levinas's complaint against Buber reaches a fever pitch when, having attacked Heidegger's "egology," he nonetheless sides with Heidegger's account of Being-with-Others:

> Buber rises in violent opposition to the Heideggerian notion of *Fursorge* (solicitude) that, to the German philosopher, would be access to Others. It is certainly not from Heidegger that one should take lessons on the love of man or social justice. But *Fursorge* – as response to an essential destitution – accedes to the alterity of the Other. It takes into account that dimension of height and misery through which the very epiphany of others takes place… One may wonder whether clothing the naked and feeding the hungry do not bring us closer to the neighbor than the rarefied atmosphere in which Buber's Meeting takes place… "The Other's material needs are my spiritual needs"… Ah! Jewish materialism![32]

Levinas jokes that giving the shirt off one's back, not money-making – much less usury! – is the essence of "Jewish materialism." But the real butt of the joke is Buber, for Levinas insinuates that Heidegger's description of "leaping in" is closer to the authentic spirit of Judaism than Buber's mutual I-You encounter.[33]

Levinas' pointed attack on Buber must have been tinged with ambivalence. Notice how, in an interview over two decades later, he criticizes Heidegger's account of solicitude almost identically to how he had previously denounced Buber's I/You relation:

> In Heidegger the ethical relation is only one moment of our presence in the world, and not the central one at that. It is not in the first instance "the face," but being-together, or perhaps even marching-together… I don't believe he thinks that feeding the hungry and clothing the naked – that is, giving – is the meaning of being, much less that it might be above the task of being.[34]

Levinas's account of the meaning of mortality highlights his distance from Heidegger and Buber alike, for, he asserts, "love of neighbor" implies that one ought to fear the death of the Other more than one's own.

> My analysis does not begin with the death of those who are 'dear to us' [read: Buber], still less in the return to 'oneself' which would bring us back to the priority of my own death [read: Heidegger]… In starting from the Holocaust, I think of "the other man" for whom one may already feel like a guilty survivor.[35]

Levinas's interviewer replies in a Buberian vein: "But surely all the others do not exist equally for us. Their lives and deaths affect us more or less, depending on how far away or close they are to our lives. And for all sorts of reasons." Levinas responds: "But the ethical attitude – the ground of sociality – regards the death of

---

[31] Levinas, "The Proximity of the Other," 218.

[32] Levinas, "Martin Buber's Thought and Contemporary Judaism," 18–19.

[33] For Heidegger's distinction between "leaping in" (or "dominating solicitude") and "leaping ahead" (or "liberating solicitude"), see <u>Being and Time</u>, 158.

[34] Levinas, "Philosophy, Justice and Love" in Is It Righteous to Be?," 177.

[35] Levinas, "The Philosopher and Death," in <u>Is It Righteous to Be?</u>, 126.

the first one to come along, not the death of a being already near and dear... When the face lays claim to me, asking not to leave it alone, the answer is, in Hebrew, "Hineni (Here I am)"...[36]

Fear for the death of the stranger must loosen the hold of the ties that bind me to "my place in the sun." Because the Other – "unique, isolated from all multiplicity and outside collective necessities" – is "beyond-the-tribal," the profoundest love – "love without concupiscence" – does NOT begin with the erotic; rather, it is "agapic" and exists "without the worry about being loved."[37] In this sense, the mutuality of Buber's "dialogical path" remains too close to the alleged "Darwinism" of Heidegger's point-of-departure: concern for one's own Being. Ethics is "against nature," according to Levinas, because the "face" commands an "unnatural" subordination of the desire-to-be for the sake of being-for-the-Other.[38]

Here's the brunt of the matter; Levinas rejects Buber's "concentric circles" model of ethical life for being too egocentric. The words of one of his teachers, the Catholic existentialist Gabriel Marcel, foreshadows Levinas's own **eccentric – or outside-in – ethic**:

> [T]he normal development of a human being implies an increasingly precise and, as it were, automatic division between what concerns him and what does not, between things for which he is responsible and those for which he is not. Each one of us becomes the center of a sort of mental space arranged in concentric zones of decreasing interest and participation. It is as though each one of us secreted a kind of shell that gradually hardened and imprisoned him. And this sclerosis is bound up with the hardening of the categories in accordance with which we conceive and evaluate the world.
>
> Fortunately, it can happen to anyone to make an encounter that breaks down the framework of this egocentric topography... What had seemed near becomes incredibly remote, and what had seemed distant feels close. Such cracks are repaired almost at once. But it is an experience that leaves us with a bitter taste, an impression of sadness and almost of anguish; yet I think it is beneficial, for it shows us as in a flash all that is contingent and – yes – artificial in the crystallized pattern of our personal system.
>
> The available soul – at the disposal of others – subverts the normal order, for it recognize[s] that it does not belong to itself; this recognition is the starting-point of its creativity... The way is undiscoverable except through love, to which alone it is visible.[39]

In following Marcel by privileging *agape* over *eros*, Levinas invites the charge, leveled time and again by critics, that he expects people to be saints. Here's his reply:

> I am not saying that men are saints or are inclined towards holiness, only that the vocation of holiness is recognized by every human being as a value and that this recognition defines the human... But the holiness of gratuitous goodness is fragile before the power of evil. It is as if the weak and simple "holy ones" want to extinguish the world conflagration with a

---

[36] Levinas, "The Philosopher and Death," 125–126.

[37] Levinas, "The Other, Utopia and Justice," 205.

[38] "Interview with Emmanuel Levinas" in Richard Cohen, ed., Face to Face with Levinas (Albany, NY: SUNY Press, 1986), 24 and 26.

[39] Gabriel Marcel, The Philosophy of Existentialism (New York: Citadel Press, 1956), 40–42.

wash-basin. Still, despite all the horrors that men have engendered, this poor goodness holds its own.[40]

In an exchange of letters written towards the end of Buber's life, Buber replies to Levinas as follows: "He who has access to the Other WITHOUT 'caring' will find it again also IN caring; but he who is devoid of that access will clothe the naked and feed the hungry in vain. He will not utter a true 'You' without great difficulty. Not until everyone has been clothed and fed will the true ethical problem become visible."[41] In other words, the confirmation of You as a full-fledged, fellow human being – aspiring to mutuality – is the essence of the ethical movement. Charity alone smacks of paternalism; one might as well be saving a wounded animal. The *telos* of generosity is to enable the beneficiary to become an equal in the common intercourse of life.

To which Levinas replies, "Once saying 'You' has been separated from giving, it is a purely spiritual, ethereal friendship. But genuinely saying 'You' operates immediately and already through my body (including my giving hands). The Other is ALWAYS, qua Other, the poor and the destitute, and so one whom I face asymmetrically."[42] Levinas would agree with Buber that the political and legal issue is one of equality. But coming to another's rescue in his hour of need is more ethically fundamental than availability for dialogue because premature concerns about mutuality will drown out the call to sacrifice.

3 Heidegger, Buber and Levinas; Three Ways of Breaking Out of Our Shell

To summarize the triangular relationship between Heidegger, Buber and Levinas: I propose that each identifies a potentiality he takes to be the defining mark of our humanity, and then defines that capacity over against a shell we devise to protect ourselves from the anxiety of breaking out of our shell and opening up to our potential.

For Heidegger, the shell is inauthenticity: losing oneself in "the Anyone." What it takes to break the shell is authenticity: facing anxiety about one's "being-unto-death" alone "unsupported by concernful solicitude." This means, in colloquial terms, pulling oneself together, struggling to find one's own voice without craving the approval of others, and having the integrity to order one's priorities in the preciousness of one's time without relying on timeless first principles or formalistic rules.

---

[40] Levinas, "The Proximity of the Other," 218.

[41] Levinas, "Dialogue with Martin Buber," Proper Names (Stanford, CA: Stanford University Press, 1996), 37.

[42] Levinas, "Dialogue with Martin Buber," 38.

For Buber, the shell is "remaining within oneself." Heidegger's account of *Mitsein* fails to crack this shell because the life of dialogue reaches its depths in "essential relations of love and friendship" – overlooked by Heidegger – where "I am not only concerned with the other, but also anxious for the other to be concerned with me." Such relationships form the core of a meaningful life, give one the strength to face death, radiate outwards to "the essential We," and animate the Golden Rule requiring one to love one's neighbor – even the stranger – as another like oneself.

For Levinas, however, the shell is the *conatus essendi*: "the natural order where beings persevere in their being." This self-centeredness lies at the heart of Heidegger's definition of *Dasein's* care as "concern for one's own being." Heidegger can never broach the radical ethical question: "Is it righteous to be in the first place?" But neither can Buber. For I-You relationships remain too egocentric, too natural: tinged as they are with my desire to be confirmed by the other. Our normal, natural attachment to our familiar circle of "essential relations" is the shell that keeps me from experiencing the Other's material needs as my spiritual needs and from ceding my place to "You first" in a "mad goodness" that renounces mutuality.

4   Balancing Authenticity and Mutuality and Holiness

"Levinasians" are inclined to interpret the Heidegger-Buber-Levinas dialectic as a story of moral progress, culminating in Levinas' *Aufhebung* of previous positions. This is a mistake, I think, for our capacities for authenticity and mutuality in love and friendship are as much "marks of the human" as what Levinas calls "holiness." And it may well be that we can't account for "holiness" without reference to the equal humanity of the Other. Still, each thinker is on to something we don't want to give up. The problem is: they pull us in different directions in our lives and can't be blended in a harmonious unity.

Charles Taylor argues that the modern ideal of authenticity – with its emphasis on living my life in my own way – need not entail hedonism or an instrumental understanding of relations with others.[43] Authenticity can't be severed from dialogue as the medium through which we seek confirmation in our private lives through identity-forming personal relationships and in public life by the equal recognition of our dignity as citizens. Taylor would join Heidegger and Buber. Nonetheless, Taylor rightly concedes, the emphasis on self-fulfillment in the ideal of living authentically tugs against long-term commitments and the stability of associations. Still, who would go back to the days when women in particular were expected to sacrifice their desire for self-fulfillment for the good of a marriage?

Furthermore, it would be dishonest to find an easy harmony between Buber's "essential relations" of love and friendship and Levinas's demand of caring for "the orphan, the widow, the stranger, and the poor." Martin Luther King's great sermon

---

[43] See Charles Taylor, The Ethics of Authenticity (Cambridge, MA: Harvard University Press, 1992).

on the Good Samaritan expresses dissonant Buberian and Levinasian undertones. In a Buberian voice, King preaches: "I must not ignore the wounded man on life's Jericho Road because he is part of me and I am part of him. His agony diminishes me, and his salvation enlarges me." Compassion reaches the neighbor's "inner humanity" regardless of "outer appearances" that might divide us. King brings Levinas's "Other" into the orbit of Buber's "essential relations" by the metaphor that we are siblings in the family of humankind.

But then King introduces a Levinasian strain as well:

> I imagine the first question the priest and the Levite asked was: "If I stop to help this man, what will happen to me?" But by the very nature of his concern, the good Samaritan reversed the question: "If I do not stop to help this man, what will happen to him?"... The good man always reverses the question... The true neighbor will risk his position, his prestige, and even his life for the welfare of others.[44]

In saying "You first," altruists like those who jumped into the fray to aid bombing victims at the recent Boston Marathon weren't acting with an eye towards getting something back in return. They displayed what Levinas calls "mad goodness."

A simple story illustrates the tension between our commitment to friends and family and our responsibility for strangers. Actor Mark Harmon yanked a teenager out of a burning car in 1996. Having saved the teen, now grown, Harmon refuses to accept the label "hero." As he put it to a reporter, "If the car blows up and I'm there next to the car, then you're talking about two young boys that don't have a father and you'd be doing this interview with my wife and talking about how foolish I was. Right?"[45]

If I'm not directly implicated in an emergency, how far ought I to go out of my way to actively help those in need? The conflict reaches its apex in the case of martyrs, who may seek out emergencies that are, after all, structural features of our deeply imperfect world. As Michael Ignatieff puts it,

> Martyrs [like Socrates and Jesus] compel us to ask why we place family values ahead of principle, why self-sacrifice has become the most distrusted of moral gestures. Since most of us are not made of stern stuff, since most of us believe – for good reason – in the bourgeois virtues, the suffering that martyrs have endured makes it all too easy to believe that anyone willing to die for what he or she believes has to be crazy or fanatical or inhumanly impervious to the claims of kith and kin.[46]

Most of us, I submit, find meaning in our lives through, as Freud simply put it, love and work. We trust that if we do the best we can in the small circle at the center of our lives, this will radiate outwards to the benefit even of those not "essential" to us. Still, shouldn't we be haunted by Levinas's survivor guilt in a world where two billion people live on less than $2 a day, where, as Richard Rorty put it, "we who sit behind desks and punch keyboards are paid 10 times as much as the people who get their hands dirty cleaning our toilets and 100 times as much as those who fabricate

---

[44] Martin Luther King, Jr., "On Being a Good Neighbor," in Introduction to Ethics, ed. Gary Perspece (Englewood Cliffs, NJ: Prentice-Hall, 1995).

[45] CBS Sunday Morning: May 5, 2013.

[46] Michael Ignatieff, "The Scandal of Martyrs" The New Republic, 9/22/97.

our keyboards in the 3rd world," and where the Western way of life depends on a level of energy-consumption that would choke the Earth if poorer nations imitated our habits?[47]

As Karsten Harries pointed out in his presentation to the Dublin conference, "Discovering the 'We,'" the problem of sacrifice today demands that we care not only for "Others" outside the shell of our privileged way of life, but also for future generations: a "future without us." The goal of sustainability presupposes that future generations have the moral authority to put the brakes on us now. A robust "We" – extending deeply into the future – must be the ground of our contemporary "We." It has proven hard enough for us to move from tribalism to global solidarity. How much harder it will be to embrace future generations as equal members of the "We" to whom we today owe obligations, especially because we value authenticity and the meaning that comes from our small circle of family and friends.

Perhaps the debate within the existential tradition over the relative priority of authenticity, mutuality and holiness has come no further than Rabbi Hillel's equivocal pronouncement in the 1st century C.E.: "If I am not for myself, who will be for me? But if I am only for myself, what am I? And if not now, when?"

References

Bauman, Zygmunt. Quality and inequality. *The Guardian*, 12/28/2001.

Buber, Martin. 1964. Interrogation of Martin Buber. In *Philosophical interrogations*, ed. Sydney and Beatrice Rome. New York: Harper and Row.

Buber, Martin. 1965. *The knowledge of man*. New York: Harper and Row.

Buber, Martin. 2002. *Between man and man*. London: Routledge.

Heidegger, Martin. 1962. *Being and time*. New York: Harper and Row.

Ignatieff, Michael. The scandal of Martyrs. *The New Republic*, 9/22/97.

Kalin, Jesse. 2003. *The films of Ingmar Bergman*. Cambridge: Cambridge University Press.

King, Jr. 1995. Martin Luther, "On Being a Good Neighbor". In *Introduction to ethics*, ed. Gary Perspece. Englewood Cliffs: Prentice-Hall.

Levinas, Emmanuel. 1986. Interview with Emmanuel Levinas. In *Face to face with Levinas*, ed. Richard Cohen. Albany: SUNY Press.

Levinas, Emmanuel. 1993. *Outside the subject*. Stanford: Stanford University Press.

Levinas, Emmanuel. 1996. *Proper names*. Stanford: Stanford University Press.

Levinas, Emmanuel. 2002. *Is it righteous to be?* Stanford: Stanford University Press.

Marcel, Gabriel. 1956. *The philosophy of existentialism*. New York: Citadel.

McConnell, Michael. 2002. Don't neglect the little platoons. In *For love of country?* ed. Martha Nussbaum. Boston: Beacon.

Mendes-Flohr, Paul. 2012. Jewish co-existentialism: Being with the other. In *Situating existentialism*, ed. Jonathan Judaken and Robert Bernasconi. New York: Columbia University Press.

Natanson, Maurice. 1970. *The journeying self: A study in philosophy and social role*. Reading: Addison-Wesley.

Taylor, Charles. 1992. *The ethics of authenticity*. Cambridge, MA: Harvard University Press.

---

[47] Zygmunt Bauman, "Quality and Inequality," <u>The Guardian</u>, 12/28/2001.

Index

© Springer International Publishing Switzerland 2016
L. Foran, R. Uljée (eds.), *Heidegger, Levinas, Derrida : The Question of
Difference*, Contributions To Phenomenology 86,
DOI 10.1007/978-3-319-39232-5